Moulton's Grammar of New Testament Greek: Volume 4

Moulton's Grammar of New Testament Greek

Volume 4: Style

Nigel Turner
With a New Critical Introduction
by
Stanley E. Porter

t&tclark
LONDON • NEW YORK • OXFORD • NEW DELHI • SYDNEY

T&T CLARK
Bloomsbury Publishing Plc
50 Bedford Square, London, WC1B 3DP, UK
1385 Broadway, New York, NY 10018, USA

BLOOMSBURY, T&T CLARK and the T&T Clark logo are trademarks of Bloomsbury Publishing Plc

First published in Great Britain 1976
This edition published by T&T Clark 2019
Paperback edition published 2025

Copyright © T&T Clark

Introduction copyright © Stanley E. Porter, 2019

Stanley E. Porter has asserted his right under the Copyright, Designs and Patents Act, 1988, to be identified as Author of this work.

All rights reserved. No part of this publication may be reproduced or transmitted in any form or by any means, electronic or mechanical, including photocopying, recording, or any information storage or retrieval system, without prior permission in writing from the publishers.

Bloomsbury Publishing Plc does not have any control over, or responsibility for, any third-party websites referred to or in this book. All internet addresses given in this book were correct at the time of going to press. The author and publisher regret any inconvenience caused if addresses have changed or sites have ceased to exist, but can accept no responsibility for any such changes.

A catalogue record for this book is available from the British Library.

A catalog record for this book is available from the Library of Congress.

ISBN: HB: 978-0-5676-0538-2
PB: 978-0-5677-1722-1
Pack: 978-0-5676-6242-2

Series: Biblical Languages: Greek

Typeset by Newgen KnowledgeWorks Pvt. Ltd., Chennai, India

To find out more about our authors and books visit www.bloomsbury.com and sign up for our newsletters.

Contents

Introduction by Stanley E. Porter	vii
Preface	xlv
Abbreviations	xlvii
Introduction	1

Chap.		Page
I.	Sources behind the Gospels	5
II.	The Style of Mark	11
III.	The Style of Matthew	31
IV.	The Style of Luke-Acts	45
V.	The Style of John	64
VI.	The Style of Paul	80
VII.	The Style of Pastoral Epistles	101
VIII.	The Style of the Epistle to the Hebrews	106
IX.	The Style of the Epistle of James	114
X.	The Style of I Peter	121
XI.	The Style of the Johannine Epistles	132
XII.	The Style of Jude and 2 Peter	139
XIII.	The Style of the Book of Revelation	145

Subject Index	161
Index of Names	163
Index of Semitic, Greek and Latin words	166
Selective Index of New Testament References	168

Nigel Turner and Greek Style

An Introduction to Moulton's Fourth Volume, *Style*

Stanley E. Porter
McMaster Divinity College

Introduction

This essay is the fourth of four, each one accompanying a reprinted edition of one of the four volumes in the New Testament Greek grammar project conceived and instigated by James Hope Moulton, *A Grammar of New Testament Greek*, along with a reprinted edition of G. B. Winer's *A Treatise on the Grammar of New Testament Greek*, translated and edited by his father, William Fiddian Moulton. Of the four volumes, James Hope Moulton was the author of the first, entitled *Prolegomena*, and much of the second, entitled *Accidence and Word-Formation*, with the second completed by Moulton's student Wilbert Francis Howard. The third volume, *Syntax*, and the fourth, *Style*, were written some time later by Nigel Turner. These introductory essays attempt to provide biographical and related information to understand the contributions of the authors and their works to the larger field of study of New Testament Greek. Readers who wish to gain a more comprehensive picture of the entire four-volume grammar, as well as the translation of Winer's grammar, will want to read each of the five introductions. Even though there is some inevitable overlap among them, each introduction is uniquely tailored to the particular volume that it accompanies. This volume, containing Turner's *Style*, discusses the author and his work that led to the production of this fourth volume in *A Grammar of New*

Testament Greek. I begin with the life and scholarly work of Turner, before offering a short summary and assessment of the volume.

The Life and Work of Nigel Turner

Nigel Turner (1916–1990) was born in Tuxford, England, on September 26, 1916, the year before Moulton died of exposure in the Mediterranean, a victim of the Great War.[1] Turner had no direct connection to Moulton, even though he lived to complete and even expand Moulton's grammar of New Testament Greek. Turner was educated at the Christ's Hospital School, a school founded in 1552 to educate the poor and that had moved from London to Horsham in West Sussex by the time Turner attended, where he received a traditional classical education with emphasis upon Greek. He proceeded to university and graduated from King's College of the University of London, where the major figure in New Testament studies was Professor R. V. G. Tasker, who, among other things, edited the Greek text used in the New English Bible, a translation project in which Turner was later involved (see below). Turner earned all three of his university degrees through the University of London, including the BD, the MTh, and the PhD, the last of which he received in 1953 while serving as a vicar. During his time at King's, Turner received a number of academic prizes. These include the Senior Wordsworth Prize for Latin in 1935 (Turner put his ability as a Latinist to good use

---

[1] There is very little readily available biographical information on Nigel Turner. I have pieced together this account on the basis of bits and pieces gathered here and there, aided by the kind and generous efforts of a number of my students and colleagues, including especially my longtime friend Robert Morgan of Oxford, who gathered information from a number of different editions of *Crockford's Clerical Directory* (apparently not always consistent in their information on Turner); Professor Edward Adams of King's College London, who pursued enquiries for me; and correspondence with Mary Turner, Nigel Turner's widow, and their daughter, Elisabeth Sheehan, who provided many further details. I have also used a number of websites for factual information.

later in his career in his work on Aquila), the Archbishop Robertson Prize in 1936 as the best second-year student, and the Plumptre Prize in 1938 for writing the best theology essay. He became an Associate of King's College in 1937 and, after an initial setback, received his BD in 1939. He then spent some time in Antigua as an assistant to the bishop of Antigua. Early in his academic career, Turner seems to have had an interest in eschatology, which was evidenced in an essay he apparently wrote on eschatology in the Old Testament.[2] His interest in eschatology was not strong throughout his career, with evidence in his further writings being relatively sparse.

Turner was educated for the Anglican ministry at Queen's College, an Anglican theological college in Birmingham, in 1938-9. He served several curacies before becoming a priest, and served in a variety of locations in the south of England especially during the war years. His younger brother, George, was a pilot during the Second World War and tragically died in a flying accident. Turner himself served as an air-raid warden during the war. His curacies during this time include Birmingham from 1939-42, Erdington (a suburb of Birmingham and also in the Birmingham diocese) from 1942-4, Aldridge (another suburb of Birmingham, but in the Litchfield diocese) from 1944-9, and Battle Abbey in East Sussex from 1949-51, near where the Battle of Hastings was fought in 1066, where Turner began his active scholarly career. Turner served as a vicar in the village of Diseworth, near Derby in Leicestershire, from 1951-8. During this time, he received his PhD for a thesis entitled "The *Testament of Abraham*: A Study of the Original Language, Place of Origin, Authorship, and Relevance" and began very

---

[2] Nigel Turner, "Eschatology in the Old Testament Literature" (1936). I secured this reference from the online catalog of the library of Nigel Turner, cataloged by author, housed in the C. S. Lewis Institute Library (to which Turner's library was donated by his widow). However, the essay now appears to be missing, so at this point nothing further can be verified (e.g., whether this is the essay for which he was awarded the Plumptre Prize), and it does not appear to have been actively followed as a major interest later in his career. I wish to thank Tyson Rallens, the current caretaker of The Kilns, for helping try to locate the essay.

actively publishing on the topic of the Greek language, the topic that would come to define his scholarly career. He then became a rector in Milton in Cambridgeshire, where he served for only two years, from 1958–60, during which time he was invited to preach a University Sermon in Cambridge in 1959. Turner left parish ministry in 1960 and settled in the ancient market town of Hitchen in Hertfordshire, where he remained until 1972. This was an important time for his scholarly career, as he published two of his major books on Greek language during this period and no doubt did work on his third. In 1972, Turner took up his only regular academic appointment, attaining the position of Reader in Theology at the University of Rhodesia in Salisbury, now the University of Zimbabwe,[3] where he remained until 1975, when he returned to England after suffering a slight stroke. He published several works that reflect his time in Africa. At that point, Turner returned to Britain and settled in Ely in Cambridgeshire, where he finished his third and fourth books on Greek and eventually died on May 21, 1990, leaving his widow, Mary, and two children, Elisabeth and Paul (to whom he dedicated the syntax volume). He is buried in the Ely Cathedral Cemetery, where his headstone succinctly describes him as both priest and scholar. This is a very apt description if it is taken in a chronological sense, as he served as a priest in the first half of his career and then devoted the second half to the publication of his major works of scholarship, especially on the Greek of the New Testament.

Turner's biblical scholarship follows two tracks, although one of the tracks is far more developed than the other. These two tracks encompass scholarship in biblical studies apart from Greek and, more importantly, scholarship in New Testament Greek. He published a significant amount

---

[3] The University of Rhodesia was founded in 1955, and at first had an affiliation with the University of London. After the country gained independence, the University of Rhodesia became the University of Zimbabwe in 1980.

of material in each area, but the second area dominated his attention throughout his scholarly career.

The area of biblical studies apart from Greek includes a number of different types of scholarly research. I enumerate three. The only major work that Turner wrote that was greatly removed from biblical topics was his book *The Art of the Greek Orthodox Church*, written while he was lecturing in Rhodesia.[4] At various points some of his extra-biblical scholarship overlaps or intersects with his Greek scholarship, but there are perhaps some hints at other areas of interest throughout his career. The first of these areas of scholarship, already mentioned, is his possible interest in eschatology and with it the book of Revelation. After his early thesis, if that is what it is, he also wrote the commentary on the book of Revelation for the revised *Peake's Commentary on the Bible*.[5] A second area of interest is some theological topics, such as the background to the use of Logos in John's Gospel being both Philonic and biblical, or the attitude of the church to the state within the New Testament where Turner sees Revelation as not as stridently anti-state as others have argued.[6] The third area is Turner's interest simply in various topics, people, and subjects within New Testament studies, what one might be tempted to call social and historical backgrounds. This interest is evidenced in the large number of dictionary entries that Turner wrote, particularly in *The Interpreter's Bible Dictionary*, on a wide variety of topics, ranging from Absalom to Trypho.[7]

---

[4] Nigel Turner, *The Art of the Greek Orthodox Church: A Study in Stylization* (University of Rhodesia Series in Humanities; Salisbury, Rhodesia: University of Rhodesia, 1976).
[5] Nigel Turner, "Revelation," in Matthew Black and H. H. Rowley (eds.), *Peake's Commentary on the Bible* (London: Thomas Nelson, 1962), pp. 1043-61.
[6] Nigel Turner, "St. John's Eternal Word," *Evangelical Quarterly* 22 (1950), pp. 243-8; Turner, "The Church's Attitude to the State in the New Testament," *Journal of Theology for Southern Africa* 2 (1973), pp. 41-52, the latter a scholarly piece published while he was in Rhodesia.
[7] See the bibliography at the end for the large number of dictionary and related entries.

INTRODUCTION: *STYLE*

Despite these interests, Turner directed his scholarship primarily toward describing the Greek of the New Testament and its relationship to other dialects of Greek used during the classical, Hellenistic, and Roman periods. Not only did Turner write four major works on Greek grammar and lexicography (see below for discussion),[8] but he also published a number of other contributions in support of his distinctive hypothesis that the Greek of the New Testament constituted a definable form of Jewish or Biblical Greek.[9] It is worth noting, however, that Turner's involvement in Moulton's *A Grammar of New Testament Greek* probably came about at least to some extent because of his interest and ability in Bible translation, an interest that he maintained throughout his scholarly career. Turner was involved in two major Bible translation projects, one organized by the British and Foreign Bible Society begun in 1954 and finally produced in 1973 as *The Translator's New Testament*,[10] and the other the revision of the Revised Version that resulted in the New English Bible (see below). Although many of Turner's articles are only indirectly concerned with translation, a number of them are specifically addressed to it, especially the translation of the Hebrew Bible into Greek, the so-called Old Greek or Septuagint. As a result, Turner wrote an article on the Greek translators of the book of Ezekiel and was responsible for revising the edition by Joseph Reider of the index to Aquila's translation of the Greek Old Testament (which also demanded

---

[8] Nigel Turner, *Syntax*, Volume 3 of *A Grammar of New Testament Greek* by James Hope Moulton (Edinburgh: T&T Clark, 1963); Turner, *Grammatical Insights into the New Testament* (Edinburgh: T&T Clark, 1965); Turner, *Style*, Volume 4 of *A Grammar of New Testament Greek* by James Hope Moulton (Edinburgh: T&T Clark, 1976); and Turner, *Christian Words* (Edinburgh: T&T Clark, 1980).

[9] See also, e.g., Nigel Turner, "The Preposition *en* in the New Testament," *Bible Translator* 10.3 (July 1959), pp. 113–20; and Turner, "Modern Issues in Biblical Studies: Philology in New Testament Studies," *Expository Times* 71 (1960), pp. 104–7.

[10] *The Translator's New Testament* (London: British and Foreign Bible Society, 1973).

INTRODUCTION: *STYLE* xiii

his ability in Latin).[11] However, Turner's interest in translation goes far beyond his interest in the Septuagint.

Turner's interest in translation is directly related to his view of the Greek of the New Testament as the special dialect of Greek of the early Christians. In reaction to the hypothesis of G. Adolf Deissmann, Albert Thumb, and Moulton regarding the Greek of the New Testament being koine or common Greek,[12] a number of scholars have argued for a Semitic substrate hypothesis as a means of accounting for the Greek of the New Testament. These scholars argue that a Semitic substrate, either Hebrew or Aramaic, underlies various books of the New Testament. One can account for Semitic language influence and interference on the basis that the Greek of the New Testament reflects some level of translation of these underlying Semitic sources. Thus, there was earlier serious scholarly discussion of whether an Aramaic Gospel underlay Mark's Gospel or whether Matthew's Gospel was originally written in Hebrew or whether John's Gospel was a translation of a Semitic Gospel, and similar theories. In their more extreme forms, these theories were

---

[11] Nigel Turner, "The Greek Translators of Ezekiel." *Journal of Theological Studies* n.s. 7 (1956), pp. 12–24; Joseph Reider, *An Index to Aquila: Greek-Hebrew, Hebrew-Greek, Latin-Hebrew, with the Syriac and Armenian Evidence* (completed and revised by Nigel Turner; Supplements to Vetus Testamentum 12; Leiden: Brill, 1966).

[12] This position is represented in such works as G. Adolf Deissmann, *Bible Studies: Contributions Chiefly from Papyri and Inscriptions to the History of the Language, the Literature, and the Religion of Hellenistic Judaism and Primitive Christianity* (trans. Alexander Grieve; Edinburgh: T&T Clark, 1901); Deissmann, *Light from the Ancient East: The New Testament Illustrated by Recently Discovered Texts of the Graeco-Roman World* (trans. Lionel R. M. Strachan; London: Hodder and Stoughton, 1910); Albert Thumb, *Die Griechische Sprache im Zeitalter des Hellenismus: Beiträge zur Geschichte und Beurteilung der KOINE* (Strassburg: Karl J. Trübner, 1901); and James Hope Moulton, *Prolegomena*, Volume 1 of *A Grammar of New Testament Greek* (Edinburgh: T&T Clark, 1906; 2nd ed., 1906; 3rd ed., 1908). For a discussion of this viewpoint, as well as the other viewpoints referred to in the discussion that follows, in conjunction with representative essays by the various proponents, see Stanley E. Porter, "Introduction: The Greek of the New Testament as a Disputed Area of Research," in Porter (ed.), *The Language of the New Testament: Classic Essays* (Sheffield: Sheffield Academic, 1991), pp. 11–38. See also the introduction to the respective volumes, "James Hope Moulton and Koine Greek: An Introduction to Moulton's *Prolegomena*" and "James Hope Moulton and Wilbert Francis Howard and Greek Phonology and Morphology: An Introduction to Moulton and Howard's *Accidence and Word-Formation*."

held by such scholars as the Yale Semiticist Charles Cutler Torrey, the Irish clergyman R. H. Charles, and the Oxford professor C. F. Burney. Torrey argued in a book entitled *Our Translated Gospels* that all four of the Gospels were translations out of Aramaic. He also argued in his *The Composition and Date of Acts* that Acts 1–15 was translated from an Aramaic source, and in *The Apocalypse of John* that it too was translated from an Aramaic original.[13] Charles in his work on the book of Revelation accounted for the well-known grammatical inconcinnities on the basis that the author thought in Hebrew while writing in Greek.[14] Burney argued for an Aramaic source for John's Gospel.[15]

A more nuanced position is taken by other, and often later, scholars such as Gustaf Dalman, Matthew Black, and Max Wilcox who argue that, while Semitic and especially Aramaic sources underlie the Gospels and especially the words of Jesus, the Gospels and Acts are not translations of these sources.[16] They nevertheless still believe that the Greek of the

---

[13] Charles Cutler Torrey, *The Composition and Date of Acts* (Harvard Theological Studies 1; Cambridge, MA: Harvard University Press, 1916); Torrey, *The Four Gospels: A New Translation* (London: Hodder and Stoughton, 1933); and Torrey, *The Apocalypse of John* (New Haven: Yale University Press, 1958).

[14] R. H. Charles, *Studies in the Apocalypse* (Edinburgh: T&T Clark, 1913), 79–102; Charles, *A Critical and Exegetical Commentary on the Revelation of St. John* (2 vols.; International Critical Commentary; Edinburgh: T&T Clark, 1920).

[15] C. F. Burney, *The Aramaic Origin of the Fourth Gospel* (Oxford: Clarendon, 1922). See also Burney, *The Poetry of Our Lord* (Oxford: Clarendon, 1925). Others to hold to similar positions were such scholars as J. A. Montgomery, *The Origin of the Gospel According to St. John* (Philadelphia, PA: John C. Winston, 1923); Klaus Beyer, *Semitische Syntax im Neuen Testament*, I (Göttingen: Vandenhoeck & Ruprecht, 1962); Frans Zimmermann, *The Aramaic Origin of the Four Gospels* (New York: KTAV, 1979); Steven Thompson, *The Apocalypse and Semitic Syntax* (Cambridge: Cambridge University Press, 1985); Günther Schwarz, *"Und Jesu Sprach": Untersuchungen zur aramäischen Urgestalt der Worte Jesu* (Stuttgart: Kohlhammer, 1985); George Howard, *The Gospel of Matthew According to a Primitive Hebrew Text* (Macon, GA: Mercer University Press, 1987); and Maurice Casey, *Aramaic Sources of Mark's Gospel* (Cambridge: Cambridge University Press, 1998), among others.

[16] Gustaf Dalman, *The Words of Jesus: Considered in the Light of Post-Biblical Jewish Writings and the Aramaic Language* (trans. D. M. Kay; Edinburgh: T&T Clark, 1909); Dalman, *Jesus-Jeshua: Studies in the Gospels* (trans. Paul P. Levertoff; London: SPCK, 1929); Matthew Black, *An Aramaic Approach to the Gospels and Acts* (Oxford: Clarendon, 1946; 2nd ed., 1954; 3rd ed., 1967); and Max Wilcox, *The Semitisms of Acts* (Oxford: Clarendon, 1965). Others to hold to a similar position were such scholars as Joseph A. Fitzmyer, "The Languages of

New Testament directly reflects various Semitic sources, sometimes to a high degree, on the basis of an underlying Semitic substrate. Turner, however, takes a view that is in a number of important ways distinct from the Semitic substrate hypothesis, even if, when examined, he too believes that the Greek in the New Testament reflects Semitic influence not because of the translation process but because of the creation of a unique Jewish and Christian dialect. Turner argues that the Greek of the New Testament does not reflect translation of underlying Semitic sources but was written in a form of Greek that encompassed Semitic influence so as to become a unified dialect of Semitic Greek used by the Jews and early Christians.[17] Hence Turner argues that the characteristics of Biblical Greek are not translationese or simply uneducated use but reflect the actual dialect used by Jews and Christians of the time. He argues this to the point where his position seems at times to hark back to the earlier Holy Ghost Greek hypothesis—that is, that the Greek of the New Testament is a special kind of theologically motivated, even if not divinely inspired, dialect of the language given for unique and even revelatory purposes. Or, to use the language of Black explicitly adopted by Turner, Biblical Greek was "a peculiar language, the language of a peculiar people."[18]

Palestine in the First Century AD," *Catholic Biblical Quarterly* 32 (1970), pp. 501-31 (and reprinted many times); and Adelbert Denaux, in Albert Hogeterp and Denaux, *Semitisms in Luke's Greek: A Descriptive Analysis of Lexical and Syntactical Domains of Semitic Language Influence in Luke's Gospel* (Wissenschaftliche Untersuchungen zum Neuen Testament 401; Tübingen: Mohr Siebeck, 2018), and, I would dare say, probably the vast majority of New Testament scholars (who, unfortunately, have not fully investigated the issue).

[17] Turner's position was held in similar ways by the Princeton Old Testament and Septuagint scholar Henry S. Gehman, "The Hebraic Character of Septuagint Greek," *Vetus Testamentum* 1 (1951), pp. 81-90, among several other articles, and more recently by Georg Walser, *The Greek of the Ancient Synagogue: An Investigation on the Greek of the Septuagint, Pseudepigrapha and the New Testament* (Stockholm: Almqvist & Wicksell, 2001), among others.

[18] Matthew Black, "The Biblical Languages," in Peter R. Ackroyd and C. F. Evans (eds.), *The Cambridge History of the Bible, Volume 1* (Cambridge: Cambridge University Press, 1970), pp. 1-11, quotation p. 111; cf. Nigel Turner, "Biblical Greek: The Peculiar Language of a Peculiar People," in Elizabeth A. Livingstone (ed.), *Studia Evangelica* VII (Berlin: Akademie-Verlag, 1982), pp. 505-12, although he alludes to this position elsewhere.

There are two important observations to make about Turner's position regarding the Greek of the New Testament, a position that he held almost from the outset of his scholarly publishing career. The first observation is that Turner's position is significantly different from the position of Moulton, whose grammar he completed. I note in the introduction to Volume 2 on *Accidence and Word-Formation* that Moulton perhaps moderated his view of the nature of Greek over the span of time from his *Prolegomena* to his *Accidence and Word-Formation*.[19] However, I also note that he did not depart significantly from his original position regarding the New Testament Greek being koine Greek, even if he admitted Semitic influence especially through the Septuagint. In increasing contrast to Moulton, however, Turner appears to have strengthened his position regarding a Semitized Jewish and Christian Greek dialect over the course of his scholarly career. In his "Preface" to the volume *Style*, Turner notes that the volumes on syntax and style have been completed by a member of a younger generation than Moulton and Howard. "Because of that, and because the enterprise reflects so wide a passage of time, it is inevitable that the viewpoint of the Grammar upon the nature of New Testament Greek is not entirely a unity, and there are traces of the radical development to be expected as the state of these studies has progressed."[20]

Despite this statement, Turner also states that he believes that "despite the passage of time I have found my own views for the most part to be consistent with those of the Grammar's originator even at the distance of seven decades from its inception."[21] Howard and then Turner both seem to treat the Semitic hypothesis as an acceptable explanation of developments in New Testament Greek. This situation may have

---

[19] James Hope Moulton and Wilbert Francis Howard, *Accidence and Word-Formation*, Volume 2 of *A Grammar of New Testament Greek* (3 parts; Edinburgh: T&T Clark, 1919–29 [one-volume edition published subsequently]), pp. 1–22.
[20] Turner, *Style*, p. vii.
[21] Ibid.

INTRODUCTION: *STYLE*   xvii

seemed to be the case at the time of Turner's writing, but already at the time of publication of the volume on style a strong movement back to the earlier koine Greek hypothesis was taking shape in the work of a number of scholars, anticipated by the writings of Joseph Fitzmyer[22] and seen more obviously in publications by more recent scholars such as Lars Rydbeck, Marius Reiser, G. H. R. Horsley, and Stanley Porter, among others, to the point where the koine Greek hypothesis is once more widely promoted.[23] The major contemporary response has been that a distinction needs to be made on the basis of the linguistic evidence in relation to the language system. Lars Rydbeck argues that the appropriate stratum of language for comparison with the Greek of the New Testament is a mid-level technical language, neither literary nor vulgar. This differentiation was more linguistically generalized by Moisés Silva in terms of *langue* and *parole*, and by Porter in terms of code and text.[24] Silva means that the *langue*, koine Greek, remained stable, even if instances of *parole*, or usage, have Semitic features, while Porter distinguishes between language as a shared meaning system or code and instances of this language or texts.

The second observation is to note how Turner outlines his developing position with regard to the nature of Greek.[25] Turner began his exploration of the topic with an essay on the question of whether

---

[22] Fitzmyer, "Languages of Palestine."
[23] Lars Rydbeck, *Fachprosa, vermeintliche Volkssprache und Neues Testament: Zur Beurteilung der sprachlichen Niveauunterschiede im nachklassischen Griechisch* (Uppsala: n.p., 1967); Marius Reiser, *Syntax und Stil des Markusevangeliums im Licht der hellenistischen Volksliteratur* (Wissenschaftliche Untersuchungen zum Neuen Testament 2/11; Tübingen: Mohr Siebeck, 1984); G. H. R. Horsley, *New Documents Illustrating Early Christianity, Volume 5: Linguistic Essays* (Sydney: Ancient History Documentary Research Centre, Macquarie University, 1989), esp. pp. 5-40, a chapter entitled "The Fiction of 'Jewish Greek'"; and Stanley E. Porter, *Verbal Aspect in the Greek of the New Testament with Reference to Tense and Mood* (Studies in Biblical Greek 1; New York: Peter Lang, 1989), pp. 141-56.
[24] Moisés Silva, "Bilingualism and the Character of Palestinian Greek," *Biblica* 61 (1980), pp. 198-219; Porter, *Verbal Aspect*, pp. 151-2.
[25] An exception to this developing theory is Nigel Turner, "The Literary Character of New Testament Greek," *New Testament Studies* 20 (1974), pp. 107-14, where he focuses upon the influence of literary Greek.

the Gospels were written in Greek or Aramaic. This paper seems to begin from Moulton's position but already with some clear Semitic modifications, while clearly rejecting the translation hypothesis.[26] Turner's position is already made stronger in his essay that speaks of the "unique character" of Biblical Greek.[27] His article on the *Testament of Abraham*, pursuing some of the research for his doctorate, is a description of the Semitic Greek of that text as an example that extends beyond the Bible.[28] His essay on Luke 1 and 2 in relation to sources and Luke–Acts argues that those two chapters drew more heavily upon Semitized Greek than the rest of Luke–Acts, rather than being a translation as some have posited.[29] Turner's essay in *Peake's Commentary on the Bible* replaced the previous essay in the first edition by Moulton and then supplemented by Howard, and reflects Turner's different perspective, more in line with Black's.[30] The volume on *Syntax* provides a short, clear summary of Turner's position regarding Greek, a position that is also briefly summarized in the volume on *Style* (see summaries below). The final chapter in Turner's *Grammatical Insights into the New Testament* is "The Language of Jesus and His Disciples." Turner acknowledges but rejects the Semitic source hypotheses for a Greek hypothesis, but a Greek that is a "hybrid" Jewish-Christian Greek, not a temporary phenomenon but the normal language used by Jesus and many others.[31] In an essay that anticipated his *Christian Words*, Turner looks to various Jewish and Christian influences on the vocabulary

---

[26] Nigel Turner, "Were the Gospels Written in Greek or Aramaic?," *Evangelical Quarterly* 21 (1949), pp. 42–8.
[27] Nigel Turner, "The Unique Character of Biblical Greek," *Vetus Testamentum* 5 (1955), pp. 208–13.
[28] Nigel Turner, "The 'Testament of Abraham': Problems in Biblical Greek," *New Testament Studies* 1 (1955), pp. 219–23.
[29] Nigel Turner, "The Relation of Luke I and II to Hebraic Sources and to the Rest of Luke–Acts," *New Testament Studies* 2 (1955), pp. 100–9.
[30] Nigel Turner, "The Language of the New Testament," in Matthew Black and H. H. Rowley (eds.), *Peake's Commentary on the Bible* (London: Thomas Nelson, 1962), pp. 659–62.
[31] Turner, *Grammatical Insights*, pp. 174–88.

of the New Testament.³² Even the characteristics of Luke's so-called literary style show the influence of various Semitisms.³³ In development of his earlier essay, Turner expands his view that both Judaism, especially through the Septuagint, and Christianity had an influence on New Testament vocabulary, giving words new and different meanings, although he seems to take the position to new lengths in his *Christian Words* (see summary below). In his final published statement, Turner responds to his critics and points to the characteristics of the Greek of the New Testament as a Semitized Greek characteristic of the early Christians.³⁴ Turner clearly represents a particular position in the study of the Greek of the New Testament, one that he had been developing since his earliest publication in 1949.

In the "Preface" to *Syntax*, Turner notes how he came to be involved in Moulton's *A Grammar of New Testament Greek*. To recapitulate the account offered in greater length in the introductions to the first two reprinted volumes of Moulton's grammar, Moulton himself was responsible for publishing the first volume, *Prolegomena*, in 1906, with two further editions soon to follow. In this grammar, Moulton, rather than continuing the grammatical thought of Georg Winer's rationalist approach or even the Semitized view of Greek that he himself had held earlier, argues that the Greek of the New Testament represents the koine or common vernacular found in the recently discovered Greek documentary papyri. Moulton began on the second volume in his grammar, *Accidence and Word-Formation*, and wrote roughly three-fourths of it before undertaking a missionary and teaching trip to India

---

[32] Nigel Turner, "Jewish and Christian Influence on New Testament Vocabulary," *Novum Testamentum* 16 (1974), pp. 149–60.
[33] Nigel Turner, "The Quality of the Greek of Luke–Acts," in J. K. Elliott (ed.), *Studies in New Testament Language and Text: Essays in Honour of George D. Kilpatrick* (Supplements to Novum Testamentum 44; Leiden: Brill, 1976), pp. 387–400.
[34] Turner, "Biblical Greek," pp. 505–12. This paper does not seem to take his view as far as the opinion expressed in *Christian Words*, but this paper was written in 1973 even though not published until 1982.

during the Great War. He unfortunately was killed on his return trip and completion of the volume was turned over to one of his accomplished students, Wilbert Francis Howard. Howard completed Moulton's preface, a major chapter in part three on suffixation, and added a very important appendix on Semitisms in the New Testament that Moulton had originally intended to coauthor with a Semiticist colleague. Howard wrote this appendix to respect Moulton's original intention to write such an appendix in response to criticisms of his position, even though his position did not change materially but had developed by recognizing more fully the possibility of some Semitisms used by some writers of the New Testament especially under Septuagintal influence. There remains some question about what Moulton himself would have written in such an appendix on the basis of his remaining writings, but Howard appears to have pushed Moulton and his position along a trajectory that was in some ways more compatible with a Semitic influence hypothesis regarding the nature of New Testament Greek. Howard was also commissioned to write the third and at that time final volume of the grammar on syntax. However, Howard died in 1952 before writing that volume.

The task of completing Moulton's grammar then fell to Henry George Meecham. Meecham, who had taught at the Methodist Hartley Victoria College since 1930[35] and lectured in New Testament in the University of Manchester, was himself a former student of Moulton (Meecham received his MA, BD, PhD, and DD from Manchester) who had revised the fifth editions of Moulton's introduction to and reader in New

---

[35] Victoria College was founded in 1881 as a Primitive Methodist institution and renamed Hartley Victoria College in 1934, and finally closed in 2015. A. S. Peake, who was also at the University of Manchester and the first holder of the position of Rylands Professor of Biblical Exegesis, was at this institution. See John James William Edmondson, "The Doctrines of Hell and Judgment and the Need for Personal Conversion as an Index to the Development of Liberal Theology within the Theological Colleges of the Methodist Church in England from 1907 to 1932" (MA thesis, University of Durham, 1990), pp. 32–68.

INTRODUCTION: *STYLE* xxi

Testament Greek³⁶ and had himself published a number of scholarly works in the area of Greek language and literature.³⁷ Meecham agreed to take on the task of writing the third volume if he were to have an assistant.³⁸ It appears that, at the time, G. D. Kilpatrick, Dean Ireland's Professor of the Exegesis of Holy Scripture at Oxford University, was on the New Testament Committee for the New English Bible, and this may have provided the link by which he knew both Meecham and Turner, who at various times worked on the translation (as did Tasker, with whom Turner must have studied in London).³⁹ At this time in the early 1950s, Turner had not yet published very many scholarly articles (to say nothing of books), even though the trajectory of his view of Biblical Greek was already emerging in those publications. In any case, Kilpatrick suggested Turner for the task of assistant to Meecham, and Turner had successfully compiled what he calls a "provisional bibliography" when in 1955 Meecham too died.⁴⁰ The publishers, who by this time must have been wondering whether anyone would live long enough to complete Moulton's grammar, commissioned Turner with the completion of the third volume, which he did, before suggesting that a fourth volume on style be included. In the "Preface" to the fourth volume, Turner notes that Moulton himself, although not specifically envisioning such a fourth

---

[36] James Hope Moulton, *An Introduction to the Study of New Testament Greek* (London: Epworth, 5th ed., 1955); Moulton, *A First Reader in New Testament Greek* (London: Epworth, 5th ed., 1955).

[37] Henry G. Meecham, *Light from Ancient Letters: Private Correspondence in the Non-Literary Papyri of Oxyrhynchus of the First Four Centuries, and Its Bearing on New Testament Language and Thought* (London: George Allen and Unwin, 1923); Meecham, *The Oldest Version of the Bible: "Aristeas" on Its Traditional Origin. A Study in Early Apologetic with Translation and Appendices* (London: Holborn, 1932) (dedicated to his teachers, Peake and Moulton, and with thanks to Howard); Meecham, *The Letter of Aristeas: A Linguistic Study with Special Reference to the Greek Bible* (Manchester: Manchester University Press, 1935); and Meecham, *The Epistle to Diognetus: The Greek Text with Introduction and Notes* (Manchester: Manchester University Press, 1949).

[38] See Turner, *Syntax*, p. v.

[39] Geoffrey Hunt, *About the New English Bible* (Oxford: Oxford University Press; Cambridge: Cambridge University Press, 1970), pp. 80, 81.

[40] Turner, *Syntax*, p. v.

volume, had in fact anticipated it in his introduction to *Accidence and Word-Formation*, in which he began to distinguish the linguistic usage of the different biblical writers (even if Howard completed this analysis drawing on other works by Moulton and others).[41] Moulton indicated his interest in style not only in that introduction but also in his major article on "New Testament Greek in the Light of Modern Discovery,"[42] in which he engaged in a much fuller exposition of what might well be called the stylistic characteristics of the various authors, as well as possibly other places in his works where he singles out the characteristics of individual New Testament writers. In any case, in 1963 Turner published the third volume on *Syntax*, followed by publication of *Style* in 1976.

Before turning to the individual grammatical volume with which we are concerned here, *Style*, we should note the other major Greek grammatical and lexicographical publications by Turner. Apart from the works on related biblical topics already noted above, Turner's major publications are directly concerned with the Greek of the New Testament. In the course of his scholarly career, he published four major volumes on Greek grammar and lexicography in its various parts.

The first of these volumes is the volume on syntax, which was his first major book publication.[43] This volume took Turner just under ten years to complete, from the time he joined the writing project as an assistant to Meecham until it was published in 1963. By this time, Turner's perspective on Greek had come to full (although arguably not its most categorical) development. He opens the volume with an "Introduction" that essentially makes two major related points regarding specifically

---

[41] Turner, *Style*, p. vii.
[42] James Hope Moulton, "New Testament Greek in the Light of Modern Discovery," in Henry Barclay Swete (ed.), *Essays on Some Biblical Questions of the Day by Members of the University of Cambridge* (London: Macmillan, 1909), pp. 461–506.
[43] For the most developed assessment of Turner's *Syntax*, along with pertinent comments on his *Style*, see Horsley, *New Documents*, pp. 49–62; cf. pp. 5–40, with his criticism of the "Jewish Greek" hypothesis as well.

INTRODUCTION: *STYLE* xxiii

the Greek of the New Testament. The first point is regarding what he calls "the almost complete absence of classical standards in nearly every author" of the New Testament.[44] His second point is that the distinctions made in the classical language have been virtually eliminated in the Greek of the New Testament. Such conclusions raise the legitimate question of how to describe the Greek of the New Testament. Turner contends that "it is not that Biblical Greek has no standards at all, but pains must be taken to discover them outside the sphere of classical Greek, even outside secular Greek altogether, although the living Koine must be kept in mind always."[45] Turner clearly positions Biblical Greek, including the Greek of the New Testament, as consciously following patterns that are recognizably Greek but moving beyond or outside of those of the secular Greek of the time. To explore this situation, Turner examines the influence of the Septuagint and of what he calls "Semitic idiom" on New Testament Greek.[46] His research as found in this volume "does suggest that Bibl[ical] Greek is a unique language with a unity and character of its own,"[47] to the point that the Septuagintal influence has resulted in the biblical books having a similar linguistic character different from that of earlier classical or contemporary documentary papyri, with some resemblances of books reflecting clear Semitic sources. After citing a number of examples, Turner closes by claiming not to wish to try to exceed the evidence in his conclusions, although he draws attention to Biblical Greek having a "remarkable unity within itself" that might well have contemporary relevance for those contemplating the question of the existence of a "Holy Ghost language."[48] This almost divine character is apparently to be expected, since both the content and the language of the Scriptures are unique. This introductory statement aptly describes

---

[44] Turner, *Syntax*, p. 2.
[45] Ibid., p. 3.
[46] Ibid., p. 4.
[47] Ibid.
[48] Ibid., p. 9.

Turner's perspective and places his subsequent description of Greek into an appropriate context.

When he turns to the description itself, Turner follows what he calls "a natural linguistic pattern: the building up of the sentence from its independent elements right to the complicated co-ordinations and subordinations of the period [meaning here compound sentence]."[49] Turner follows this linguistic pattern of building the sentence, a feature not found in many other Greek grammars, except perhaps for Edwin Mayser's grammar of the papyri.[50] However, his abbreviated discussion seems to assume basic knowledge of standard Greek syntax as he discusses how the Greek of the New Testament differs from either classical Greek or other Hellenistic or extra-biblical Greek. The resulting grammar is divided into two portions or what are called books. The first book—the larger of the two—concerns building up the sentence and is what Turner calls analytical. This first book is divided into three parts. Before he begins part one, however, Turner dedicates the first chapter to various types of substitution for nouns, including the article with various other elements. Some may find this initial chapter oddly placed, as none of the linguistic components of the sentence have yet been discussed. Part one in ten chapters addresses words used to build the sentence, with chapters on gender and number of nouns, comparison of adjectives and adverbs, vocatives, substantival use of the article and pronoun, and then six chapters on the verb, with chapters on voice, aspect and tense, the indicative and subjunctive moods, optative mood, infinitive as noun form of the verb, and participle as adjective form of the verb. This chapter treats the major parts of speech as components within the

---

[49] Ibid., p. 1.
[50] Edwin Mayser, *Grammatik der griechischen Papyri aus der Ptolemäerzeit* (3 vols.; vol. 1.1 rev. Hans Schmoll; Berlin: de Gruyter, 1906-1970), volume 2 (in three parts). See Horsley, *New Documents*, pp. 50-2.

sentence. A number of the categories within this section seem to reflect similar categories as are found in earlier grammars influenced by comparative philology, although at places Turner is cognizant of more recent twentieth-century developments. This is evident in the chapter on aspect and tense, in which Turner refers to both verbal aspect and lexical aspect. He claims that the Greek tense-forms express both "kind of *action*" or *Aktionsart* and "the state of the subject" or aspect (he uses the German "Aspekt"). However, he states that *Aktionsart* or "kind of action" is used to express the notion that "the tense-stems indicate the point of view from which the action or state is regarded,"[51] apparently conflating the two concepts under the term *Aktionsart*. The subsequent descriptions of use of verbs utilize a mix of both *Aktionsart* and aspect terminology, including "continuous" ("linear") and "instantaneous" ("punctiliar") as the major kinds of action, and traditional categories.[52] However, the voice and mood systems are not linguistically defined, with, instead, categories of usage being exemplified.

Part two in four chapters addresses word-groups used to define nouns or adjectives. Turner apparently divides the major parts of speech into nominals and verbals and in this chapter treats expansion of the nominal category. This includes chapters on adjectival and predicative use of the article (Turner uses the term "definite article" in the title but simply "article" in most other places), and then three relatively short chapters on the attributive relationship, with one chapter each for adjectives and numerals, for pronouns and pronominal adjectives, and for substantives. The third and final part of book one concerns words

---

[51] Turner, *Syntax*, p. 59. See note 1, where Turner includes a relatively full bibliography including Jens Holt, *Études d'Aspect* (Copenhagen: Universitetsforlaget I Aarhus, 1943), during Turner's time one of the only and latest books on aspect. The only other was Martin Sánchez Ruipérez, *Estructura del Sistema de Aspectos y Tiempos del Verbo Griego Antiguo: Análysis Funcional Sincrónico* (Salamanca: Colegio Trilingue de la Universidad, 1954).
[52] Turner, *Syntax*, p. 59 and following.

used to define a verb, with four chapters. This part is concerned with expansion of the verbal category. These chapters include predicative usage, cases without a preposition in relation to a verb, cases with a preposition in relation to the verb, and negatives. Thus, book one describes words and word-groups and how they are related to each other.

Book two—roughly only one-fifth of the entire volume—is concerned with the complete sentence, what Turner calls synthetic. There are two parts. Part one on the simple sentence contains five short chapters. These chapters focus upon subject and predicate without a subject, subject and predicate without a form of the verb "be," congruence, clausal subordination, and inconsistencies in complex sentences. Part two concerns connections between sentences. These three short chapters address coordinating particles, irregular subordination, and word order. Thus, book two concerns sentences and sentence compounding, along with the semantic relationships between and among these sentences. With that, the volume closes with indexes. Throughout the volume Turner makes clear his perspective on the nature of the Greek of the New Testament, by drawing attention to various Semitic elements at various points.

Turner's second scholarly volume on matters of Greek was entitled *Grammatical Insights into the New Testament*, published in 1965, only two years after *Syntax* and clearly benefiting from the research that he had completed on the previous volume. Turner frames this second volume as designed both for the interested person without technical competence in Greek (hence he uses transliteration as a means of ostensive accommodation) and for the specialist. His overriding purpose in the volume is to address the relevance and importance of matters of Greek grammar, including finer points of syntax, especially as they may inform Biblical Theology. Turner claims to share the perspective of James Barr that theology does not occur at the level of the word but at the level of the sentence,[53] with Turner emphasizing that the Semitic influence upon the use of Greek by the early Christian authors is even greater in syntax than in the language's lexicon. Turner makes clear that he is not advocating either a fundamentalist or neo-fundamentalist approach and he is certainly not advocating for an approach that takes an approximate view of the text through relying upon translation. Turner cites an appropriate quotation from the Manchester Old Testament scholar H. H. Rowley made already in 1963 concerning the importance of knowledge of the Greek or Hebrew language for study of the Bible: "One who made it his life's work to interpret French literature, but who could only read it in an English translation, would not be taken seriously; yet it is remarkable how many ministers of religion week by week expound a literature that they are unable to read save in translation!"[54] In a statement as timely in 1960 as it would be today, Turner cites R. A. Ward as stating that "he has been told by ministers that there is no need to 'waste time on Greek. It is all in the commentaries.'"[55] Turner's book is an attempt to show the value of Greek grammatical study by offering insights into the text by means of sometimes focused and specific and other times more general grammatical observations.

Turner includes forty-six relatively short studies, most of them subdivided into a number of even smaller studies, under six major chapter headings, before concluding with a chapter on "The Language of Jesus and His Disciples." It is impossible here to summarize even a small number of these short articles, although virtually all of them contain

---

[53] See James Barr, *The Semantics of Biblical Language* (Oxford: Oxford University Press, 1961), p. 233.
[54] H. H. Rowley, "Recent Foreign Theology," *Expository Times* 74 (September 1963), p. 383, cited in Turner, *Grammatical Insights*, p. 3.
[55] R. A. Ward, "The Preacher's Use of the Aorist," *Expository Times* 71 (June 1960), pp. 267–70, here p. 267, cited in Turner, *Grammatical Insights*, p. 3. Ward taught at Wycliffe College in Toronto, Ontario, Canada. One might, in this day and age, indeed think that "it is all in commentaries" on the basis of their size and attempt to be comprehensive in scope in virtually all regards (apart possibly from Greek, one notes), but we know from simple examination of them that this is hardly the case.

matters of interest to the Greek student. Some of the positions advocated by Turner have become well known, while others arguably merit further consideration than they have received to date. The first section is on what he calls the "grammar of God." In this chapter, with three studies included on "God," "Jesus is God," and "A holy spirit and the Holy Ghost," Turner discusses a variety of grammatical constructions that have implications for understanding God, many of them related to the use of the article.[56] He directly responds to modern theology as represented by the biblically conservative but theologically liberal scholar J. A. T. Robinson[57] by showing how the use of the Greek article is important for establishing the subject and predicate of a Greek clause, all in the service of clear theology. In a discussion of Jesus as God, Turner sees Greek grammar supporting such a notion in several key passages (although he does not refer to Granville Sharp). Chapter two concerns Jesus of Nazareth. The largest chapter, this one includes fifteen subordinate studies. The first is on the census in Luke 2, where Turner argues that the word often translated "first" should be translated "before," indicating that the Lukan census is the one before Quirinius's in AD 6. This is an argument that merits further consideration. Turner argues for a reformulation of Mark 1:1 and 4 by placing vv. 2–3 in parenthesis. He also argues for a reformulation of Mark 1:9 as "Jesus of Nazareth in Galilee came." Turner claims that John 2:4 should be "Madam, leave this to me" on the basis of Semitic influence and implication. His survey of the meaning of the ἵνα clause in Mark 4:12 is insightful, as is his conclusion regarding human deliberation. He argues for the kingdom of God being a human condition in Luke 17:21, and for "he went outside" for the verb ἐπιβαλών in Mark 14:72, based on the parallel in Matthew. Jesus may not have given a clear "yes" to

---

[56] I note that many times, although not always, Turner refers to the "definite article" in *Grammatical Insights*, whereas in *Syntax* he usually refers simply to the "article." One wonders if this is inadvertent, or whether there is some theological significance he is attaching to the terminology in *Grammatical Insights*.

[57] John A. T. Robinson, *Honest to God* (London: SCM, 1963).

the question of his identity at his trial, thus maintaining the messianic secret despite his personal beliefs (Matt 26:64). Turner argues for a past and present understanding of the perfect in Matt 16:19 as a means of alleviating human responsibility.

Chapter three contains five shorter studies. The first concerns Acts 22:3 and 26:4, where Turner believes they both point to Tarsus as the place of Paul's upbringing, not Jerusalem. He is probably correct on this point. Turner also takes the reference to "I" in Romans 7 and elsewhere as a rhetorical device. He believes that a distinction can be made regarding "hearing" on the basis of case in Acts 9:4. He further argues that Paul's purpose for going to Rome was to preach his own point of view (Rom 1:15). Turner even entertains the idea that Gal 6:11 in context implies that Paul had literally rather than metaphorically been crucified. Chapter four on Paul's teaching contains twelve shorter studies. He sees Paul as arguing for reconciliation or freedom from an unbelieving spouse in 1 Cor 7:10–16, and 1 Cor 7:21 indicating a slave should take the opportunity to be free. Turner argues for both objective and subjective genitive in "faith of God." He also argues for Pauline soteriology being corporate, and so the conjunction in Rom 5:12 is "in" or "by whom," not "because." He further argues for a mystical use of the preposition ἐν. 2 Corinthians 5, Turner argues, is about being unclothed in an intermediate state. Chapter five has six subunits on John. Turner argues here that in John 1:40 the Other Disciple is John the son of Zebedee, the traditionally ascribed author of the Gospel. As for John 1:3–4, Turner follows the early church fathers in rendering it "as to that which has been made, he was its life," interpreting the construction as an independent nominative. "Born of bloods" in John 1:13 refers to a joint contribution to birth, either of both male and female or of human and spiritual. John 3:16 using the indicative rather than the infinitive with ὥστε is about the incarnation rather than about God's love. Turner argues for an imperatival use of ἵνα in John's Gospel (e.g., in John 9:3).

The contrast in 1 John 2:1 and 3:9, based upon tense-forms, is between committing a sin and becoming a sinner. Chapter six has five subsections on other New Testament writers. However, Turner returns to Acts 4:2 to find unity in use of the preposition ἐν. He also examines two instances from Revelation, three from James, several from 1 Peter, and one from Hebrews. Some of Turner's explanations are concerned with lexical items, some with entire clauses, some with verbal aspect, and some with the rendering of idioms, and a number with other grammatical issues. Sometimes he argues for Markan parenthesis, and sometimes he is not certain of the linguistic significance, even if he observes the usage, as in the rendering of the perfect imperative in Mark 4:39.

Turner concludes his grammatical insights with his essay on the language of Jesus and his disciples, in which he argues that the disciples certainly spoke Aramaic but they also spoke and wrote in a dialect of Greek with sufficient Semitic influence, especially from the Septuagint, to be called Jewish Greek. As a result, Jesus may have spoken Greek in such situations as his conversation with the Syro-phoenician woman, his encounter with the Roman centurion, and his trial before Pilate. Rather than this being a sign of bilingualism or only a temporary linguistic situation, Turner argues for this usage as what he calls "the normal language of Jesus, at least in Galilee—rather a separate dialect of Greek than a form of the Koine, and distinguishable as something parallel to classical, Hellenistic, Koine and Imperial Greek."[58] He is skeptical about how much Hebrew Jesus would have known and used. Turner is more inclined to accept the view of T. K. Abbott from 1891 that Greek was Jesus's primary language, based upon the argument that selective and limited instances of use of Aramaic in Mark's Gospel probably reflect those occasions when Jesus used Aramaic, possibly with those who

---

[58] Turner, *Grammatical Insights*, p. 183.

only spoke Aramaic.[59] The fact that this Greek has resemblances to the documentary papyri may be because the papyri themselves reflect Semitic influence. However, none of the papyri have the sustained style of usage found in the Greek of the New Testament. This language has its own linguistic unity and consistency and character whose effect is "to evoke a sense of the holy and to point the reader beyond," with the book of Revelation reflecting this "hieratic tongue" most sublimely.[60] *Grammatical Insights* draws upon examples from the Greek New Testament informed throughout by Turner's findings in his *Syntax*, which relies upon his theory of Jewish Greek used by early Christians, a position summarized in his final essay in the volume. This volume is worth revisiting, whether one agrees with Turner's conclusions or not, to benefit from his provocative analyses.

In his *Style*, published in 1976, Turner produced the fourth and final volume in Moulton's *A Grammar of New Testament Greek*. This also represents the third and final book by Turner on Greek grammar excluding lexicography. A summary and discussion of the volume is found in the next section of this essay, after completing the treatment of Turner's last major scholarly work.

Turner's fourth and final book on Greek language, as well as his last written book, is entitled *Christian Words* and was published in 1980. As mentioned above, this volume seems to contain in some ways the most categorical of Turner's statements regarding the Greek of the New Testament. He lays out his viewpoint in his "Introduction." Turner begins where he left off with his earlier statement from Barr in *Grammatical Insights* regarding a syntactical over a lexicographical approach to New Testament theology, by claiming that exegesis must take into account the larger context (what he calls the "total environment"): "The paragraph

---

[59] T. K. Abbott, *Essays, Chiefly on the Original Texts of the Old and New Testaments* (London: Longmans, Green, 1891), pp. 129–82, esp. 147–61.
[60] Turner, *Grammatical Insights*, p. 188.

determines the gist of the individual words within it."[61] However, Turner then takes a turn toward endorsing the value of the individual word, especially a word of Holy Scripture. His concern is with Christianity communicating in the context of the contemporary world, a context in which, at least figuratively speaking, there are conflicting biblical and secular languages, and the Christian must be knowledgeable about the language of the Bible. Turner, endorsing an infalliblist view of the Scriptures, argues that those who were inspired to write the Bible were given the task of conveying God's language through the earthly language of Biblical Greek, which we must understand to understand the Bible. "More than fifteen years ago," Turner states, "my studies in syntax led me to ask whether the Biblical language was not unique, and since then investigation of the style of Biblical Greek has confirmed that impression."[62] Turner thus reinforces his view of the unique Greek of the Bible, a position tied very closely to his view of inspiration and coming exceptionally close to advocacy of Holy Ghost Greek. Having dealt with syntax and style, he continues: "Now, in turn, the vocabulary of the same kind of Greek has come under discussion, only to strengthen it."[63] This volume contains examples of what he calls Christian Words. He deals with a surprisingly large number of words within this volume (although it is difficult to specify the number, as his headings are English concepts, under which Greek words are listed and treated—the estimate on the back cover is over 450; see below on this mixing of concepts and words).

For this volume, Turner defines his Christian Words under four categories.[64] At the outset, he states, "By 'Christian words' I have in

---

[61] Turner, *Christian Words*, p. viii.
[62] Ibid., p. ix.
[63] Ibid.
[64] For an assessment of Turner's view of Christian words, see Stanley E. Porter, "Is *dipsuchos* (James 1,8; 4,8) a 'Christian' Word?," *Biblica* 71 (1990), pp. 469–98, which I draw upon here. Some of the criticisms raised include Turner's disregard of Barr's admonitions regarding biblical theology and lexical fallacies (such as confusion of word and concept, among others), his not noting other linguistic explanations of semantic shifts, and his apparent lack

mind Greek terms which so far as I know the first believers devised for themselves."[65] Turner recognizes that recent New Testament Greek lexicography (he cites Walter Bauer, but this actually goes back much further to Deissmann) has reduced the number of such words to a very small number. He offers as examples (in English rendering) newly formed compounds such as "little-faith," "eye-service," "double-minded," and "respect of persons."[66] Turner, however, has three further categories that greatly re-expand the categories. The second category includes words "which acquire a deeper sense and a new consecration within the Christian vocabulary."[67] He includes here the words "truth," "church," "parable," "way," "covenant," "Word," "saint," and "angel." He also includes words heightened in frequency, such as "goodness," "reverence," "evangelist," and "beloved." Finally, he includes words used with a different sense than in their secular sources, such as "Bishop," "Presbyter," "Deacon," "brother," "gospel," "koinōnia," "parousia," and "salvation." The third category is reserved for those words that, "through their Biblical association, had deployed a new level of meaning in addition to their gist hitherto."[68] Words included by him here include *doxa* adding the meaning of "glory," *homologō* adding "praise," *glōssai* adding "nations," and *diathēkē* adding "covenant." The fourth and final category that Turner posits is where Christian usage has "quite changed their former meaning."[69] Examples here include "hypocrite" not being used of an actor, "peace" not being used to indicate the ceasing of strife, "tender mercies" not indicating one's intestines, and "parable" not being a maxim.

---

of differentiation between *langue* and *parole* or code and text, along with some questions of whether his analyses of individual words are correct.
[65] Turner, *Christian Words*, p. ix.
[66] Ibid., p. x. Turner concedes Hellenistic influence even upon these words, although he seems to confine it to spelling.
[67] Ibid.
[68] Ibid.
[69] Ibid.

The question becomes how one determines such meanings. Turner posits several steps. The first, he claims, is to return to the notion of context or "their immediate linguistic environment."[70] However, this proposal is intriguing, as Turner wishes to call into question, to the point of virtual outright rejection, both Jewish usage contemporary with that of the New Testament and, perhaps more importantly, the evidence from the Greek documentary papyri especially from Egypt. The theological reason for this is clear: God chose not to communicate in this way. In explicitly rejecting Moulton's position on koine Greek,[71] Turner directly states, "God seems not to have used the contemporary vernacular speech [as Moulton believed, and before him J. B. Lightfoot posited][72] without revolutionizing it, whether in style (or lack of it), whether in sentence construction [as evidenced in Turner's *Syntax* and *Style*], or whether in vocabulary."[73] Turner thus claims that "the early Christians had their own form of speech, and I account it to be as 'sacred' in vocabulary as I found it in syntax and style."[74]

Turner recognizes, however, that the language he is examining is still recognizably Greek, with many words still used with recognizably Greek meanings. This leads him to attempt to tie his view of Greek to the view promoted by Deissmann and Moulton. He states that what he is calling "Christian Greek is essentially the old Attic dialect of the secular language extended and popularized by contact with other dialects and by its employment among the conquered peoples of the Greek

---

[70] Ibid.
[71] Ibid., p. xi, quoting and rejecting Moulton, *Prolegomena*, p. 5. One cannot help but notice that this calls into question the continuity that Turner posits between Moulton's and his views of Greek, as stated in Turner, *Style*, p. vii. See further below.
[72] Turner cites the well-known statement by J. B. Lightfoot, who wrote before the discovery of the Greek documentary papyri in Egypt, that "if we could only recover letters that ordinary people wrote to each other without any thought of being literary, we should have the greatest possible help for the understanding of the language of the New Testament" (J. B. Lightfoot from notes of lectures given in 1863, cited by Moulton, *Prolegomena*, p. 242).
[73] Turner, *Christian Words*, p. xi.
[74] Ibid.

and Roman empires."[75] Such a position, as advocated by Deissmann, Moulton, and others who have followed them, is supported by abundant papyrological evidence—although such a position, Turner argues, is also directly linked to a socioeconomic view of early Christianity that links vernacular language with the lowest socioeconomic classes. Rather than looking to such secular origins for the nature of Greek, Turner posits, one must look to the religious environment of early Christianity formed by the Greek Old Testament, which itself preceded the Greek of the New Testament and had already evidenced religious transformation. The basis of determining the Christian vocabulary of the New Testament is not its socioeconomic or any other secular environment but its Christian thought-world that was already thoroughly biblical in its orientation. In the numerous examples that follow, Turner proceeds alphabetically—in English—through the vocabulary of the New Testament. Although he often recognizes the meaning of the word in secular Greek, he then proceeds to examine the word as Biblical or Christian Greek.

Style

In his *Style*, Turner produced the fourth and final volume in Moulton's *A Grammar of New Testament Greek*. This volume, his last, was published in 1976. In the "Preface" to *Style*, Turner recognizes that his perspective is different from that of Moulton and even Howard, and hence does not represent a unified position on the nature of New Testament Greek within the set of grammar volumes.[76] However, as mentioned above, Turner rightly notes that Moulton did in some ways envision not just a third volume on syntax, which he himself had originally intended to

---

[75] Ibid., p. xii.
[76] Turner, *Style*, p. vii.

write, but also a fourth volume on style. Turner also claims, however, that his views have, despite the passage of seven decades from the origination of the grammar project, been consistent with Moulton's, to the point that Moulton's son, Harold K. Moulton, had approved of the fourth volume on style being included within *A Grammar of New Testament Greek*. Turner does not reconcile these positions.

The first and most important matter for a volume on style is definition of it. For his treatment, Turner begins his "Introduction" with the question regarding the nature of the Greek of the New Testament, that is, regarding the "dialect" of its Greek, and whether that dialect is unified.[77] For Turner, this question is inextricably joined to the question of what he defines as style. He also notes that style is closely related to syntax and admits that some duplication between the two is inevitable. Style, for Turner, "concerns itself with grammatical and other linguistic features which distinguish the work of one author from that of another," that is, he attempts "to isolate comparative tendencies and differing techniques."[78] To this point, style appears to be a reconfiguration of syntax. However, it is more than this. It also involves "wider categories, such as word-order, rhetoric, parallelism and parenthesis."[79] He continues by noting that it also involves "the irregularities in sentence-construction which result from Semitic influence," in order "to investigate the ways in which the dialect or variety of Greek found here is distinctive from the main stream of the language."[80] He believes that there is much evidence of such Semitic influence at every turn, due to the fact that early Christians were probably bilingual with Aramaic and Greek, and possibly Hebrew. Turner recognizes that there is the possibility of confusion over his

---

[77] Ibid., p. 1.
[78] Ibid. Turner favorably quotes the definition by K. J. Dover "that style is 'a group of aspects of language,' a contrasting of linguistic facts among various authors" (*Greek Word Order* [Cambridge: Cambridge University Press, 1960], p. 66).
[79] Turner, *Style*, p. 1.
[80] Ibid.

definition of style, and so he clarifies by noting that, even though each biblical author has a distinct style, "the styles are not so far apart as to impair the inner homogeneity of Biblical Greek," that is, the unity of his Jewish Greek is not compromised by authorial variation.[81] Further, he notes that he rejects the notion of Semitic sources, apart from in rare instances. Turner concludes the introduction with a brief summary of his findings for the New Testament authors.

The rest of the volume on style is organized around thirteen chapters. The first concerns sources behind the individual Gospels, followed by chapters on the sub-corpora of the New Testament: Mark, Matthew, Luke–Acts, John, Paul, the Pastoral Epistles, Hebrews, James, 1 Peter, the Johannine letters, Jude and 2 Peter, and Revelation. The first chapter, on sources for the Gospels, constitutes in many ways a defense of the author's Jewish Greek hypothesis. Turner first gives credence to various circumscribed theories arguing for written Semitic sources behind various parts of the New Testament (but dismissing those that claim this for the entire New Testament), to the point that he accepts a multilingual, possibly even a trilingual, linguistic environment, certainly with Aramaic among the Jews of Palestine, with Greek at least for trade with Gentiles, and possibly with Hebrew being used in the time of Jesus. Turner moves from this to his Jewish Greek hypothesis: "Since the quality of New Testament Greek is decidedly Semitic in varying degrees, there may well have been a spoken language in common use among these trilingual Jews which would render superfluous the hypothesis of source-translation as an explanation of certain phenomena in New Testament Greek," to the point of suggesting that what he calls "uncommon Greek idioms" are common in Aramaic and Hebrew and indicate "that such a body of idiom, as is exposed everywhere in this volume [*Style*], comprised a distinct dialect or

---

[81] Ibid., p. 2.

branch of the Koine Greek."[82] He extends his theory further by noting ancient evidence of the use of Greek, indicating that "Greek was a living tongue among first-century Jews even around Jerusalem."[83] This came about as a result of the conquests of Alexander in the fourth century BC including Palestine, with a range of epigraphical and literary evidence in support. "It should not be considered improbable, therefore, that Jesus normally spoke in Greek, albeit a simple Semitic kind of speech."[84] This Semitic Greek was influenced by both Hebrew and Aramaic. Whereas Jesus's language may reflect Aramaic, the evangelists sometimes reflect both. Turner's "Semiticized Biblical Greek" as a unified dialect, he claims, may remove the feeling of certainty sought by some interpreters who wish to go back to original Aramaic sources, but it is what Turner believes is to be found in the New Testament.[85]

In discussing the individual books of the New Testament, Turner often follows a common pattern. That pattern is, usually after a relatively short introductory section, to discuss Aramaisms, Hebraisms, and then Semitisms, before concluding with discussion of features of the subcorpus. This general pattern is followed, for example, for Mark, Matthew, Luke–Acts, John in a slightly different configuration, James along with several other prior discussions, the Johannine letters again with several other prior discussions, and Revelation again with several other prior discussions. The treatment of Mark includes an extended discussion of Mark's so-called "mannered style" and Latinisms mostly in Mark. The chapter on Matthew compares the Semitic "quality" of Matthew and Mark, arguing for Matthew's "smoother style" and some distinctive Matthean features. Discussion of Luke–Acts includes treatment of Lukan

---

[82] Ibid., p. 7. Turner claims as his ally in this position Gerhard Mussies, *The Morphology of Koine Greek* (Leiden: Brill, 1971), pp. 96–7.
[83] Turner, *Style*, p. 8.
[84] Ibid.
[85] Ibid., p. 9. He refers in particular to Vincent Taylor, *The Gospel According to St. Mark* (London: Macmillan, 1955), p. 65, as one of those expositors.

sources, literary features, a section on Semitisms where Luke is least likely to have originated with sources, and a final section on Christian elements of Lukan style (see Turner's subsequent book on this topic, *Christian Words*, treated above). The study of John includes discussion of sources, the influence of the Septuagint, then discussion of types of Semitisms, before concluding with brief discussion of such elements as clause ordering, particles, prepositions, John's constrained vocabulary, and what Turner thinks are needless stylistic varieties. James treats authorship, several form-critical issues, and its close relationship to wisdom literature, before discussing types of Semitisms and concluding with another chapter on Christian style. Treatment of the Johannine letters discusses authorship, unity with the Gospel, and its own integrity, before discussion of Semitic elements. Finally, examination of Revelation begins with sections on sources, grammatical solecisms, redundant expressions, and discussion of various views of the Greek found in Revelation, before discussing types of Semitisms.

By contrast with these chapters, the chapters on the other sub-corpora are arranged individually. The chapter on Paul excludes the Pastoral Epistles and divides the remaining ten letters into four groups, with group two being the four main letters. The character of this group is treated first, seeing them as private letters but with literary features, and then the style of Ephesians is contrasted with this major group. After a chapter on harsh elements in Paul's style, Turner refutes a Hellenistic hypothesis regarding Paul and discusses Paul's Semitic style. He treats Paul's biblically influenced syntax, biblical vocabulary, Biblical Greek word order, and Biblical Greek style, before concluding with discussion of Paul's amanuensis. The Pastoral Epistles are treated separately, beginning with a discussion of what Turner characterizes as an elevated koine style relatively free from Semitic influence, even if it is not elegant Greek. Turner's discussion of Hebrews begins with such literary characteristics as rhythm and other features, but he still discerns an underlying influence of Jewish Greek, which is tied to speculation on authorship by a Jew or Jewish proselyte. Treatment of 1 Peter discusses the issues of integrity, the role of an amanuensis, and some literary features along with significant Semitic characteristics. Finally, the chapter on Jude and 2 Peter includes a section on Jude's literary language and Jewish features, and then 2 Peter's literary features and Jewish character, before comparing the two. One sees a number of common major areas of discussion within Turner's examination of sub-corpora of the New Testament, such as various types of Semitisms, the issue of Christian language including both syntax and vocabulary, and debate over literary features and their relationship to Jewish Greek. Turner also includes a number of other features not always treated in every book, usually in support of his Jewish Greek hypothesis.

The criticisms of Greg Horsley of Turner's *Syntax* in many ways apply to Turner's *Style*.[86] Horsley notes in particular that Turner's work was already dated at the time of its appearance. Since Turner relies heavily upon the approach of his *Syntax* for his *Style*—in some ways simply taking the broader data and individualizing them for the New Testament authors according to sub-corpus—his comparative and often diachronic approach neglects attention to synchronic elements of the language as system. The comparative data that Turner seems to rely upon are inadequately reported and differentiated, leading to imprecise and potentially misleading conclusions. Turner's Semitic Greek hypothesis, including his assertion of its unique character, remains firmly in place, even though further research has called such a conclusion into question. One must also note the lack of concord between Moulton's and Turner's views of how to describe Greek. The character of the Greek of the New Testament continues to be central to this volume, to the point that both the third and fourth volumes represent a recognizably different approach to Greek than is represented in the first two volumes. Turner

---

[86] Horsley, *New Documents*, pp. 49–62.

takes into consideration adequate definitions of what constitutes style in the introduction to his work, but his application often focuses upon a limited range of topics, in particular a variety of Semitic elements (although he also often treats issues not clearly germane to a notion of style), rather than examining style as the situationally or literarily located instances of usage by individual authors in relation to the language system.[87] His discussion seems to focus upon those issues that he believes reinforce his description of Biblical Greek as Jewish Greek, rather than differentiating instances of usage in relation to the language system. In other words, Turner seems to not make a useful distinction between *langue* and *parole*, or code and text. Nevertheless, in light of the history of discussion of Moulton's grammar and Turner's having not just brought it to completion but also extended it to a fourth volume, we should be grateful and beholden to Turner for his diligence in writing this volume on style.

Nigel Turner Select Bibliography

This bibliography is organized roughly chronologically, so that one can trace the progress of Turner's intellectual thought. As a result, some works without his authorship appear within this list.

Turner, Nigel. "Eschatology in the Old Testament Literature." Unpublished paper, 1936.
Turner, Nigel. "Were the Gospels Written in Greek or Aramaic?" *Evangelical Quarterly* 21 (1949), pp. 42–8.
Turner, Nigel. "St. John's Eternal Word." *Evangelical Quarterly* 22 (1950), pp. 243–8.

---

[87] See David Crystal, *A Dictionary of Language* (Chicago, IL: University of Chicago Press, 2nd ed., 1999), p. 323.

Turner, Nigel. "The Unique Character of Biblical Greek." *Vetus Testamentum* 5 (1955), pp. 208–13.

Turner, Nigel. "The 'Testament of Abraham': Problems in Biblical Greek." *New Testament Studies* 1 (1955), pp. 219–23.

Turner, Nigel. "The Relation of Luke I and II to Hebraic Sources and to the Rest of Luke–Acts." *New Testament Studies* 2 (1955), pp. 100–9.

Turner, Nigel. "An Alleged Semitism." *Expository Times* 66 (1955), pp. 252–4.

Turner, Nigel. "The Translation of Μοιχᾶται ἐπ' Αὐτήν in Mark 10:11." *Bible Translator* 7.4 (1956), pp. 151–2.

Turner, Nigel. "The Greek Translators of Ezekiel." *Journal of Theological Studies* n.s. 7 (1956), pp. 12–24.

Turner, Nigel. "The Style of St. Mark's Eucharistic Words." *Journal of Theological Studies* n.s. 8.1 (1957), pp. 108–11.

Turner, Nigel. "The New-Born King (Matthew ii. 2)." *Expository Times* 68 (1957), p. 122.

Turner, Nigel. "The Preposition *en* in the New Testament." *Bible Translator* 10.3 (July 1959), pp. 113–20.

Turner, Nigel. "The Minor Verbal Agreements of Mt. and Lk. against Mk." In *Studia Evangelica*. Texte und Untersuchungen 73. Berlin: Akademie-Verlag, 1959. pp. 223–34.

Turner, Nigel. "Modern Issues in Biblical Studies: Philology in New Testament Studies." *Expository Times* 71 (1960), pp. 104–7.

Turner, Nigel. "The Language of the New Testament." In Matthew Black and H. H. Rowley (eds.), *Peake's Commentary on the Bible*. London: Thomas Nelson, 1962. pp. 659–62.

Turner, Nigel. "Revelation." In Matthew Black and H. H. Rowley (eds.), *Peake's Commentary on the Bible*. London: Thomas Nelson, 1962. pp. 1043–61.

Turner, Nigel. "Absalom" (I, pp. 22–3), "Acraba" (I, p. 28), "Agia" (I, p. 55), "Alexander" (I, pp. 77–8), "Alexandra" (I, pp. 78–9), "Asphar" (I, p. 260), "Attharias" (I, p. 317), "Calamolalus" (I, p. 482), "Callisthenes" (I, p. 490), "Chadiasans" (I, p. 549), "Chaereas" (I, p. 549), "Chaphenatha" (I, p. 552), "Charax" (I, p. 552), "Cos" (I, p. 701), "Daphne" (I, p. 769), "Dathema" (I, p. 771), "Delos" (I, p. 815), "Dionysia" (I, p. 844), "Elasa" (II, p. 71), "Epiphanes" (II, p. 123), "Esdras, Books of" (II, pp. 140–2), "Eumenes"

INTRODUCTION: *STYLE* xliii

(II, p. 179), "Eupolemus" (II, p. 181), "Gymnasium" (II, p. 502), "Hanukkah" (II, p. 523), "Hasmoneans" (II, pp. 529–35), "Hyrcanus" (II, p. 669), "Indian Driver" (II, p. 700), "Joakim" (II, p. 909), "Joseph, Prayer of" (II, p. 979), "Kedron" (III, p. 5), "Ladder of Tyre" (III, pp. 57–8), "Lysias (Syrian)" (III, p. 193), "Maccabeus" (III, p. 215), "Machaerus" (III, pp. 217–18), "Menelaus" (III, pp. 349–50), "Myndos" (III, p. 478), "Nicanor" (III, pp. 546–7), "Orthosia" (III, p. 609), "Phaselis" (III, p. 781), "Sampsames" (IV, p. 198), "Seat, Moses" (IV, p. 260), "Seleucia" (IV, pp. 263–4), "Seleucia in Syria" (IV, pp. 264–6), "Seleucus" (IV, pp. 266–7), "Sicyon" (IV, p. 343), "Side" (IV, p. 343), "Symeon" (IV, p. 476), "Tephon" (IV, pp. 573–4), "Toparchy" (IV, pp. 672–3), "Touch" (IV, p. 675), "Tribune" (IV, p. 710), "Trypho" (IV, p. 717). In George Arthur Buttrick (ed.), *The Interpreter's Dictionary of the Bible*. 4 vols. New York: Abingdon, 1962.

Turner, Nigel. *Syntax*, Volume 3 of *A Grammar of New Testament Greek* by James Hope Moulton. Edinburgh: T&T Clark, 1963.

Turner, Nigel. "The Transmission of the Text: B. New Testament." In T. W. Manson (ed.), *A Companion to the Bible*. Second edition edited by H. H. Rowley. Edinburgh: T&T Clark, 1963. pp. 163–82.

Turner, Nigel. "Beatitudes" (pp. 93–4), "Beloved" (pp. 95–6), "Love" with GGF (pp. 593–5), "Lovely" (p. 595), "Lover" (p. 595). In Frederick C. Grant and H. H. Rowley (eds.), *Dictionary of the Bible*. Edinburgh: T&T Clark, 1963.

Turner, Nigel. "Second Thoughts: VII. Papyrus Finds." *Expository Times* 76 (1964), pp. 44–8.

Turner, Nigel. *Grammatical Insights into the New Testament*. Edinburgh: T&T Clark, 1965.

Reider, Joseph. *An Index to Aquila: Greek-Hebrew, Hebrew-Greek, Latin-Hebrew, with the Syriac and Armenian Evidence*. Completed and revised by Nigel Turner. Supplements to Vetus Testamentum 12. Leiden: Brill, 1966.

Turner, Nigel. "Q in Recent Thought." *Expository Times* 80 (1969), pp. 324–8.

Turner, Nigel. "The Church's Attitude to the State in the New Testament." *Journal of Theology for Southern Africa* 2 (1973), pp. 41–52.

The Translator's New Testament. London: British and Foreign Bible Society, 1973.

Turner, Nigel. "Jewish and Christian Influence on New Testament Vocabulary." *Novum Testamentum* 16 (1974), pp. 149–60.

Turner, Nigel. "The Literary Character of New Testament Greek." *New Testament Studies* 20 (1974), pp. 107–14.

Turner, Nigel. *The Art of the Greek Orthodox Church: A Study in Stylization*. University of Rhodesia Series in Humanities. Salisbury, Rhodesia: University of Rhodesia, 1976.

Turner, Nigel. *Style*, Volume 4 of *A Grammar of New Testament Greek* by James Hope Moulton. Edinburgh: T&T Clark, 1976.

Turner, Nigel. "The Quality of the Greek of Luke–Acts." In J. K. Elliott (ed.), *Studies in New Testament Language and Text: Essays in Honour of George D. Kilpatrick*. Supplements to Novum Testamentum 44. Leiden: Brill, 1976. pp. 387–400.

Turner, Nigel. *Christian Words*. Edinburgh: T&T Clark, 1980.

Turner, Nigel. "Biblical Greek: The Peculiar Language of a Peculiar People." In Elizabeth A. Livingstone (ed.), *Studia Evangelica* VII. Berlin: Akademie-Verlag, 1982. pp. 505–12.

PREFACE

The appearance of the various volumes of this Grammar spans the greater part of a century. The first volume (Prolegomena) was the work of Dr. J. H. Moulton himself in the first decade of the century, the second (Accidence) was the work of both Dr. Moulton and his eminent disciple, Dr. W. F. Howard, but the volumes on Syntax and Style have been entirely the work of one of a younger generation. Because of that, and because the enterprise reflects so wide a passage of time, it is inevitable that the viewpoint of the Grammar upon the nature of New Testament Greek is not entirely a unity, and there are traces of the radical development to be expected as the state of these studies has progressed. Although Dr. Moulton did not visualize a fourth volume, nevertheless the Introduction to volume Two demonstrated his deep concern with questions of Style as well as with Accidence and Syntax. I am therefore glad that despite the passage of time I have found my own views for the most part to be consistent with those of the Grammar's originator even at the distance of seven decades from its inception, and I am also glad that Dr. Harold K. Moulton has kindly approved the suggestion that this fourth and final volume be added to his father's Grammar.

I would wish to express appreciation once again of the expertise of our printers, Morrison and Gibb, Ltd., in dealing so smoothly and competently with complex problems of typography.

Of my renowned and distinguished Publishers I cannot adequately speak the praise due from myself and fellow-students in this field, but I pay this humble tribute to T. & T. Clark's large share in producing a rising generation of scholars who, with reverent devotion, keep the light of Biblical Greek erudition shining in a dark world.

NIGEL TURNER
Epiphany 1975   Cambridge

ABBREVIATIONS

The works most often mentioned are abbreviated thus:

Bauer : W. Bauer, *Griechisch-Deutsches Wörterbuch* . . .[4], Berlin 1952.
Beyer : K. Beyer, *Semitische Syntax im Neuen Testament*, I Satzlehre i, Göttingen 1962.
Black[3] : Matthew Black, *An Aramaic Approach to the Gospels and Acts*, 3rd ed., Oxford 1967.
Grammar I : J. H. Moulton, *A Grammar of New Testament Greek*, vol. I, Edinburgh, 3rd ed. 1908.
Grammar II : J. H. Moulton, W. F. Howard, *A Grammar of New Testament Greek*, vol. II, Edinburgh 1919-1929.
Grammar III: Nigel Turner, *A Grammar of New Testament Greek*, vol. III, Edinburgh 1963.
Grammatical Insights : Nigel Turner, *Grammatical Insights into the New Testament*, Edinburgh 1965.
Helbing : Robert Helbing, *Die Kasussyntax der Verba bei den Septuaginta*, Göttingen 1928.
LXX : Septuagint.
MM : J. H. Moulton, G. Milligan, *Vocabulary of the Greek New Testament*, London 1930.
Mayser : E. Mayser, *Grammatik der griechischen Papyri aus der Ptolemäerzeit*, Berlin and Leipzig, II 1 1926 ; II 2, 3, 1934.
NT : New Testament.
Pernot : H. Pernot, *Études sur la Langue des Évangiles*, Paris 1927.
Radermacher[2] : L. Radermacher, *Neutestamentliche Grammatik*, Tübingen, 2nd ed. 1925.
S.-B. : H. L. Strack, P. Billerbeck, *Kommentar zum Neuen Testament aus Talmud und Midrasch*, Munich, III, 4th ed. 1955.
TWNT : *Theologisches Wörterbuch zum Neuen Testament*, ed. G. Kittel and others, Tübingen 1933ff.

Periodicals

Biblica : *Biblica*, Rome.
BJRL : *Bulletin of the John Rylands Library*, Manchester.
CBQ : *Catholic Biblical Quarterly*, Washington.
ET : *Expository Times*, Edinburgh.
JBL : *Journal of Biblical Literature*, Philadelphia, PA.
JBR : *Journal of the Bible and Religion*, Bethlehem, PA.

JTS NS : *Journal of Theological Studies*, New Series, Oxford.
Nov.T : *Novum Testamentum*. Leiden.
NTS : *New Testament Studies*, Cambridge.
ZAW : *Zeitschrift für die alttestamentliche Wissenschaft*, Berlin.
ZNT : *Zeitschrift für die neutestamentliche Wissenschaft*, Berlin.

Other works are cited in full at their first mention, and other abbreviations are as in vols. I–III.

The bibliography at the end of each chapter is intended only to be selective, and apologies are offered to authors whose works do not appear.

INTRODUCTION

The characteristic components in the style of divergent New Testament authors have some practical pertinence for exegesis and for textual criticism, both in adjudging which alternative exposition of any verse conforms with the same author's style elsewhere throughout his work, and also in determining which of several variant readings has the highest internal probability on account of stylistic consistency.

In itself, too, the nature of the Greek in the New Testament demands close attention, raising the question as to what kind of " dialect " it is, and whether it is even a unity within itself. Each style is different, as the student discovers when he turns to the language of the Apocalypse after revelling in the charms of the Epistle to the Hebrews.

In the investigation, I do not seek to drive a rigid distinction between syntax, which was the subject of our third volume, and style. Since style, in our view, involves the same considerations as syntax, there must be some duplication, but this fourth volume rather concerns itself with grammatical and other linguistic features which distinguish the work of one author from that of another. Here we are attempting to isolate comparative tendencies and differing techniques. The reader is referred to the perspicuous distinction between style and syntax made by Professor K. J. Dover, when he claims that style is " a group of aspects of language," a contrasting of linguistic facts among various authors. There could be no clearer definition of the dichotomy between volumes three and four (*Greek Word Order*, Cambridge 1960, 66).

This does not restrict the theme to matters of syntax in different arrangement, or merely viewed in a new light. Close attention is given to wider categories, such as word-order, rhetoric, parallelism and parenthesis. Moreover, the irregularities in sentence-construction which result from Semitic influence will be particularly observed, in order to investigate the ways in which the dialect or variety of Greek found here is distinctive from the main stream of the language.

I cannot discern any telling evidence for Latin impression on New Testament style. Rather I am assured of the direct influence of Aramaic and Hebrew everywhere, together with that of the synagogue and the Septuagint, and the likelihood that many of the very earliest Christians in Palestine possessed Greek and Aramaic, and perhaps also Hebrew.

In particular, two conclusions may incite challenge, and therefore I have provided the supporting evidence rather fully. First, though there is a comparative style for each author, I believe that the styles are not so far apart as to impair the inner homogeneity of Biblical Greek ; even the extremes of, say, Mark and James share a stylistic generic likeness. Secondly, I find the hypothesis of Aramaic or Hebrew sources, except perhaps in limited areas which concern the teaching of Jesus and others, to be less credible than the use of a kind of Greek which was inoculated with Semitic syntax and style.

For instance, the language of Mark is a unity, rich in Aramaisms, perhaps based on an Aramaic catechism for converts, but here, as in all the New Testament books, exclusive Aramaisms and exclusive Hebraisms co-exist, even in the same passage, making less likely the use of Aramaic or Hebrew documents in the composition of the Gospel. However, the probability that Aramaic or Hebrew sources for the teaching of Jesus did exist at an earlier stage, cannot be excluded.

The style of Mark recalls parts of the Septuagint, e.g. Genesis, in some respects, and is as simple, stereotyped (as to set rules), and as patterned as that of the Apocalypse. The style of both Mark and the Seer is numinous and evocative, like their theology. The Greek of the Apocalypse is not *sui generis*, but rather it has more of the same qualities of Semitic Greek that are shared by other writers. It is also more provocatively barbarous in tone, a language of " anti-culture," neither inarticulate nor inartistic, however, which reads strangely at first after 2 Peter, dynamic and expressive, yet never very subtle. At his place of exile, the Seer may have missed the services of a revising amanuensis, which was enjoyed by some other authors. Even so, his Greek is not on the level of vernacular papyrus letters.

All the Gospels have considerable Semitic features, and Matthew cannot be said to be " improving " the style of Mark in this respect, for sometimes he is Semitic when Mark is not. Neither Matthew nor Luke take pains to avoid Mark's Jewish Greek, but they write more smoothly, less vividly and with less heavy redundancy. Matthew is less picturesque, resorting to mnemonic devices, and his style resembles in certain respects that of Hebrews, James, 1 Peter and Luke-Acts.

Even excluding his obvious sources, Luke has a style which varies from the same kind of Jewish Greek as Mark and Matthew to a more non-Biblical style, and this variation may either be contrived, a deliberate adaptation of language to narrative, or else it may have something to do with the date at which the author composed some parts of Acts. At times Luke displays that distinctively Christian style which is conspicuous elsewhere in the New Testament, and which has much in common with the Jewish Greek of the Septuagint and pseudepigraphical literature.

I find the style of the Fouth Gospel to be homogeneous, revealing no sources, and at one with that of the Johannine epistles. While the Gospel alone is directly influenced by the Septuagint, the Johannine style generally teems with Aramaisms, Hebraisms and Semitisms. It is a simple language, distinguished by transparent sincerity; it is an attractive expression of the influence of the synagogue upon the new Christian community, remarkable especially for its new Christian use of the preposition *en* which it shares with Paul. Having the eurhythmic balance of Hebrew parallelism, it lacks the vigour and passion of other examples of Christian speech, notably Revelation.

A contrasting style must be distinguished for each of Paul's main groups of epistles, of which the least literary and most direct in expression is Thessalonians. The epistle to the Ephesians and the Pastorals stand apart, but not so very far, and merely on grounds of style it would be gratuitous to deny their authenticity. The Greek of the Paulines is Jewish, much influenced by the Septuagint. Its verbosity may derive from Paul's predilection for chiasmus and Old Testament parallelism.

The scope of the amanuensis in New Testament composition, gives rise to baffling perplexity, and on the general question I believe that some authors enjoyed varying degrees of help with their Greek, sometimes with an Atticizing trend.

For instance, the style of the Pastorals is much nearer to the higher Koine than most New Testament writing, not so closely Jewish and moulded less on the Septuagint. Nevertheless, it is not completely free from Semitisms, nor is it the most elegant style in the New Testament, never rising to the level of some of Paul's literary flights.

The epistle to the Hebrews affects an elegance memorable in the New Testament, and yet there is in it a layer of basic Jewish Greek. The author is less dexterous than appears at first sight, but his script reaches the parity of a pleasantly rhythmical sermon. The epistle of James, too, is of a cultural quality, recalling the philosophical diatribe. Yet this author is less careful of style than the author to the Hebrews and falls far short of Paul at his best. The Greek is inherently Jewish, and the vocabulary smacks of the Old Testament, to such an extent that here may be yet another example of the peculiarly Christian dialect.

Rather less elegant than these is 1 Peter, firmly Septuagintal and Semitic, despite the likely efforts of a lettered amanuensis, and again exhibiting the characteristic vocabulary, solemn liturgical style and the haunting loveliness, of the peculiarly Christian variety of Greek. On grounds of style at least, it cannot be divided into two parts at 4^{11}.

A later example of the Christian style appears with the epistles of Jude and 2 Peter. Jude's is an elevated diction, tolerably heavy with redundancy, but rhythmical, not altogether innocent of Semitism,

Jewish in recollection, and echoed to some extent in 2 Peter. Both authors borrow terms from renowned classical and Hellenistic writers, but 2 Peter is more Semitic in style, more patently influenced by the Septuagint, and a degree more pompous. In my opinion, the help of a professional amanuensis is plausible again in these two works.

In this volume, much of the Greek has been transliterated, especially where a single word was reproduced, and this resort has assisted to keep the cost of the book within a moderate range.

The absence of footnotes arises because matter not immediately serving the argument is avoided, and digressions, however intriguing, have been resisted; but the citations of authors, usually placed in footnotes, are retained in the text. Where there is a large number of supporting references, smaller type is used, but not to imply that they are a digression.

CHAPTER ONE

SOURCES BEHIND THE GOSPELS

Two distinct questions arise and are not to be confused : 1. whether any of the New Testament was originally written in a Semitic language, 2. how much influence from Semitic languages is discernible in the New Testament itself. The assessing of that influence occupies a considerable part of this volume, but in the Gospels especially the question of sources is important, and the question which immediately arises from it : how much Hebrew or Aramaic was used by Jesus and his disciples ?

Students of an extreme persuasion have discerned Aramaic written sources behind the whole of the New Testament, for instance, G. M. Lamsa (*New Testament Origin*, Chicago 1947). M.-J. Lagrange and C. C. Torrey made the more modest claim that all four gospels were written at first in Palestinian Aramaic. The evidence from style will suggest that this view also is too extreme. It is safer to look sceptically, with Dr. Matthew Black, on the thesis of written Aramaic originals and to accept his proposition that some sources of the gospels were at one point extant in Aramaic (Black[3] 271-274). However, that would not be true of the hypothetical documents, Q, M, and L.

Matthew Black confirms that the Aramaisms are mainly confined to the teaching of Jesus himself and John the Baptist and are not spread through the whole narrative. There are, for instance, *talitha cum*, *ephphatha*, *eloi eloi lama sabachthani*, *abba* and *rabboni* (said to Jesus). Paul alone is found with *marana tha*.*

There is some reason to think that the apostle Matthew wrote an Aramaic gospel which was later rendered into Greek and, having been lost, was then replaced by the Greek version. St. Jerome referred to a " Gospel according to the Hebrews," written in Aramaic, as the original Matthew. Scholars continue to review the idea, and among theories more recent than those of Torrey and the like are those of B. C. Butler (*The Originality of St. Matthew*, Cambridge 1951) and P. Parker (*The Gospel before Mark*, Chicago 1953). The latter has in mind an original Aramaic gospel, probably by the apostle Matthew, which the authors of our present Matthew and Mark translated and

---

* By Aramaisms, Hebraisms and Semitisms respectively, are intended those Greek idioms which owe their form or the frequence of their occurrence to Aramaic, Hebrew, or an influence which might equally well apply to both languages.

revised. Parker regards Mark as a compression of the material, disjointed and episodic. It is consistent with the Papias tradition that the words of Jesus were first written down in a Semitic language, but it does not do justice to Matthew's style of Greek to suppose that it was a translation of Aramaic.

As to the Fourth Gospel, while few to-day claim that the whole of it is an Aramaic translation, some are reluctant to deny the possibility of Aramaic sources, especially since the discovery at Qumran of Aramaic writings comparable with the Fourth Gospel, and some critics are beginning to see a Jewish environment of thought behind the Gospel consistent with the underlying Semitic idiom. An interesting review is presented by S. Brown, " From Burney to Black : The Fourth Gospel and the Aramaic Question," *CBQ* 26 (1964) 323–339. E. C. Colwell's statement against Aramaic influence is too extreme (*The Greek of the Fourth Gospel*, Chicago 1931) : cf. below pp. 64, 70.

There is some evidence to support the claim that Mark and perhaps John and Revelation and Acts 1–11 were originally composed in the Galilean or northern dialect of a contemporary Semitic language, spoken daily by Jesus and his disciples, perhaps the northern branch of Levantine Aramaic, distinguishable from the dialect centred at Jerusalem, for Peter's way of speaking was conspicuous to the serving maid in the south (Mt only).

Hebrew had been displaced as the national tongue of Judaea, probably as early as Hezekiah's reign : Neh 8[7f] provides evidence of the need of Aramaic in Nehemiah's day. One may assume that Aramaic continued in use at least until the time of Jesus and that sacred books of a faith beginning at Jerusalem would be issued in a native Aramaic dialect, even if Greek was spoken in Palestine at large and even by the rabbis (for there are Greek loan-words in their writings, although they are of uncertain date). It is argued that the Aramaic of the Palestinian Pentateuch Targum and other Targums is the very language of the time of Jesus, " when Palestinian Aramaic was spoken in a hellenistic environment " (Black[3] 22f). It is urged that the many Greek borrowings in it suggest this early date, but the borrowings may have taken place at any time during a very long period of hellenization in Palestine, as is pointed out by J. A. Fitzmyer (" The Languages of Palestine in the First Century A.D.," *CBQ* 32 (1970) 524f). We do not know how far the Jews of Palestine ever used Greek at all except for commerce and social intercourse with Gentiles. It may be dangerous to assume that Greek was restricted to upper-class Jews and government officials under the Romans. There is some evidence that even Hebrew had been revived as a spoken language by the time of Jesus, as M. Bobichon argues (" Grec, Araméen et Hébreu : les langues de Palestine au premier siècle chrétien," *Bible et Terre Sainte*, Paris 58

(1963) 4–5). Most of the Qumran texts so far discovered are in Hebrew, but they are too early in all probability to be significant. At any rate, it looks as if the first-century Jews may have been trilingual. Since the quality of New Testament Greek is decidedly Semitic in varying degrees, there may well have been a spoken language in common use among these trilingual Jews which would render superfluous the hypothesis of source-translation as an explanation of certain phenomena in New Testament Greek. In the most characteristic form of this language, which is found in Mark (especially the D-text) and the Seer, there was a strong tendency towards uncommon Greek idioms which happened also to be idiomatic in the two Semitic languages. The tendency is only less slight in some other New Testament authors. Our suggestion is that such a body of idiom, as is exposed everywhere in this volume, comprised a distinct dialect or branch of the Koine Greek. Reference must be made to our *Grammatical Insights* (183ff). One or two scholars have been found hesitatingly to agree; for instance, G. Mussies has this to say, " In our opinion it is even conceivable that original Greek works were composed in some kind of Biblical Greek which imitated Semitizing translation . . ." (*The Morphology of Koine Greek*, Leiden 1971, 96f). We believe our view to be supported by the possibility of the bilingual or even trilingual nature of much of contemporary Palestine. The author of the Epistle of James was bilingual, according to A. Schlatter (*Der Brief des Jakobus*, 1956, 84). A man living in Galilee would be likely to be bilingual for he would be in contact with Gentile culture. Moreover, from certain hellenistic towns, namely the league of Decapolis, Caesarea, Antipatris, Phasaelis and Sebaste, which were Greek-speaking, the influence would spread to the surrounding area and would produce a bilingual population.

Nevertheless the belief in the existence of Aramaic sources has been widely held. Irenaeus spoke of " the Gospel " as being at first in Hebrew (Aramaic intended ?), and there is Jerome's reference to an Aramaic Gospel. On the face of it, the view seems likely enough. If Greek was understood well enough in Palestine to warrant issuing the Gospels in that language, it is strange that Palestinians who later became Christians needed to have their Scriptures in a Palestinian Aramaic version, the " Palestinian-Syriac " which was provided by Byzantine emperors for the Christianized Palestinians. Moreover, Eusebius seems to indicate that in the third century at Scythopolis parts of the Christian service were rendered into Aramaic for the benefit of peasants who were unversed in Greek. All this, however, is to assume that the same linguistic state of affairs existed two centuries earlier. More significant perhaps is the following contemporary evidence.

Josephus claims to have written some books in Aramaic and to have rendered them later into Greek, so he tells us in the preface to *de Bello Iudaico* (ed. B. Niese, Berlin 1895, vol. VI, i 3), and one passage in his *Antiquities* implies that a Jew in Palestine rarely acquired Greek, Josephus himself making the effort to master the elements, but pronunciation giving him difficulty. " I have also taken a great deal of pains to obtain the learning of the Greeks, and understand the elements of the Greek language, although I have so long accustomed myself to speak our own tongue, that I cannot pronounce Greek with sufficient exactness ; for our own nation does not encourage those that learn the languages of many nations. . . ." (W. Whiston, *The Works of Flavius Josephus*, London 1875, vol. II, 143 ; Niese, vol. IV, *Antiqu. Iud.* xx 263, 264). The meaning of Whiston's translation is not always perfectly clear, and one should consult the discussion of the meaning of Josephus in J. N. Sevenster, *Do You know Greek ? How much Greek could the Early Christians have Known ?* Leiden 1968, 67–71). It is doubtful whether such information as Josephus gives is reliable, in face of contrary evidence that Greek was widely used even in southern Palestine. The language of the *Jewish Wars* does not read like translation-Greek, but it is in fact " an excellent specimen of the Atticistic Greek of the first century," according to Thackeray (*Josephus the Man and the Historian*, New York 1929, 104). But Josephus may have had help in the translation if we are to believe *contra Apionem* I 50. Still, Jews did take pains to learn Greek, as Josephus admits, though the practice may have been frowned upon.

There is evidence that Greek was a living tongue among first-century Jews even around Jerusalem, for on Mount Olivet it has been found that eleven out of twenty-nine ossuaries which were discovered there were written in Greek, and two articles by P. Kahane (" Pottery Types from the Jewish Ossuary-Tombs around Jerusalem. An Archaeological Contribution to the Problem of the Hellenization of Jewry in the Herodian Period," *Israel Exploration Journal* 2 (1952) 125–139 ; 3 (1953) 48–54) and one by R. H. Gundry (" The Language Milieu of First-Century Palestine. Its Bearing on the Authenticity of the Gospel Tradition," *JBL* 83 (1964) 404–408) are very informative in this respect.

The hellenization by Alexander and his successors included Palestine, synagogues in Jerusalem catered for the needs of Greek-speaking Jews (Ac $6^{1.9}$), and copies of the Greek Bible were found at Qumran. Greek papyri dating from our period have been found in Judaea, as is noted by B. Lifshitz (" Papyrus grecs du désert de Juda," *Aegyptus* 42 (1962) 240–256). It should not be considered improbable, therefore, that Jesus normally spoke in Greek, albeit a simple Semitic kind of speech, such as is revealed in the subsequent enquiry in this volume, and that he used Aramaic on certain occasions. The isolation of *talitha cum* and *ephphatha* and the like, as Aramaic phrases surviving in the Greek gospels, might then be explained as rare instances where patients of Jesus comprehended only Aramaic. H. Birkeland is among those who see the force of this, although he himself holds that Hebrew, slightly Aramaicized, was the normal language of Jesus (" The Language of Jesus," *Arhandlinger utgitt av et Norske Videnskaps-Akademi* i Oslo, II *Historisk-Filosofisk Klasse* 19, 54). To suggest that it is due to " inadvertance " that Aramaic words are left untranslated is a needless charge against the final redactor of Mark. Nor is the presence of Aramaic transliterations in the vocabulary of the New Testament (*Boanerges, Barnabas, Cephas, pascha, abba, marana tha*) evidence that the first Christians lived in an Aramaic-speaking community any more than the survival of *amen* and *alleluia* proves that they lived in a Hebrew-speaking community. Presumably Jesus addressed the Syrophoenician woman, the Roman centurion, and Pilate in Greek ; we hear of no interpreter on any of the occasions. Some inner-Greek alliterations are further evidence that at least some of his teaching was in Greek. Some of these alliterations were mentioned in *Grammatical Insights* (181f), and Dr. A. J. B. Higgins criticizes the suggestions concerning some of these alliterations, on the grounds that it is very improbable that Jesus used the Greek words *ecclesia* and *Son of Man* (*BJRL* 49 [1966] 375f). In an interesting note, A. W. Argyle shows that the word *hypocrite*, occurring 17 times in the synoptic gospels, has no appropriate Aramaic parallel (*ET* 75 [1964] 113f). Reserve is needed, however, as subsequent research may unearth such a parallel ; the good Greek idiom of a noun in the genitive following a noun with pronominal suffix (τὸ αἷμά μου τῆς διαθήκης) has been found in an Aramaic Targum (J. A. Emerton, *JTS* NS 15 [1964] 58f).

As the volume proceeds, it will be shown that there are instances enough in the evangelists' Greek to suggest that they were influenced by idioms of an exclusively Hebrew kind, and in another place by idioms of an exclusively Aramaic kind. Unless Hebrew and Aramaic sources were used side by side, we must in consequence rule out the source-hypothesis, adopting instead the suggestion that the evangelists for the most part used Jewish Greek.

They may have used sources for the words of Jesus, on the occasions when he addressed people in Aramaic, but this cannot explain why the language of the evangelists is both Aramaized and Hebraized at the same time. It is not enough to say that some idioms are common to both languages, for some of them are not. The suggestion of a Semiticized Biblical Greek may remove the assurance felt by some expositors that " a Gospel so deeply coloured by Semitic usages must, in the main, bear a high historical value," for we presume that such expositors set high store by the presence of Aramaic sources (Vincent Taylor, *The Gospel according to St. Mark*, London 1955, 65). The Aramaisms are not all primitive survivals of the original teaching of Jesus, but they may rather be a part of the evangelists' Greek style.

Other Literature :

J. C. James, *The Language of Palestine*, Edinburgh 1920.
S. Lieberman, *Greek in Jewish Palestine*, New York 1942.
F. Büchsel, " Die griechische Sprache der Juden in der Zeit der Septuaginta und des Neuen Testaments," *ZAW* 60 (1944) 132–149.
Articles in *ET*, " Did Jesus Speak Aramaic ? "
   56 (1944) 95–97, 305, 327–328 ;
   67 (1955) 92–93, 246, 317, 383 ;
   68 (1956) 121f.
S. M. Patterson, " What Language did Jesus Speak ? " *Classical Outlook* 23 (1946) 65–67.
R. O. P. Taylor, *The Groundwork of the Gospels*, Oxford 1946, 91–105.
M. Black, " The Recovery of the Language of Jesus," *NTS* 3 (1957) 305–313.
M. Smith, " Aramaic Studies and the Study of the New Testament," *JBR* 26 (1958) 304-313.
J. M. Grintz, " Hebrew as the Spoken and Written Language in the Last Days of the Second Temple," *JBL* 79 (1960) 32–47 [Mishnaic Hebrew, not Aramaic, was the language of Palestine in 1st century A.D.].
J. A. Emerton, " Did Jesus Speak Hebrew ? " *JTS* NS 12 (1961) 189–202.
S. Lieberman, " How Much Greek in Jewish Palestine ? " *Biblical and Other Studies*, ed. A. Altmann, Massachusetts 1963, 121–141.
M. Black, " Second Thoughts. IX. The Semitic Element in the New Testament," *ET* 77 (1965) 20–23.
H. Ott, " Um die Muttersprache Jesu ; Forschungen seit Gustaf Dalman," *Nov.T.* 9 (1967) 1–25.
H. P. Rüger, " Zum Probleme der Sprache Jesu," *ZNW* 59 (1968) 113–122.
J. Barr, " Which Language did Jesus Speak ?—Some remarks of a Semitist," *BJRL* 53 (1970) 9–29.

CHAPTER TWO

THE STYLE OF MARK

§ 1. Literary Sources in Mark

Although scholars of various schools have sought to detect literary sources in Mark and to distinguish them by means of linguistic tests, the attempt has never succeeded because the various stylistic features cut right across the boundaries of any literary divisions that have yet been suggested. In consequence, it seems that although there may have been literary sources to begin with a final redactor has so obliterated all traces of them that Mark is in the main a literary unity from the beginning to 16^8, as the foregoing analysis of the stylistic features will show.

We must except both the Longer and Shorter endings ($16^{9\cdot20}$) which are full of non-Markan words and phrases : e.g. *he appeared (ephanē)*[9], *first day of the week*[9] (i.e. the normal Greek *prōtē* instead of Semitic *mia* as in 16^2), *after this (meta tauta)*[10] and so on. Cf. V. Taylor, *Mark* 610-615.

§ 2. Aramaic Influence on the Style of Mark

On the one hand, it is felt that Mark's style is unpretentious, verging on the vernacular ; on the other, that it is rich in Aramaisms. The latter are so much in evidence that early in this century scholars were convinced that Aramaic sources had been translated. Torrey followed them, adducing mistranslations to support the hypothesis (C. C. Torrey, *The Four Gospels*, Oxford 1922 ; *Our Translated Gospels*, London 1933). To Burney the Aramaic flavour of Mark was not so strong as that of the Fourth Gospel, and he found no mistranslation in Mark (C. F. Burney, *The Aramaic Origin of the Fourth Gospel*, Oxford 1922, 19). Rawlinson thought that the Paralytic narrative might be a translation (2^{1-12}), but anything further was " highly improbable." (A. E. J. Rawlinson, *The Gospel according to St. Mark*, London 1925, xxxiii.) Howard concurred with Lagrange that the Greek was translation Greek but he left open the question whether the evangelist translated or whether he was subsequently translated ; he inclined to the view that Mark was here and there translating an Aramaic catechetical system of instruction (*Grammar* II 481). Since

Papias indicates that Mark was a catechist, it is conceivable that the Gospel was based on Aramaic catechetical teaching given by the evangelist to Palestinian converts.

Sentence Construction. *Asyndeton.* This is probably where Aramaic influence is strongest in the style of Mark (Taylor, *Mark* 49f, 58; Black[3] 55-61). The same is true of the Fourth Gospel. C. H. Turner found 38 examples of asyndeta in Mark, and although many of these may not be abnormal in Greek the number is significant ("Marcan Usage," *JTS* 28 [1929] 15-19; Lagrange adds others: M.-J. Lagrange, *Évangile selon Saint Marc*, 5th ed. Paris 1929, LXXf).

Active impersonal plural. This Markan mannerism may well evince an Aramaic way of expressing a substitute for the rare passive voice. Thus, *Does the lamp come?* for *Is the lamp brought?* due to misunderstanding the Aphel or Ittaphel of '*t*' (*bring*).

Mk4^{21} B-text 6^{14} 7^{19} 9^{43} 10^{13} 13^{26} 15^{27}. It is not exclusively Markan: Mt 5^{15} (Mt's Q) 9^2 (from Mk) 17^{27} (M), Lk 4^{41} (add. to Mk) 8^2 (L) 12^{20} (L). Cf. "Marcan Usage," *JTS* 25 (1926) 377-386; M. Wilcox, *The Semitisms of Acts*, Oxford 1965, 127ff; *Grammar* II 447f; III 292f; Black[3] 126-128; Taylor, *Mark* 47f, 62; L. Rydbeck, *Fachprosa*, Uppsala 1967, 39-42.

Similar is the impersonal plural with vague subject, e.g. *they were astonished* for *people were astonished* (which is strictly a Semitism, for it reflects a Hebrew idiom in the LXX, as well as Aramaic).

Mk 1$^{22.30.32.45}$ 2$^{3.18}$ 3$^{2.21.32}$ 5$^{14.35}$ 6$^{33.43.54}$ 7^{32} 8^{22} 10$^{2.49}$ 13$^{9.11}$ 14^{12} 15^{14}.

Another kind of impersonal plural seems to reflect the eye-witness account of a group of disciples, as C. H. Turner suggested ("Marcan Usage," *JTS* 26 [1927] 228-231). Others find difficulty in accepting the suggestion, e.g. V. Taylor, *Mark* 47f; Black[3] 127. To Black, such a plural seems to be "characteristic of simple Semitic narrative."

Mk 1^{21} (*they went into Capernaum*) 2^{9f} 5$^{1.38}$ 8^{22} 9$^{14f.30.33}$ 10$^{32.46}$ 11$^{1.11}$ v.l.$^{12.15.19.21.27}$ 14$^{18.22.26f.32}$. However, this plural is quite characteristic of Semitic speech.

Use of Participle for a main verb. Rare in the papyri, it is characteristic of Aramaic and it occurs in the Western text of Mark: 1^{13} 3^6 7^{25} 9^{26} (also Mt 2^{41}D). *Grammar* I 224; D. Daube in E. G. Selwyn, *I Peter*[2], London 1947, 471ff; Lagrange, *Marc* XC.

Proleptic Pronoun. Black classes as a genuine Aramaism the proleptic pronoun followed by a resumptive noun (e.g. *he, Herod, had sent*). However, the construction is wider than Mark, and need not indicate the translation of a document unless the non-Markan instances do too.

It occurs particularly in the D-text: Mk $6^{17.18}$D 5^{15}D Mt 3^4 12^{45}D Lk 1^{36} 4^{43}D 10^7 24^{10}D Ac 3^2D 6^7D 7^{52}D 11^{27}SB. (Black³ 96–100; *Grammar* II 431; Taylor, *Mark* 59f; Burney, *Aramaic Origin* 85ff). However, in Mk 6^{22} where AC read αὐτῆς τῆς Ἡρῳδιάδος, the Old Latin texts understand αὐτῆς (*ipsius*), i.e. *of Herodias herself.*

Conjunctions. In Aramaic the conjunction '*illâ* (*but*) has both exceptive and adversative force, which may explain how the Greek *alla* and *ean mē* can appear together in 4^{22}, and it may account for the textual variants in 9^8. Greek *alla*, in 10^{40}, may have been chosen for its similarity to Aramic '*illâ* in form and sound, instead of the more appropriate *ean mē*. Thus the sense should clearly be: *To sit . . . is not mine to give* (to anyone) *unless it has been prepared for him. . . .* The Biblical Greek confusion of *ei mē* and *alla* is further seen in 13^{32} = Mt 24^{36}, as also in Paul: cf. below pp. 92, 150

We must dismiss Burney's suggestion that Aramaic translation or influence accounts for the peculiar use of Greek *hina mē* as meaning *lest* five times in Mark, instead of the more normal *mēpote*. His grounds are that Aramaic has a similar composite term of two words *lᵉmâ dî* (Dan 2^{18} $6^{9.18}$) where Hebrew has the single word *pen*. However, the suggestion of direct translation is weak when it is considered that on many occasions Paul wrote *hina mē* when *lest* was meant (e.g. I Cor $1^{10.15.17}$); he was not translating but his Greek may well have been Semitic in style. The Testament of Abraham is not likely to have an Aramaic original, yet recension A 87^7 has *hina mē* where recension B 109^{23} has *mēpote*. Cf. *Grammar* I 241, and the additional note in J. H. Moulton, *Einleitung in die Sprache des Neuen Testaments*, Heidelberg 1911, 269 n. 1; *Grammar* II 468.

Other Syntax. Howard has reminded us of *pros*=*with*, reminiscent of Aramaic *lᵉwāth*, though similar to the classical usage (*Grammar* II 467): Mk 6^3 9^{19} 14^{49}. One must reject this as evidence for translation, unless one makes the claim also for Paul, where it occurs more than a dozen times: cf. below pp. 71, 93. It may well be an Aramaic element in this type of Greek, however.

Black quotes a Targum to illustrate a construction parallel with *katenanti* in Mk 6^{41}D; cf. also 11^2 12^{41} 13^3 (*Grammar* II 465; Black³ 116f).

The use of Greek *hen* as multiplicative or distributive in the D-text of Mk 4^8 recalls the same use of Aramaic *ḥadh* (e.g. Dan 3^{19}); cf. Black³ 124; Taylor, *Mark* 60, and *in loc.* 4^8.

A Markan and Pauline mannerism is adverbial *polla* (Mk 1^{45} 3^{12} $5^{10.23.38.43}$ 6^{20} 9^{26} 15^3), the frequency of which induced Howard to concede as Aramaic, a parallel to *saggî* (=*many, greatly*); cf. *Grammar* II 446; Lagrange, *Marc* XCVIII. However, the adverbial accusative of extent is quite normal in Greek. If this were direct translation from an Aramaic source, why not also Paul and James? (Rom $16^{6.12}$ 1 Cor $16^{12.19}$ Jas 3^2). Another adverbial expression is *loipon* (esp. 14^{41}) with weakened meaning, which Torrey suggested was an over-literal rendering of *mikkᵉ· an* (= *from now*), which itself was weakened in Aramaic to little more than *presently, now* (C. C. Torrey, *The Four Gospels*, 303) ; it is found in Test.Abr., which is probably innocent of Aramaic sources (84^{27} $92^{19.21}$ 111^{12} 113^{16}).

Vocabulary. A. J. Wensinck's unpublished work (Black³ 302) pointed out the unattested Greek use of *poiein* in Mk 4^{32}, instancing the Onkelos Targum of Gen $49^{15.21}$. Further, as Black suggests, Greek *oros* in 3^{13} may correspond to Aramaic *ṭura*, with its double meaning of *mountain* and open *country* (Black³ 133, 299). He further suggests that the name *pîsteqâ* (Palestinian Talmud) was " simply transliterated, and then taken into the sentence as an adjective " 14^3 (Black³ 223-225), but it may in fact be a loan-word, naturalized in Greek, and not a translation.

In 2^{21} the sense required of *pleroma* is *patch*, and Black's suggestion of a Syriac word which has the double meaning of *patch* and *fill* (*mᵉla*) is interesting ; perhaps it may be granted that here, as elsewhere, Semitic usage has enriched the vocabulary of Biblical Greek. This may be said of the next suggestions too. Black notes that the Greek verb *hupagein* in the sense *to die* (Mk 14^{21} and John) has no Greek or LXX parallel, but there was the Aramaic parallel *'zl* ; however, the Hebrew *hlk* might also have sufficed. In Mk 14^{41} Black rejects Torrey's theory of mistranslation and substitutes his own, based on the reading of the D-text : confusion of *r* and *d* means that the D-text is a mistranslation of, " the end and the hour are pressing " (Black³ 225f).

Mistranslation of Aramaic *dᵉ* has frequently been adduced, for *dᵉ* has a wide variety of usages, and sometimes an obscurity is cleared on the theory of mistranslation of this ubiquitous particle (C. F. Burney, *The Poetry of Our Lord*, Oxford 1925, 145n ; *Aramaic Origin* 70 ; Grammar II 434-437 ; Black³ 71-81 ; Taylor, *Mark* 58f). T. W. Manson's explanation of the difficult 4^{12} (*so that they may see but not perceive . . .*) is well known, based on confusion of *who* and *in order that*, both *dᵉ* (*The Teaching of Jesus*, Cambridge 1936, 76-80).

In Mk 4^{22} it has been suggested, not wholly convincingly, that *for there is nothing hid except with the purpose of being revealed* should read, *for there is nothing hid which will not be revealed* ; it is claimed that Mark or one of his sources has failed to note that *dᵉ* might be relative in this context (Burney, *Aramaic Origin* 76). For the same reason the *hos* of the D-text in 9^{38} may preserve the true sense of *dᵉ*, and in 4^{41} we ought to understand a relative (Old Lat. *cui*) : *whom even the wind and sea obey* (Moulton, *Einleitung* 332 ; Grammar II 436 ; Black³ 71). Black has accepted Torrey's suggestion that *ti* in Peter's words 14^{68} is a mistranslation of the relative pronoun and we should read : " I am neither a companion of, nor do I know at all, *him of whom* (*dᵉ*) *you speak* " (Torrey, *Four Gospels* 303 ; Manson, *Teaching* 16f ; Black³ 79f). Three mistranslations suggested by Wellhausen are of great interest : 1. *Son of Man* for Aramaic *man*, 2. *uncovered the roof* 2^4 for *brought him to the roof*, 3. the improbable *to Bethsaida* 6^{45} should be *through Sidon* (W. C. Allen, *The Gospel according to St. Mark*, London 1915, in loc.).

There is considerable evidence favouring influence of an exclusively Aramaic kind upon the style of Mark, but the case for the translation of documents is somewhat weakened by the fact that here in the same gospel are instances both of exclusive Aramaisms and exclusive Hebraisms existing side by side. This occurs even within a single verse, e.g. 4^{41} where there is the influence of the Hebrew infinitive absolute together with a misunderstanding of Aramaic d^e by the use of ὅτι for ᾧ. Therefore unless we can suppose that the sources were composite, parts in Aramaic, parts in Hebrew, the source-hypothesis fails to account for all the Semitic features of style.

§ 3. Hebraic Influence on the Style of Mark

The style is not free from Hebraism, in spite of Howard (*Grammar* II 446), although the exclusively Hebraic influence is less than that which is common to Hebrew and Aramaic.

Syntax. When partitive expressions are used as nominal phrases, without either definite or indefinite article, as subject or object of a verb, then the style ceases to be characteristic of normal Greek. It is rare in the non-Biblical language and seems to have originated with the LXX (Gen 27^{28} 2 Kms 11^{17} 1 Mac 6^{48} A, etc).

As object of a verb : Mk 6^{43} (*they took up . . . some of the fishes*), 9^{37}W 12^2 (*receive some fruit*), 14^{23} (*they all drank some of it*). *Grammar* I 72, 102, 245 ; II 433 ; III 7, 208f ; *Grammatical Insights* 57f ; H. B. Swete, *The Gospel according to St. Mark*³, London 1909, 158 ; E. Lohmeyer, *Das Evangelium des Markus*, Göttingen 1937, 147n.

The auxiliary use of the verb *add* may reflect Aramaic influence. Cf. G. B. Winer-W. F. Moulton, *A Treatise on the Grammar of New Testament Greek*⁸, Edinburgh 1877, 587-590 ; *Grammar* I 233 ; II 445 ; III 227 ; H. St. J. Thackeray, *A Grammar of the Old Testament in Greek according to the Septuagint*, I Cambridge 1909, 52f ; Allen, *Mark* 169 ; Taylor, *Mark* 61. However, its common occurrence in the LXX (109 times) argues for its being an idiom of Biblical Greek (Hebrew *ysp*) : Mk 14^{25}D (the same construction of the idiom as is found in the LXX).

The addition of a cognate noun or participle to the main verb, which is very rare in Aramaic, is more likely to be a Hebraism such as is found in the LXX, through the influence of the infinitive absolute.

Mk 4^{12} (*seeing see* and *hearing hear*), ⁴¹ (*fear with fear*), 5^{42} (*amazed with amazement*). Also Mt Lk Jn Jas 1 Pet Rev LXX e.g. Gen 2^{16f} Jon 1^{10} 1 Mac 10^8 (108 times). Cf. below pp. 47f ; Thackeray, *Grammar* 48f ; G. Dalman, *The Words of Jesus*, E. T. Edinburgh 1902, 34f ; *Grammar* II 443-445 ; Taylor, *Mark* 61.

Sometimes the aorist indicative is found in a context which is unusual for Greek but which is explained by the influence of Hebrew Stative perfect in the LXX, e.g. *rsh* in Isa 42^1, *haphēṣ b^e* in Isa 62^{4}B.

Mk 1^8 *I baptize* (Mt corrects to pres. tense), ^{11} *I am well pleased*, also in Mt Ac. Cf. W. C. Allen, *A Critical and Exegetical Commentary on the Gospel according to St. Matthew*, ICC Edinburgh 1907, 29; Grammar I 134f; II 458; III 72; Black^3 128–130; Taylor, *Mark* 64.

The articular infinitive, very common in the LXX, characteristic of Luke, but rare in the secular papyri, is clearly influenced by the Hebrew *b^e* with infinitive, and is a fairly clear instance of the influence of the LXX upon the Greek of the NT.

It occurs in Mk with four cases: 1. Nom. 9^{10} 10^{40} 12^{33}. 2. Acc. 1^{14} 4$^{5.6}$ 5^4 13^{22} 14$^{28.55}$B. 3. Gen. 4^{3}v.l. 4. Dat. 4^4 6^{48}B. As *during* it occurs (but rarely) in Thucydides. *Grammar* I 14, 215, 249; II 448, 450f; III 140–142; L. Radermacher, *Neutestamentliche Grammatik*^{2}, Tübingen 1925, 189.

The prolepsis of the subject of a subordinate clause is widespread throughout the NT (Mark, Matthew, Luke-Acts, John, Paul, Revelation), and although it has a few parallels outside Biblical Greek it is clearly a Hebrew idiom, e.g. " God saw *the light*, that *it* was good " Gen 1^4.

Mk 1^{24} (*I know thee who thou art*), 7^2 (*seeing some of the disciples, that they ate*), 11^{32} (*all considered John, that he was a prophet*), 12^{34} (*seeing him that he had answered*).

Certain Hebrew words are literally rendered. The word *nephesh* has a reflexive function, in Greek replacing the normal pronoun with *psuchē*. It is " a pure Semitism " (Black^3 102) in Mk 8^{36}, which Luke alters to more normal Greek. The Hebrew word *liphnê*, literally rendered in the LXX of Am 9^4 etc., becomes the Biblical Greek *pro prosōpou* Mk 1^2. The Hebrew *bayyāmîm hāhēm* (in those days), a very common LXX phrase, is literally rendered in Mk 1^9, and the Hebrew *l^e'olām* (for ever) becomes logically εἰς τὸν αἰῶνα 3^{29}, since '*ōlām* (age) has become identical in meaning with αἰών.

Much has been written on the phrase *believe in the gospel* 1^{15}, but in view of the massive Semitic complexion of Mark's language it would seem less appropriate to quote classical and vernacular precedents than to suspect the Hebrew phrase *he'^{e}mîn b^e* (to trust in) as the real inspiration. Neither verb nor noun with *en* are anything but rare outside Biblical Greek, but the noun with *en* is frequent in Paul. However, it does appear from Pauline usage that *to trust in* involves the prepositions *eis* and *epi*, and so *en* may carry quite a different sense in the primitive Church's terminology, especially as the important formulae, *en Kurio* and *en Christo*, have a theological implication of their own, and so *en* may be taken in sense very closely with Christ and Gospel.

Grammar III 262f; A. Deissmann, *Die NT Formel " in Christo Jesu"*, Marburg 1892; A. Oepke, in *TWNT* II 534-539; M. Zerwick, *Graecitas Biblica*³, Rome 1955, § 88; N. Turner, " The Preposition *en* in the New Testament," *Bible Translator* 10 (1959) 262ff.

A difficult phrase for translation is τί ἐμοὶ καὶ σοί (= Heb. *mah-lī wālāk*) : Mk 1²⁴ 5⁷ Mt 8²⁹ Lk 8²⁸ Jn 2⁴.

The nominative case indicating time is a Hebraism borrowed by Mk and Lk from the LXX (Josh 1¹¹A Eccl 2¹⁶ emended in A S^{c.a}) Mk 8².

Word-order. 1. *Position of attributive genitive.* Mark's style is conspicuously different from the Ptolemaic Papyri and closer to the LXX, following the order : article—noun—article—genitive (54 times). He never has the position which is common in non-Biblical Greek : article—article—genitive—noun (*Grammar* III 217). Further influence of the Hebrew construct state appears, when the noun in the genitive case follows immediately upon its governing noun, in contrast with the tendency of literary style which is to precede (*Grammar* III 349).

The table will help to appreciate how the matter stands relatively to Biblical and secular Greek. The number of examples are given for some representative material, and it will be seen that there is a considerable difference between even the more " stylish " parts of the NT and a selection of non-Biblical Greek.

	Genitive before noun	Genitive after noun
Mk 1-5	none	50
Mt 1-5	1¹⁸	46
Ac (We sections)	16¹² 21¹⁴ 27²³·³⁴·⁴² 28³·¹⁷	28
Jas	3	50
Thucyd. I 89-93	9	7
Philostratus *Vit. Ap.* cc. 1-5	7	7

2. *Co-ordinating particles.* The abundance of *kai* and *de* in Mark reflects Hebrew rather than Aramaic use. Moreover, because *waw* must occupy first place in the sentence, Mark prefers *kai* to the second-place conjunctions *gar, ge, de, men, oun, te,* and Mark has a *kai : de* proportion of 5 : 1 (*Grammar* III 332). Mark shares this characteristic with the vernacular too, but this is not to deny that the tendency is Hebraic.

3. *Position of the verb in nominal sentences.* Following Hebrew, the copula is almost always in first-position after the connecting conjunction; the subject immediately follows, and after that the predicate, as in the normal unemphatic and non-interrogative nominal sentence of Hebrew prose.

Exceptions: copula not in first-position 5^5 7^{15} 13^{25} 14^{49}. Subject not immediately following 7^{15} 10^{32} 13^{25}. Where the copula is very closely taken with a ptc, we may be able to distinguish a periphrastic tense from the predicate ptc. e.g. 5^5 10^{32}. Other exceptions are: the placing of a pronoun, etc., first in the sentence for emphasis, where (as in Hebrew) it avoids becoming " a mere appendage to a subject which consists of several words " (e.g. 2 Kings 2^{19} "*good* is the word of Yahweh which you have spoken "); E. Kautzsch, *Gesenius' Hebrew Grammar*, 2nd English ed. by A. E. Cowley, Oxford 1910, § 141n. Also exceptions to the primary position of the verb are 4^{38} 13^{25} 15^{23}, but they are not exceptions to the Hebrew order in nominal sentences without the copula (subject–predicate). Nor is 14^{49} an exception, because *daily* represents the adverbial phrase which may stand at the beginning of a Heb. nominal sentence (e.g. Gen4^7).

4. *Position of the verb in verbal sentences.* Contrary to the usual way in non-Biblical Greek, the NT verb tends towards the beginning of the sentence. For instance, the verb in Herodotus has mainly the middle-position, according to Kieckers (initial/middle/final: 47/167/71). It is a matter of tendency only. In good prose of the fifth and fourth centuries, the subject tends to precede its verb (K. J. Dover, *Greek Word Order*, ch. III), but classical authors vary so much that no principle appears to lie behind their choice of word-order; it is rather a matter of emphasis in each particular context. So it is, to some extent, in Biblical Greek; however, here there is definite influence from the normal Hebrew pattern of verbal sentences: verb—subject —object (*Grammar* III 347f). The Biblical Greek verb is followed by personal pronoun, subject, object, supplementary participle—often in that order, which owes everything to Hebrew and nothing to Aramaic, where the verb tends to end the clause, viz. subject—object—verb. Normally in Hebrew the subject immediately follows the verb unless a pronominal object is involved, for that will be inseparable from the verb and will precede the subject.

On our view that Mark's style is largely Hebraic, therefore, a radical change is probably involved in the rendering of Mk 2^{15t}, which will have to be: " For they were many. There followed him also some scribes of the Pharisees. They noticed him eating. . . ." The only translation, to our knowledge, which takes this point is the British and Foreign Bible Society's *Mark. A Greek–English Diglot for the Use of Translators*, London 1958, 6.

Also preceding the subject will be a prepositional phrase which includes a pronominal suffix, for that too goes closely with the verb. However, a prepositional phrase which includes a noun will follow the subject, which makes probable the translation of Mk 6^{26} as : " he was grieved because of his oaths and guests " (*Diglot* 15 ; *Grammar* III 350). A relative phrase with '*asher*, and a genitive of quality, occur after the noun they qualify ; so in Biblical and translation Greek, a prepositional phrase immediately follows the noun which it qualifies, usually with repetition of the definite article ; i.e. it does not occur between article and noun as in secular Greek, and even in the free Greek books of the LXX to some extent (M. Johannessohn, *Der Gebrauch der Präpositionen in der LXX*, Berlin 1926, 362ff).

§ 4. Semitic Influence on the Style of Mark

By " Semitic " we understand those features of syntax which may be either Hebrew or Aramaic ; it is not always possible to decide which is the more likely when they are common to both Semitic languages.

Parataxis. Except in $5^{4.25.27}$, Mark rather studiously avoids subordinate clauses, in the way of vernacular Greek. The tendency would be Hebraic and Aramaic too ; indeed, *kai* is so commonly used in the LXX to render the Hebrew subordinating *waw* that Mark's *kai* may probably be said to have a subordinating function too.

E.g. 4^{27} " *while* he rises night and day, the seed sprouts," 8^{34} " *if* he will take up his cross, let him follow me," 15^{25} " *when* it was the third hour, they crucified him." Perhaps add $1^{6.11}$ 4^{38} 5^{21} 7^{30} 6^{45}D. A. B. Davidson, *Hebrew Syntax*³, Edinburgh 1901, § 141 ; S. R. Driver, *A Treatise on the Use of the Tenses in Hebrew*³, London 1892, § 166ff ; E. Kautzsch, §§ 116,u, 142,e ; *Grammar* II 423 ; Black³ 66f.

Redundancy. Mark's style tends to be diffuse (cf. Lagrange, *Marc* LXXII–LXXV ; *Grammar* II 419f ; Taylor, *Mark* 50–52). It tends to repeat apparent synonyms, as also do some other NT authors to a less extent : e.g. *the house's householder* (Lk 22^{11}), *straightway immediately* (Ac 14^{10}D), *again a second time* (Ac 10^{15}), *return again* (Ac 18^{21} Gal 1^{17} 4^9), *again the second* (Jn 4^{54}), *then after this* (Jn 11^7v.l.). This, it has been suggested, is an Aramaic mannerism, but it belongs to Hebrew too, corresponding to the parallelism of Semitic speech.

Here are some examples of Mark's redundancy : 1^{28} *everywhere, in all the district,* ^{32} *when evening was come, when the sun was set,* ^{35} *early morning, very early,* 2^{25} *he had need, and was hungry,* 4^2 *he taught, and said in his teaching,* ^{39} *be quiet, be muzzled,* 5^{15} *the possessed man, the man who had the legion,* ^{19} *to your home, to your family,* ^{39} *why . . . distressed, why . . . weeping?* 6^4 *family, relatives, home,* ^{25} *immediately, with haste,* 7^{21} *from within, from the heart,* ^{33} *away from the crowd, on his own* 8^{17} *know, or understand,* 9^2 *privately, alone,* 12^{44} *all that she had, all her livelihood,* 13^{19} *the creation, which God created,* ^{20} *the predestined, whom he predestined,* 14^1 *the Passover, and*

Unleavened Bread, [18] *at a meal, and eating,* [30] *to-day, to-night,* [61] *he was silent, and answered nothing,* 15[26] *the superscription, which was superscribed.*

The Pleonastic Auxiliary. Mark is fond of the redundant auxiliary *began to* ; it occurs 26 times, and a further three times in D, easily seen in the concordance, and evenly distributed throughout the Gospel. Matthew reduces these instances to six ; Luke to two ; yet Luke adds 25 others, and it is a Lukan stylistic feature, since 13 are in Proto-Luke. Since Aramaic used *shārî* as an auxiliary verb the idiom has been claimed as a pure Aramaism for the Gospels, and yet the matter cannot be decisive since we have the Hebrew *y'l* hiph. and the late Hebrew *thl* hiph. as well as the Latin *incipere*. The verb is relatively frequent in the Testament of Abraham, rec. A (82^{19} 83^{34} 110^{25}), on each occasion as pleonastic as in the Gospels, without any trace of direct Aramaic influence, but rather of Hebrew.

Black[3] 125f ; J. H. Hunkin, *JTS* 25 (1926) 390–402 ; 28 (1929) 352f ; Allen, *Mark* 49f ; *Grammar* I 14f ; II 455f ; Taylor, *Mark* 48, 63f ; Lagrange, *Marc* XCIII.

The Historic Present. Mark has 151 examples, although there are 151 also in John ; and 52 of Mark's concern verbs of speaking. Thackeray suggested that, except with verbs of speaking, Mark indicates thereby a new scene and fresh characters (*The Septuagint and Jewish Worship*, Oxford 1923, 21). The tense is characteristic of vivid narrative in most languages ; it may owe something to Aramaic influence in Mark, but it should be noted to the contrary that the historic present occurs some 330 times in the LXX, and thus Hebrew influence is very apparent. As well as Semitic influence, there may have been something theological behind the large use of this tense in Mark. T. A. Burkill reviews with approval Trocmé's view that from Mark's post-resurrection theological viewpoint the past record of Jesus' doings are "construed in terms of the present," and the acts and words of the Crucified One are now being said and done by the living and risen Christ (*New Light on the Earliest Gospel*, Ithaca, N.Y., 1972, 185f).

Periphrastic Tenses. Though these proliferate in Mark, they were not favoured in vernacular Greek (cf. MM 184f), nor by subsequent copiers and correctors of the NT text, for there are variant readings at Mk 1^{39} 2^4 3^1 $5^{11.40}$ 9^4 13^{25} 14^4 15^{26}. They were, however, characteristic of Aramaic and of Hebrew, as witness the LXX. In Biblical Greek they abound more than anywhere else.

Periphrastic imperfect : $1^{6.13.22.39}$ACDW $2^{4.6.18}$ 3^1 4^{38} $5^{5.11.40}$ 9^4 $10^{22.32}$bis $14^{4.40.49.54}$ $15^{40.43}$. Present : 5^{41} 7^{15} $15^{22.34}$. Perfect or Plupf. : $1^{6.33}$ 6^{52} 14^{21}D $15^{7.26.46}$. Future : $13^{13.25}$. M.-J. Lagrange, *Évangile selon Saint Matthieu*[8], Paris 1948, XCI ; J. de Zwaan, "The Use of the Septuagint in Acts," *The Beginnings of Christianity*, ed. F. J. Foakes Jackson, K. Lake,

London 1922, II 62 ; P. Chantraine, *Histoire du Parfait Grec*, Paris 1907, ch. IX.

The Article. 1. Aramaic *nāsh* and Hebrew *'ish* are rendered literally in Mark as indefinite article 1^{23} 7^{11} etc. (cf. concordance under *anthrōpos*). 2. The use of the definite article displays some inconsistency in Mark. Black, following Wensinck, considers that the anomalous practice of all the evangelists may have been influenced by the disappearance of the formal distinction between definite and indefinite nouns in Aramaic, and makes the credible suggestion that Aramaic influence led to some confusion in the normal speech of Greek-speaking Jews. It can further be seen in Paul (cf. p. 91). Black[3] 93.

Pronouns. 1. The incidence of a resumptive personal pronoun, used after a relative, is too widespread in the Gospels to be explained as vernacular Greek without Semitic influence. It is due either to the d^e construction of Aramaic or, just as likely, to *'asher . . . lô* in Hebrew.

Mk 1^7 7^{25} share the idiom with Biblical Greek in general, e.g. LXX Gen 28^{13} Mt 3^{12} 10^{11}D 18^{20}D Lk 8^{12}D 12^{43}D Jn $1^{27.33}$ 9^{36}? 13^{26} 18^9 Rev 3^8 $7^{2.9}$ $12^{6.14}$ $13^{8.12}$ 16^{19} 17^9 20^8.

2. The construction which allows an expression in casus pendens to be followed by a resumptive personal pronoun is to some extent secular but, alongside all the other evidence for Semitisms, it is more probable that a Semitic idiom lies behind the Greek of Mark and John. While it is possible in Aramaic, it is more likely to have come by way of the LXX, as in Mark's own quotation at 12^{10} (cf. also Gen 31^{16}).

Mk 1^{34}D (*and those who had devils he cast them out of them*), 6^{16} (*John whom I beheaded, he is risen*), 7^{20} (*that which goes out, this defiles*), 13^{11} (*whatever is given you, this speak*). For rabbinical parallel, cf. below, p. 71.

3. The high incidence of the oblique cases of *autos* is a Semitic tendency due to the pronominal suffix, although the similar tendency in the vernacular doubtless exerted some influence. Arranged in order of Semitic (or vernacular) influence in this respect, Mark, Matthew and John rank the highest in the NT (cf. below p. 72), with a figure of one occurrence of superfluous cases of *autos* every two lines, whereas the papyri have one every 13 lines.

Prepositions. 1. The repetition of the preposition before two or more phrases is a prominent feature of Biblical Greek, based on the Semitic practice. It is very pronounced in the style of Mark and Revelation, and least in evidence in that of Luke–Acts and the Pastoral Epistles.

It is particularly marked in the Western text: 3^7 *from Galilee and from Judaea and from Jerusalem and from Idumaea*, 5^1, 6^{26}D *because of his oaths* and because of his guests, ³⁶D into the fields and into the villages, ⁵⁶, 8³¹D of the elders and of the chief priests, 11¹, 14⁴³D from the chief priests and from the scribes. Grammar III 275; Black³ 114f.

2. **Instrumental en.** Although in the vast majority of instances *en* has its fundamental spatial meaning of *in* or *among*, yet there are undoubtedly some important exceptions, not the least of which is the peculiarly Christian usage of this powerful word. Indeed, Mark correctly and more normally has *eis* after *dip* 14²⁰ where Matthew has pregnant *en* (Mt 26²³). But in Mk 4³⁰ *en* must be instrumental ($=b^e$), as in both Semitic Greek and the Koine (*with what parable shall we set forth the kingdom?*). Sometimes Mark's *en* is temporal: in *rowing* 6⁴⁸. The *en dolo* of 14¹ shows how close we are to the instrumental sense: *by means of guile*. In 1²³ 5² the man is *with* an unclean spirit, but here we may meet the Christian sense of spatial *en* in a spiritual dimension: the man was *in the sphere of* the demon. This is more frequent in the Johannine writings.

En is not likely to express motion in Mk. Except for *epi* c. acc. twice, Mark's rule is invariable for expressing motion after *erchesthai*: i.e. *eis* (22 times) or *pros* (12 times), and so in 5²⁷ 8³⁸ 13²⁶ the preposition will not express *motion* from place to place, but rather the accompanying circumstances or the sphere in which the motion occurs.

Adjectives and Numerals. In Semitic languages the positive degree does duty for the comparative and superlative. The only analogy to this in the vernacular is the occasional use of comparative for superlative, but the Biblical Greek use of positive for comparative and superlative has come from the LXX. The use of the cardinal for the ordinal is recognized as Semitic, in Mk 16² (=Mt 28¹=Lk 24¹= Jn 20¹·¹⁹), coming into Biblical Greek by way of the LXX (Taylor, *Mark* 60).

Mk 9⁴³ *good* (=*better*) *to enter the Kingdom mained* ⁴⁵·⁴⁷ 14²¹ *good* (=*better*) *for him if he had not been born.* LXX instances: Exod 25³³ *the first tabernacle* for *the former*, quoted at Heb 9²ᶠ, Can 1⁸ *fair amongst women* for *fairest*. Cardinal for ordinal: Gen 8¹³ Exod 40² Ps 23 (24)ᵗⁱᵗ *one* for *first*.

Other Parts of Speech. 1. Wensinck and Black have observed that there is a characteristic way of using the interrogative particle, *What?* to express sarcasm in Semitic languages (Black³ 121f). Although most of their parallels are Aramaic it is also a Hebrew feature. The fact that almost all instances are in the words of Jesus is not significant for, as Black concedes, ordinary narrative does not lend itself to questions.

Wensinck had noted its appearance in Lk (especially the D-text): Lk 5²²D ⁴¹D 6². Black adds the following from Mk: 2⁷ *What? Does this man so speak?* ⁸ *What? Are you discussing these things...?* ²⁴ 4⁴⁰ 10¹⁸. (LXX Gen 44¹⁶ *What? Shall we justify ourselves?* etc.).

2. The pleonastic *thus* after verbs of speaking (Mk $2^{7.8.12}$) is more likely to be influenced by the Hebrew *kāzôth* (LXX Jg 13^{23} 15^7 19^{30} Isa 66^8 etc.) than the Aramaic *kidnâ* (e.g. Dan 2^{10}), because it occurs in books with a Hebrew background, e.g. T.Abr. 85^{15} 86^{25} 87^8 cod. 88^{16} $96^{8.10}$ 103^{31}.

3. The imperatival *hina*, a Biblical rather than a secular idiom (*Grammar* III 94f), occurs once or twice in Mark. The evangelist uses *hina* in a non-final sense at least as often as a final. It belongs to post-classical Greek but never occurs in so large a variety and concentration as in Biblical books. It may derive from Hebrew or Aramaic. The evidence for this is given below, pp. 73f. Cf. also the informative article by W. G. Morrice, " The Imperatival ἵνα," *Bible Translator*, 23 (1972) 326–330.

Imperatival: Mk 5^{23} *Come and lay your hands. . . !* 10^{51} (= Mt Lk) *Let me see again!* 14^{49} *Let the Scriptures be fulfilled!* Epexegetical, after a variety of verbs of command and speaking: $3^{9.12}$ $5^{10.18.43}$ $6^{8.12.25}$ $7^{26.32.36}$ $8^{22.30}$ $9^{9.18.30}$ $10^{35.87.48}$ $11^{16.28}$ 12^{19} $13^{18.34}$ $14^{35.38}$ 15^{21}. Ecbatic: 6^2D *so that mighty deeds are wrought by his hands* 11^{28} *who gave you authority so that you do this?*

Word Order. 1. *Position of the adjective.* The practice of joining the article and its noun closely together reflects the Semitic necessity to join them as one word. Thus it happens that in a kind of Greek which is influenced by Semitic forms, any matter which qualifies the noun tends to be placed in a separate and subsequent articular phrase, in contrast with secular style which avoids this almost completely.

	Between art. and noun	In subsequent articular phrase	Proportion
Papyri of ii–i/BC	140	4 or 5	28 : 1
Philostratus (sample)	27	1	27 : 1
Hebrews	15	10	1,5 : 1
Acts (We)	4	4	1 : 1
James	7	8	1 : 1
Rev 1–3 LXX	5	16	1 : 3,2
Gen 1–19	17	56	1 : 3,3
Mark	7	27	1 : 3,8
Lk 1,2	2	8	1 : 4
Rev 4–22	21	107	1 : 5

The table on page 23, arranged in descending order, will illustrate the closeness of Mk's style to that of Rev and the LXX (Gen), and its contrast with that of the vernacular. (The table includes adjectival phrases but not cardinal numerals. Papyri statistics are from Mayser II 2, 54 and involve pap. Tebtunis nos. 5–124).
The close link between def. art. and noun is a feature of the LXX, where separation occurs in only 4% of the incidence of the art. in translated books; in 11% of the incidence in non-translated books, and in 18% of the incidence in the NT epistles (according to the research of J. M. Rife, " The Mechanics of Translation Greek," *JBL* 52 [1933] 247). The NT epistles thus stand half-way between the LXX on the one hand and non-Biblical Greek on the other (Philostratus *Vit. Ap.* 28%; Thucydides I 89–93 39%). On these estimates, Mk, Mt, Lk's Infancy, document L, and Rev 1–3 stand very much nearer to Semitic Greek than do the epistles (Mk 1–3: 4,7%; Mt $1^8\text{-}4^{end}$: 14%; Lk's Infancy: 3,3%; L: 6,5%; Rev 1–3: 9,4%).

2. *The post-position of demonstrative adjectives.* Again Biblical Greek follows the precedent set by Semitic word-order, and invariably places the adjective after its noun. But this is not as significant as the figures above, because it is only in the translated books of the LXX that there is a spectacular difference between Biblical and non-Biblical Greek in this respect. However, in the frequency of the demonstrative adjective itself there is a marked difference between Biblical and non-Biblical Greek, especially in the attributive use, which is very rare in the Ptolemaic papyri (Mayser II 2, 79–82).

	Pre-positive	Post-positive	Proportion
Mark	14	31/32	1 : 2
Matthew	23/24	76/79	1 : 3
Luke	28	95	1 : 3
John	32/33	36/38	1 : 1
Revelation	5	12	1 : 2,4
LXX : Gen Exod	1	54	1 : 54
Judith	1	10	1 : 10
2–4 Mac	4	8	1 : 2
Philostratus *Vit. Ap.* I	9	22	1 : 2
Thucyd. II 1–34	9	15	1 : 1,6

In the following two tables, the figures for the NT agree closely with the LXX, except that Paul, John and Wisdom are less Semitic in this respect. With these exceptions the figures differ markedly from the secular papyri. Even as early as the third century B.C., thirteen examples of independent *ekeinos* were discovered by Mayser for only two attributive (N. Turner, " The Unique Character of Biblical Greek," *VT* 5 [1955] 208–213).

THE STYLE OF MARK

Use of *ekeinos* (LXX)			
	Independent	Attibutive	Proportion
Minor Prophets	1	59	1 : 59
Judges	—	36	—
Early Kingdoms	2	69	1 : 35
Chronicles	—	30	—
Jeremiah	1	30	1 : 30
Isaiah	2	56	1 : 28
Daniel LXX	—	28	—
1 Maccabees	2	56	1 : 28
2 Esdras-Nehemiah	—	26	—
Late Kingdoms	—	25	—
Pentateuch	8	159	1 : 20
Ezekiel	2	24	1 : 12
Daniel Th.	2	23	1 : 11,5
Joshua	2	22	1 : 11
Judith	2	11	1 : 5,5
Esther	—	3	—
1 Esdras	3	8	1 : 3
Job	3	8	1 : 3
Tobit S	2	5	1 : 2,5
Psalms	1	2	1 : 2
Ecclesiastes	—	1	—
Tobit B	1	1	1 : 1
2–4 Maccabees	14	13	1 : 1
Proverbs	3	2	1 : 0,6
Wisdom	12	6	1 : 0,5
Sirach	1	—	—

Use of *ekeinos* (NT)			
	Independent	Attributive	Proportion
Matthew	4	50	1 : 12
Luke–Acts	6	50	1 : 8
Mark	5	18	1 : 3,6
Revelation	—	2	—
Heb, Jas, 2 Pet.	6	6	1 : 1
Pastorals	4	3	1 : 0,75
Paul	9	4	1 : 0,5
John and 1 John	59	18	1 : 0,3

§ 5. Mark's Mannered Style

Apart from the redundancy which we have already noticed in discussing Semitic features of style, there are other stylistic features of a stereotyped nature which are not necessarily Semitic.

His mannered style is most conspicuous perhaps in his over-use of participles, which incidentally is often reminiscent of Semitic style. The concordance should be consulted for such redundant words as *coming, leaving, rising, answering*, and *saying*.

Accumulation of particles : Mk $1^{31.41}$ 5^{25ff} *there being a woman . . . having suffered . . . having spent . . . not having benefitted . . . coming . . . hearing . . . coming* 14^{67} 15^{43} (*Grammatical Insights* 66).

Redundant negatives are another contribution to Mark's distinctly heavy style, though several other NT authors share this habit, and it is common in earlier secular authors.

Mk 1^{44} *see you say nothing to no one* 2^2 *room for no one not even at the door* 3^{20} *not able not even to . . .* ^{27} *no one was not able to enter . . .* 5^3 *no one had been able to bind him not yet not even with chains* ^{37} 6^5 7^{12} 9^8 11^{14} $12^{14.34}$ $14^{25.60}$ 15^5 16^8.

Mark is particularly fond of clumsy parentheses, often delayed to such an extent that the reader is confused and sometimes entirely misled. Thus, in 2^{15}, if the parenthesis is restored to its rightful place, the sentence will read : " While Jesus was dining at home many publicans and sinners (There were many such who followed him) came and joined Jesus and his disciples. There followed him also the scribes of the Pharisees." We may do the same for 6^{15} : " John the Baptist is risen and therefore mighty powers are at work in him, like one of the prophets (some said that he was Elijah and others that he was a prophet)."

Parentheses are very common ; we give but a selection : 1^{2f} $2^{10f.15.22.26b}$ 5^{42} 6^{14f} $7^{2f.11.19.25-26a}$ $8^{15.38-41}$ 11^{32} 12^{12a} $13^{10.14}$ 14^{36} $16^{3f.7f}$. C. H. Turner, " Marcan Usage," *JTS* 26 (1927) 145–156 ; M. Zerwick, *Untersuchungen zum Markus-styl*, Rome 1937, 130–138 ; *Grammatical Insights* 64–66.

Another factor contributing to heaviness of style is Mark's inclination to alternate the normal imperfect (220 times) with the sonorous periphrastic imperfect (25 times). C. H. Turner suggested that the periphrastic imperfect was intended to be the true imperfect, referring to continuous action in the past, and that Mark uses the normal imperfect-form as the equivalent of an aorist (doubted by V. Taylor, *Mark* 45). Swete's view was that the normal imperfect-form is used when an eyewitness is vividly describing events which took place under his very

eyes, especially 5^{18} 7^{17} 10^{17} 12^{41} 14^{55}. Just as plausible is the view that the normal imperfect-form represents the conative imperfect, since it is appropriate at 9^{38} *we tried to forbid* 15^{23} *they tried to give him.*
In addition to the heaviness of style, and germane to it, is what we choose to call the iconographic nature of Mark's Greek. To some extent all the NT authors share it, but especially Mark and Revelation. They eschew literary virtuosity, conventional rules of Syntax, and they succeed in evoking a numinous sense to point the reader upwards by the unclassical barbarism of the style. This is seen particularly in a feature which we must now consider, the over-use of stereotyped expressions and the preference for a set formula. Vincent Taylor assumed that such features were part of the ancient tradition which Mark received (*Mark* 53), but they are characteristic of the evangelist himself and they abound throughout his work. In this respect the language does justice to his somewhat stereotyped theme : viz. to explain the humiliation and passion of Jesus by showing that " the true status of Jesus was a predetermined secret " (T. A. Burkill, *Mysterious Revelation*, Ithaca, N.Y., 1963, 319 ; cf. also the sequel, *New Light on the Earliest Gospel*, Ithaca 1972, especially 184f, 198f, 214f, 263). This is the theological standpoint which will be found most helpful for the understanding of Mark's mysterious iconographic language. Theologically and linguistically all is predetermined, nothing left to human art or device, all conforming to an iconographic pattern.

Rigidity of style is apparent in some of the repeated expressions : 3^{12} 8^{30} *he charged them to*, 5^{43} 7^{36} 9^9 *he strictly charged them to*, $3^{5.34}$ 10^{23} *he looked around* . . . *and said*, 1^{31} 5^{41} 9^{27} *he took* . . . *by the hand*, 7^{17} $9^{28.33}$ 10^{10} *he entered the house*, 8^{27} 9^{33} 10^{32} *on the road*.

This poverty of expression must be deliberate, for it is not due to lack of skill in Greek composition on the part of Mark : he can properly employ his tenses (e.g. 5^{15ff} 6^{14ff} 7^{35} 9^{15} 15^{44}), preserving the correct distinction between perfect and aorist, imperfect and aorist, which was quite beyond the powers of some contemporary writers.

The aor. is correctly followed by impf. at 6^{41} *he broke* (aor.) *the loaves and kept giving* (impf.). Cf. 5^{15} *he is in process of being possessed* (pres.), *because he has received the devils* (perf.). In 5^{18} the aor. ptc. (*the once possessed*) represents the man who in 5^{15} was constantly possessed (pres. ptc.). The distinction of aor. and perf. is carefully preserved in 5^{19} (*what the Lord has done for him*, as a finished work, *and did have mercy upon him*, a single act in the past), and 15^{44} (*Pilate marvelled that he was already dead* (perf.) . . . *and asked if he died* (aor.) *very long ago*). Swete, *Mark* xlix ; *Grammar* III 69.

So when Mark economizes, it is deliberately, and not through inadequate knowledge of syntax. Rather than resort to proper names unduly, he will economize with *ho de* and *hoi de*, often to the reader's confusion, and thus marks a change of subject which might have been done more clearly by the use of a proper name. But here he is imitating a classical Greek device, though doubtless the classical writers would have been less ambiguous. The only exception to Mark's rigid use of the *ho de/hoi de* device for change of subject is at 10^{32}, as far as can be discovered, and then it is only apparent, for the witnesses which read *kai* or *kai ho* are probably correct (A, fam^{13}, etc.), as against *hoi de* in S, B, fam^1, 565, etc. This rigid feature of style is not so much " harsh " (Rawlinson) as " iconographic."

Quite as economical and enigmatic is the phrase καὶ ἰδὼν αὐτὸν τὸ πνεῦμα συνεσπάραξεν αὐτόν (9^{20}), which seems to defy the laws of language, but Mark may have had some such model as LXX Exod 9^7 in mind : ἰδὼν δὲ Φαραώ ... ἐβαρύνθη ἡ καρδία Φαραώ, and perhaps Herm. M. V 14 ; VII 5.

The vocabulary is economical, too, limited to 1270 words, and specially weak in particles (another feature of Semitic Greek). He has only 80 NT hapax, and only five words entirely peculiar to himself. These are all words compounded with a preposition, of which he is specially fond : ἐκπερισσῶς and ὑπερπερισσῶς, ἐπιράπτω, ἐπισυντρέχω, προμεριμνάω. Whether Mark invented such words it is impossible to say ; they may have belonged to the vocabulary of this circle of iconographic writers, whose habit it was to build up new words from old ones. To us it seems unlikely that he would be much given to invention, for variety is not to his taste : he overworks certain words and expressions, *immediately, which is, why ?, again, much, amazed, bring*. In some ways we can detect a tendency towards the vernacular, in that he uses some diminutive words which bear no diminutive force : *little daughter, little fish, little girl, small child, little shoe, small morsel, small ear*, but perhaps *little dog* and *little boat* are true diminutives ; and he has the vernacular *krabattos*.

One striking example of the economy of vocabulary is the load which *eis* is made to carry, being used 165 times. The overworked preposition appears in some very interesting contexts : viz. with *baptize IN, descend UPON, preach TO, sit ON, beat IN the synagogues, to be AT home* or *IN the field, speak IN the village, become (into) one flesh, spread ON the road, blaspheme AGAINST*. Nevertheless the idea of motion seems to be included in most of the instances of *eis*, and it is not simply a case of confusion with *en*.

In conclusion, the impression derived from a survey of Mark's style is that he is manipulating none too skilfully but with a curious overall effectiveness, a stereotyped variety of Greek, rather inflexible and schematized, adhering to simple and rigid rules.

Thus, if he uses *pros* with verbs of speaking, it is always before *heautous* and *allēlous* : 4^{41} 10^{26} ADW 12^7 16^3 ; in the two apparent exceptions, it

really goes with the preceding verb 11³¹ 12⁶ and once it means *against* 12¹².
His use of *palin* and *euthus* follows rigid rules : at the beginning of the clause they are mere conjunctions, but adverbial elsewhere (*Grammar* III 229). His use of recitative *hoti* is no less rigid ; his rule apparently is not to employ it after a recitative *legōn*, avoiding two recitatives in juxtaposition, for to his mind they both perform the same function, that of quote marks. When in fact they occur together, some 11 times, the *legōn* is not recitative for the main verb is other than one of speaking ; where it seems to be recitative (i.e. with *answer, glorify, cry, bear false witness*) then there is always a variant omitting *hoti* and this will probably be correct—unless we are presuming to invent Mark's own rules for him.

§ 6. Latinisms in the Gospels

Some features of Markan style recall Latin constructions and vocabulary. That they are probably more frequent in Mark than in other NT texts, except the Pastoral epistles, may raise the question whether Mark was written in Italy in a kind of Greek that was influenced by Latin. However, supposing that his language is influenced in that way, we presume that it could have happened as well in the Roman provinces.

Syntax. Whereas Latin influence is possible but improbable in certain simplifications within the Greek language itself, the aoristic perfect, the omission of the definite article, the use of subjunctive to replace optative, the periphrastic tenses, yet the following constructions have some probability, inasmuch as they tend to occur in the particularly Roman parts of the Gospel.

2²³ *make a way* may be *iter facio*, but it may as well be a Hebraism *'sh derek*, LXX Jg 17⁸, which seems more likely in view of the considerable Hebraic evidence above. 3⁶S 15¹B *making consultation* may be *consilium facere* (*capere*), 14⁶⁵ *received him with blows* may be *verberibus recipere*, 15¹⁵ *make satisfaction* may be *satisfacere* (cf. also Hermas Sim. 6.5.5), 15¹⁹ *place the knees* may be *genua ponere* (= Lk 22⁴¹ Ac 7⁶⁰ 9⁴⁰ 20³⁶ 21⁵ Herm. Vis. 1.1.3 ; 2.1.2 ; 3.1.5). But some have found a non-official Latinism in 5⁴³ : *he commanded to be given her to eat* may be the construction *duci eum iussit*.

Vocabulary. Several of Mark's words are obviously transliterations from Latin, and some of them are in other gospels too, but there is nothing very remarkable about transliterations and loan-words, for they occur in all languages.

Aitia = *causa* (papyri). *Census* (papyri). *Crabattus* (papyri). *Denarius* (papyri). *Phragelloō* = *fragellare*. *Praetorius* (papyri). *Kodrantēs* = *quadrans*. The following words are found only in Mk among the gospels : *centurio, xestēs* = *sextarius, speculator*. Luke has avoided some Latin words of Mk but he still has *assarion* (= Mt), a Greek diminutive of the Roman *as* (one-sixteenth of a denarius), *sudarium* (= Jn, Ac), *legio* (Mt Mk Lk), and *modius* (Mt Mk Lk).

Extent of the Latinism. In addition to these Matthew has *mille*, *custodia* and *rationes conferre* 18^{23} (cast up accounts). Luke has *satis accipere* Ac 17^9, *fora aguntur* 19^{38} (cf. also the D-text of Acts, 19^{34,35} marked *ex lat?* in Nestle). Some others are sometimes cited, but their resemblance to Latin would seem to be incidental. The integrity of Hellenistic Greek, outside the NT, was not seriously contaminated by Latinisms, and this is not really surprising, for we would expect subject peoples to avoid aping the conqueror's language. T. A. Burkill very plausibly considers that the use of *legiōn* in connection with the demoniac (Mk 5$^{1-20}$) betrays anti-Roman feeling (*Mysterious Revelation* 93, n. 12), and we would not consider the extent of the borrowing to be much more significant than this. Rather, external influence on Greek would tend to be other than Latin. Greek language and civilization deeply influenced the Romans; the Romans did not influence the Greek language very much (F.-M. Abel, *Grammaire du Grec Biblique*, Paris 1927, XXXVI).

Codex Bezae. A question which calls for consideration is whether some of the characteristic Semitisms of the Western text are in reality Latinisms: asyndeta and parataxis may perhaps be in this category. Theoretically, asyndeton is as much a Latinism as an Aramaism, especially perhaps when it occurs in Greek books written in Rome, e.g. the *Acts of Pilate* and *Shepherd* of Hermas. Black at any rate thinks not, because the reading involving parataxis will often occur in non-Western MSS alongside the witness of D; moreover, in several instances, it is the Westcott-Hort text which has parataxis and not D (Black^3 67).

E. P. Sanders, *The Tendencies of the Synoptic Tradition*, Cambridge 1969, 251; Taylor, *Mark* 45; P. L. Couchoud, "L'Évangile de Marc a-t-il été écrit en Latin?" *Revue de l'Histoire des Religions* 94 (1926) 161–192. The main argument of the latter, which concerns MSS and versions, we do not find wholly convincing.

Other Literature:

J. W. Hunkin, "Pleonastic *archomai* in the New Testament," *JTS* 25 (1926) 390ff.
J. R. Harris, "An Unnoticed Aramaism in St. Mark," *ET* 26 (1915) 248ff.
C. H. Bird, "Some *gar*-clauses in St. Mark's Gospel," *JTS* NS 4 (1953) 171–187.
R. Morgenthaler, *Statistik des neutestamentlichen Wortschatzes*, Zurich–Frankfurt 1958.
J. C. Doudna, *The Greek of the Gospel of Mark*, Philadelphia P.A. 1961.
R. Bultmann, *The History of the Synoptic Tradition*, ET Oxford 1963, 339ff.
J. G. Williams, "A Critical Note on the Aramaic Indefinite Plural of the Verb," *JBL* 83 (1964) 180–182.
J. J. O'Rourke, "Critical Notes: A note concerning the use of *eis* and *en* in Mark," *JBL* 85 (1966) 349–351.

CHAPTER THREE

THE STYLE OF MATTHEW

It is widely granted that the first evangelist uses sources, certainly Mark, and probably also Q and other documents. However, we are specially concerned with the stylistic matters belonging peculiarly to the evangelist himself rather than to his sources. We shall take special note of the editorial additions and corrections of Mark, and of Matthew's special material, designated M, and of Matthew's special version of Q. We must first consider how Semitic is Matthew's own peculiar style, apart from any features he may take over from Mark.

§ 1. Aramaic Influence

Asyndeta. Although this prominent feature in Mark is relieved by Matthew on some thirty occasions, yet there are still 21 instances of asyndeta in Matthew's Markan sections where Mark has no asyndeton. Mt remedies Mk's asyndeta on the following occasions:

Mk 1^8 (=Mt 3^{11}), 2^9 (=9^5), ^{17} (=9^{13}), ^{21} (9^{16}), 3^{35} (=12^{50}), 5^{39} (=9^{24}), 6^{36} (=14^{15}), 8^{15} (=16^6), ^{29b} (=16^{16}), 10^{14} (=19^{14}), ^{25} (=19^{24}), ^{37} (=19^{26}), ^{28} (=19^{27}), ^{29} (=19^{28}), 12^{17} (=22^{21}), ^{20} (=22^{25}), ^{22} (=22^{27}), ^{23} (=22^{28}), ^{24} (=22^{29}), ^{36} (=22^{43}), ^{37} (=22^{45}), 13^6 (=24^5), ^{7} (=24^6), ^{8b} (=24^{7b}), ^{8d} (=24^8), ^{9} (=10^{17}), ^{34} (=25^{14}), 14^6 (=26^{10}), ^{9} (=26^{22}), 16^6 (=28^6). But the following asyndeta are in Markan sections where Mk has no asyndeta: Mt 12^3 $13^{13,34}$ 16^{15} $19^{7,8,20,21}$ $20^{21,22,23,26,33}$ 21^{27} $22^{21,32}$ $26^{34,35,42,64}$ 27^{22}. For these references I am indebted to the careful work of E. P. Sanders, *The Tendencies of the Synoptic Tradition*, Cambridge 1969, 240f.

The asyndetic *he says/they say* is presumably based on the Aramaic ptc. '*āmar*, '*āmᵉrîn*. Asyndetic *legei* never occurs in Mk, but all the following are peculiar to Mt: 9^{28} 13^{28b}D $19^{7,10}$ $20^{7,22,33}$ $21^{31,41}$ $22^{21,42}$ 27^{22}. Although Mk has asyndetic *ephē* three times (9^{38} 10^{29} 12^{24}), the following are peculiar to M or Mt's Q or to his editorial adjustments to Mk: 4^7 19^{21} not B 21^{27} 22^{37}D $25^{21,23}$ 26^{34} 27^{65} not D.

Excluding *he says/they say*, notable instances of asyndeton in Mt are 6^{14} 19^{22}D (which are alterations in Markan sections) 25^{14}D ^{22} (Mt's Q) 12^{42} (Q) 22^{25}D (also in Mk).

Therefore while it is true that Matthew's use of particles is actually the highest in the NT (cf. below), yet asyndeton in Matthew is considerable, occurring both within and without the teaching of Jesus. Despite his wide use of particles, asyndeta may still be said to be a feature of the styles of Matthew and Mark.

Other Aramaic Features. *1. Reflexives.* Black[3] (102ff) urges that 23^{31} (*bear witness to yourselves*) and 23^9D (*do not call you*), as well as Mk 7^4D, Jn 19^{17}, are Semitic forms of reflexives, the Aramaic ethic dative, which in non-Biblical Greek would be expressed by the middle voice. Black gives convincing examples from the Elephantine papyri, e.g. *I went me home, he went him up to the roof, he fell him asleep.*

2. Adverbial *palin* in the gospels probably represents the Aramaic *tubh* (*then*) which occurs 26 times in Mark, but only a few times in non-Markan parts of Matthew.

Mt sometimes copies *palin* from Mk (21^{36} $26^{42.43.72}$), and sometimes he uses it independently, although most of these instances are better understood in the normal sense of *again* (4^7 *again it is written*, 5^{33} *again you have heard*, perhaps also 13^{45} 19^{24} 20^5 22^1 $26^{43.44.72}$ 27^{50}). Only on the following occasions has it certainly the Aramaic sense : 4^8 *then the devil takes him* (Mt's Q), 18^{19} *then verily I say to you* (M), 22^4 *then he sent other servants* (Mt's Q). Black[3] 112f.

3. The redundant *begin to* is an Aramaism which Matthew has reduced from Mark's 26 instances to his own 13, but that is not the complete picture. In view of the following evidence it cannot be urged that Matthew was trying to improve the style of Mark by eliminating the auxiliary *begin to*.

Mt found this Aramaism in Mk 26 times and retained it only six times (12^1 $16^{21.22}$ $26^{22.37.74}$) ; nevertheless Mt found it also in Q and retained it three times ($11^{7.20}$ 24^{49}), and even more significantly (unless *begin* is not redundant here) he once added it to Mk quite gratuitously (at 4^{17}) ; on a further three occasions it was either in his special M-source or was part of his own editorial work (14^{30} 18^{24} 20^8).

4. *From that hour* 9^{22} 15^{28} 17^{18} (in these Markan sections, the phrase is always peculiar to Mt) is a rabbinical Aramaism. Black[3] 110 n.1.

5. The act. impers. plural is found in Mt as well as in Mk (cf. above p. 12) : Mt 5^{15} (Mt's Q) 9^2 (from Mk) 17^{27} (M) (sing.).

That, we suggest, is the extent of exclusively Aramaic influence upon the peculiarly Matthaean style. It is considerable, but probably not as much as it is in Mark.

§ 2. Hebraic Influence

Sentence Construction. 1. The anarthrous partitive expression as the object of a verb is found in Mark, but independently also in Matthew. One instance he shares with Luke (Q), 23^{34} *some of them you will slay*, and one is from his M-source 25^8 *give us some of your oil*, both with *ek* and both in the teaching of Jesus.

2. Prolepsis of the subject of a subordinate clause occurs in the teaching of Jesus 10^{25} *it is enough for the disciple that (hina) he should be as his Master* (M), when more naturally we should read : *it is enough that the disciple should be as his Master*, 25^{24} *I knew you that you were* (Mt's Q). This is widely used in the NT.

The Verb. Perhaps the Greek aorist, on occasions when the present tense might be more appropriate, is an unconscious substitute for the Hebrew Stative perfect, which is not actually a past tense. The instances occur in the teaching of Jesus and raise the question what language he used. If they reflect the Stative perfect, then he did not use Aramaic on these occasions. However, it is no more likely that he used Hebrew either, but this idiom is a part of free Jewish Greek.

These are all peculiar to Mt : 6^{12} *as we forgive* (i.e. have reached a stage of habitually forgiving), 10^{25} *if they called* (i.e. habitually call) *the householder Beezeboul*, 14^{31} *why did you doubt* (i.e. get into a state of doubting)?, 23^2 *the scribes sat* (do sit) *in Moses's seat*, 13^{24} 22^2 *the Kingdom of Heaven was likened* (is like).

The Noun. 1. Perhaps the omission of the definite article on occasions when normal Greek requires it betrays the habit of thinking in terms of the construct state : 1^{20} $2^{13,19}$ [the] *angel of the Lord* (Mt's free composition), 12^{42} [the] *Queen of the South* (both forms of Q), 12^{35} [the] *good treasury* (both forms of Q).

2. However, sometimes Hebrew idiom will influence the Greek writers towards a needless insertion of the article, reflecting the emphatic state in which a noun is made more definite in order to denote a special person or object.

Mt 5^{15} *under the measure . . . upon the lampstand* (both forms of Q), $12^{24\cdot 27}$ *the demons* (for *some demons*) (Mt Mk Lk), 15^{29} *to the mountain* (add. to Mk), 12^{12}B *a man better than the sheep* (add. to Mk), 18^{19}D* *all the matter* (for *any matter*) M.

3. Literal translation of Heb. infin. absol. is a Septuagintism in Biblical Greek. It occurs in Mt's own work : 2^{10} *rejoiced with joy*. Also in Lk Jn Jas 1 Pet Rev.

The Negative. The strong negative *ou mē* is restricted to the teaching of Jesus. In denials it is usually taken over by Matthew from Mark (16^{28} $24^{2,21,34,35}$ $26^{29,35}$), but occasionally it is peculiarly Matthaean, being added to the Markan material (16^{22} 21^{19}) or taken from Q (5^{26}) or from Matthew's special material ($5^{18,20}$ 15^5). This double negative is a Septuagintal feature of Matthew, Mark, and John.

Thus, the peculiarly Hebrew influence is not considerable. However, any of the instances in the following section may just as well indicate Hebrew influence as Aramaic.

§ 3. Semitic (Hebrew or Aramaic) Influence

Sentence Construction. *1. Parataxis.* Generally, Matthew reduces the Semitic nature of Mark's style in this respect : Luke on 23 occasions, and Matthew on 19, have eliminated Mark's parataxis by the substitution of a participle.

E.g. Mk 1^{41} *he touched and says* = Mt 8^3 *he touched saying*. However, there are four instances of the reverse process, where Mt has the parataxis and Mk is without it : Mt 14^6 *she danced and pleased* = Mk 6^{22} *dancing she pleased*, Mt 17^{11} *Elijah comes and will restore* = Mk 9^{12} *Elijah coming restores*, Mt 21^{12} *he entered and cast out* = Mk 11^{15} *entering he cast out*, Mt 26^{69} *Peter sat outside and she came up* = Mk 14^{16} *while Peter was below she comes*. I owe these instances to E. P. Sanders, 238f.

It cannot therefore be urged that Matthew was " improving " the style of Mark in this respect, nor that Matthew felt that parataxis was alien to his own style.

2. Casus Pendens. This too is a genuine feature of Matthew's style, but it must be admitted that, since all the examples are from the words of Jesus, the casus pendens may be due to literal translation from the Semitic language of Jesus.

Mt 24^{13} has borrowed from Mk *he that endureth . . . he shall be saved*, the remainder being from M (13^{38} *the good seed, these are . . .*, 19^{28} *you that have . . . you shall . . .*) or Mt's additions to Markan sections ($13^{20,22,23}$ *that sown . . . this is*, 15^{11} *not that which enters . . . this defiles the man*, 26^{23} *he that dips . . . this man shall*). To these examples of Burney (*Aramaic Origin* 65), Black adds 6^4D *and thy Father . . . he shall recompense*, 12^{36} *every idle word . . . he shall account for it* (M), 5^{40}D *he that wishes . . . let him*, 12^{32} *whosoever shall speak . . . it shall be forgiven him* (Q). Cf. Black³ 53. Black observes that in this respect D has preserved the " primitive text " better than SB. It should be noted that in this Semitic construction *ekeinos* or *houtos* is equally possible, but that Mt favours the latter.

3. Questions as protasis of a conditional clause. Black points out that in Semitic languages a question may be a substitute for a condition, as in Ps 25^{12} *who is the man that fears the Lord* (= if a man fears the Lord). In Hebrew, " in lively speech aided by intonation almost any direct form of expression without particles may be equivalent to what in other languages would be a conditional " (A. B. Davidson, *Hebrew Syntax*³, Edinburgh 1901, § 132, rem. 2). In Mt there is a possible instance : 24^{45} *if a faithful and wise servant has been made overseer . . . blessed is he when his lord returns and finds him so doing* (Q).

The Verb. 1. Periphrastic tenses when found in Mark are nearly always changed by both Matthew and Luke, but Matthew leaves unaltered the periphrastic tenses at 7^{29} 10^{21} 13^{30} 19^{22} 26^{43} $27^{33,55}$. In addition he retained 24^{40t} *shall be grinding* from Q (Mt and Lk's), and quite independently added 5^{25} 10^{30} 24^{38} (in Mt's Q), and 1^{23} 9^{36} 12^4 16^{19} $18^{18,20}$ 27^{61} (special source M or Mt's editorial work). The love for periphrastic tenses is therefore not peculiar to Mark.

2. The auxiliary verb *take* is very common in Matthew, who takes it from Mark only four times.

From Mk : Mt 21³⁵ *taking he beat,* ³⁹ *taking they cast,* 26²⁶·²⁷ *taking the bread/cup, he blessed/gave thanks.* The only other instances are Mt's own work (17²⁷ 25¹ 27²⁴·⁴⁸·⁵⁹) or else from Q (13³¹·³³). It corresponds to Heb. *lāqaḥ, nāṭal,* Aram. *nᵉṣab.*

3. The auxiliary *come* (Heb. *lek,* Aram. *'ᵃzal*) is sometimes taken from Mark (9¹⁸ 15²⁵ 26⁴³), and Matthew uses it independently at 2⁸·⁹·²³ 4¹³ 5²⁴ 18³¹ 20¹⁰ 27⁶⁴ 28¹³ (all M), 8⁷ 12⁴⁴ 24⁴⁶ 25²⁷ (Q), 8¹⁴ 9¹⁰·²³ 13⁴ 14¹² 16¹³ (additions to Mark).

4. Use of the impersonal plural is Semitic, though it has been claimed as an Aramaism (cf. pp. 12, 89). It was frequent in Mark, but Matthew has it quite independently at 1²³ *they shall call his name* (M), 5¹⁵ *do they light* (Q), 7¹⁶ *they gather* 9¹⁷ *they put new wine* (Matthew only).

5. True, Matthew has changed Mark's historic present 78 times (Sanders 246), not because he found it alien to his style, for he has the tense 23 times when it is absent from Mark's parallel. However, it is doubtful whether the excessive use of historic present can certainly be claimed as a Semitism; " modern Aramaic scholars seem not to consider it an Aramaism, and it is not included in their discussions " (Sanders 253). As Sanders observes, the use is probably a matter of taste, but, we suspect, strongly affected by Jewish influence (above p. 20).

Pronoun. 1. *Substitutes for indefinite pronoun (tis). Heis* is the equivalent of Heb. *'aḥadh,* Aram. *ḥadh.* Although Mt retains Mk's *heis* on two occasions (19¹⁶ 22³⁵ = Mk 10¹⁷ 12²⁸), yet on three other occasions he supplies *one* where Mk does not (21¹⁹ 26⁵¹ 27⁴⁸) ; sometimes he has conflated Mk and Lk (9¹⁸ v.l. 22³⁵ 26⁶⁹), and once he has taken it from Q (8¹⁹). Twice otherwise it is peculiar to Mt (12¹¹ 18²⁴). On another occasion, 27⁴⁸ *one of them (heis* as pure pronoun), he has altered Mk's more normal *tis* in the Semitic direction.

Other substitutes for the indefinite pronominal adjective include *anthrōpos* : 7⁹ *what man of you* (Q), 9³²D *dumb man* (M), 11¹⁹ *gluttonous man* (Q), 12¹¹ *what man of you* (Mt only), 13²⁸ *an enemy man* (M), ⁵² *a householder man* (M), ⁴⁵D *a man a merchant* (M), 18²³ *a king man* (M), 21²³ *a householder man* (Mt and Lk have only *man*), 25²⁴ *a hard man* (Q), 27³² *a man a Cyrenian* (Mt's add.), ⁵⁷ *a rich man* (Mt's add.).

Also *anēr* : 7²⁴ *wise man* (Q), ²⁶ *foolish man* (Q), 12⁴¹ *Ninevite man* (Q). Also *anthrōpos* as an indef. pronoun proper : 8⁹ *one under authority* (Q), 9⁹ *one sitting* (Mt only), 11⁸ *one clothed* (Q), 12⁴³ *out of someone* (Q), 13³¹ *someone sowed* (Q), ⁴⁴ *someone hid* (M), 17¹⁴ *someone kneeling* (Mt only ; Lk *anēr*), 21²⁸ *someone had* (M), 22¹¹ *someone without a wedding garment* (Mt's add.).

We see then that this idiom occurs in Mt's own work and must be part of his style.

2. *Superfluous pronoun.* Instances of oblique cases of *autos* occur throughout all strata of the Gospel : M 1²·¹¹·¹⁸ 5¹·²²·²⁸·³⁵ Markan 3³·⁴·⁶·¹³

Q 4^6 $5^{2.25.32.45}$ and so on. For parallel passages of Mt, Mk and Lk, E. P. Sanders examines Mt's occurrences of the superfluous genitive pronoun where Mk is lacking it, and vice versa, with these results : proportion Mt : Mk :: 14 : 16, proportion Mt : Lk :: 15 : 7, illustrating that Mk is most addicted to this superlative pronoun and Lk the least. However, " the difference is not large enough to be of significance " (Sanders 167f, 184) ; " and the Semitic Matthew's usage is no more abundant than Mark's or Luke's " (*Grammar* III 38).

3. *Resumptive pronoun after a relative.* This characteristic Semitic feature, found in Mk, is used independently by Mt or taken over from Q by Mt ; 3^{12} *of whom the fan is in his hand*, 10^{11}D *into whatsoever city . . . you enter into it*, 18^{20}D *among whom I am not in the midst of them.*

4. *Proleptic nominative pronoun.* Used by Mk 6^{17} $12^{36.37}$, it is also added to a Markan section by Mt (3^4 *he, i.e. John*). It is " evidence for a very primitive kind of translation or Semitic Greek. It would not, of course, be understood by Greek readers who were not Jews or Greek-speaking Syrians. . . . Many other examples were probably removed [by revising scribes] from the primitive text " (Black[3] 100).

5. *Distributive pronoun* : *heis . . . heis* for *one . . . another*. Some of the Markan instances (Mk $4^{8.20}$ 9^5 10^{37} 14^{19} 15^{27}) Mt has adopted 20^{21} 27^{38}, but in Mt's Q we find the same idiom $24^{40.41}$. However, he seems to have left Q unaltered at 6^{24} where Q has the normal Greek (*one . . . another*) in both Mt's and Lk's version, and he has altered Mk 4^8 into less Semitic Greek (13^8).

6. *Reflexive pronoun.* In common with other NT authors, Mt is prone to use the simple pronoun where a reflexive would be more normal : 6^{19} *treasure up treasure for you* (= yourselves), 17^{27} *for me and you* (= myself and yourself), 18^{15} *judge between you and him* (= yourself).

The reflexive pronoun tended to fall out in Biblical Greek, in favour of simple pronoun. " The confusion has a Semitic explanation, in that Hebrew-Aramaic pronominal suffixes allow no distinction between personal and reflexive " (*Grammar* III 42).

Conjunctions. Epexegetical *hina* : the use of *hina* in Matthew is not considerable compared with some NT authors (cf. below pp. 73f), but the epexegetical *hina* occurs fairly often. Matthew takes it directly from Mark, but twice (with Luke) from Q (4^3 7^{12}), once from Mt's Q (18^{14}), once from M (28^{10}). On the whole, Matthew tends to substitute an infinitive expression for Mark's *hina*.

Prepositions. An instance of interest and difficulty concerns *pros* at 27^{14} *he answered him TO not even a word* (πρὸς οὐδὲ ἓν ῥῆμα). Black (117) tentatively suggests the Aramaic *l^equbhla* but with hesitation. In fact, the idiom is a Septuagintism, although it does not directly correspond with a parallel Hebrew construction, occurring at Job 9^3 (μὴ ἀντείπῃ πρὸς ἕνα λόγον), and the idiom may belong not to translation Greek but to Jewish Greek. On the whole, Matthew is not as Septuagintal in style as Luke.

But the citations peculiar to Mt are akin to the LXX, and even when they differ do not correspond with the Hebrew (K. Stendahl, *The School of St. Matthew and its Use of the Old Testament*, Uppsala 1954). The following citations seem to be free renderings from the Hebrew : 2^6 8^{17} 13^{35} 14^{15f} 27^{9f}. Citations taken from Mk are either left unchanged or else brought nearer to the LXX.

§ 4. Relative Semitic Quality of Matthew and Mark

It is sometimes assumed that Matthew writes Greek of a less Aramaic quality than Mark, and that he tends to soften the Semitisms in general. That is not always true : we have found already many Semitisms which may be attributed to Matthew independently of Mark. Nevertheless, besides those already noted there are some general Semitic-type phrases which have been put forward to show that Mark is more Semitic than Matthew.

E.g. Mk 3^{28} *the sons of men* (Mt 12^{31} *the men*), Mk 4^{20} τὴν γῆν τὴν καλήν (Mt 13^{23} adj. placed between art. and noun, and in other ways the style of this passage in Mt is more elegant), Mk 4^{22} *nothing is hid, unless in order that* (Mt 10^{26} *nothing is hid which shall not*), Mk 7^{20} *that which* . . . *that defiles* (Mt 15^{18} less Semitic), Mk 8^{36} *gain the whole world AND forfeit* (Mt 16^{26} *but for and*), Mk 9^9 *unless when* (Mt 17^9 *until* less Semitic), Mk 11^{24} *it shall be to you* (Mt 21^{22} *you shall receive*), Mk 11^{29} *answer me AND I shall tell you* (Mt 21^{24} first part conditional), Mk 11^{32} *BUT we say* (Mt 21^{26} *IF we say*), Mk 12^2 partitive expression as obj. of verb (Mt 21^{34} altered to accus.), Mk 12^{19} *die and leave* . . . *and not leave* (Mt 22^{24} participle).

It is true that in these instances Matthew has substituted an expression which has a normal Greek sound for one with a Semitic flavour. Yet if we examine the Markan sections of Matthew we shall find the contrary evidence, suggesting that Matthew has altered Mark to something more Semitic, confirming what we have already found.

E.g. Mt 12^{24} *this one does not cast out demons unless by Beezeboul* (Mk 3^{22} less Semitic : *he cast out demons by Beezeboul*), Mt 12^{25} *every city* . . . *shall not* (Mk 3^{25} *if a house*). . .), Mt 13^{19} *everyone hearing* (Mk 4^{15} *when they hear*), Mt $13^{20.22.23}$ *that which* . . . *this is* (Mk $4^{16.18.20}$ less Semitic), Mt 15^{11} *that which comes* . . . *this* (Mk 7^{15} *the things which*), Mt 26^{23} *the one dipping* . . . *this one* (Mk 14^{20} no Semitism), Mt 27^{42} *let him come down AND we will believe* (Mk 15^{32} . . . *in order that*. . . .)

It would seem then that there is very little to choose between the relative Semitism of Mark's and Matthew's style. Neither Matthew nor Luke discloses any significant tendency to avoid the Semitisms of Mark. Mark is no more likely to be an Aramaic translation than Matthew or Luke ; in some respects (e.g. parataxis) Mark may be more Semitic, but even this does not suggest direct translation. Matthew's Greek is assuredly not a translation, in spite of its Semitic idiom, for its style is too smooth, too much interspersed with subordinate clauses and genitives absolute, one of the latter appearing every twenty verses.

Men ... de, not at all characteristic of translation Greek, occurs in the teaching of Jesus, his disciples, and the Baptist. The Greek puns are too complex to have been transmitted in a translation.

E.g. even in the teaching of Jesus we have 6^{16} ἀφανίζουσιν ... φανῶσιν (they disfigure ... to appear), 16^{18} (the Peter-Rock pun), 21^{41} κακοὺς κακῶς. Thus, " it would have been pointless for early translators of the Lord's words to indulge in clever adornments, and interest in language for its own sake could not have been very high on their list of priorities " (Grammatical Insights 181).

§ 5. A Smoother Style than Mark

Particles. Matthew's usage is the most considerable in the NT, with one particle every three lines of Nestle, closely followed by Luke-Acts with one in four lines; but although Matthew uses men ... de twice as frequently as Mark pro rata (once in 100 lines for Matthew; once in 212 for Mark), he still falls behind all other NT authors in this respect, except for the Johannine epistles and Revelation.

Mt retains two instances of Mk's men ... de ($26^{24.41}$), one he shares with Lk from Q (9^{37}), and the rest are either from Mt's Q (16^3 $22^{5.8}$ $23^{27.28}$ 25^{15}) or Mt's source M and his editorial additions (3^{11} 10^{13} $13^{4.8.23.32}$ 16^{14} 17^{11} 20^{23} 21^{35} 25^{33}).

The frequence of gar is about the same as in Mark (one in 15 lines), less frequent than Paul and Hebrews, more so than Luke-Acts and the Johannine writings. The frequence of oun is about the same as Paul's (one in 35 lines), of alla slightly more than Luke-Acts (one in 54 lines) but substantially less than the Johannine epistles, Paul, and 1 Peter.

Change to less vernacular speech.

a. *Doubtful instances of this.* Hina after a verb of command (Mk 6^8) is absent from Mt 10^{10}, perhaps because Matthew did not favour the emerging popularity of hina. W. C. Allen presented its absence as an instance of Matthew's correction of Mark's harsh syntax (Mark ICC xxvii). More probably there is no significance in the change, for Matthew failed to correct Mark at 16^{20} 20^{31}, and he has hina after commands several times: in Q-sections 4^3 14^{36}, in M 28^{10}, or simply added gratuitously to Mark 26^{63}.

The removal of some of Mk's favourite words may be a bid to make the style more literary: *immediately, again,* adverbial *polla,* and recitative *hoti.* It is true that Mt has reduced 42 instances of Mk's euthus to seven, 28 instances of palin to 16, 27 instances of recitative hoti to about 13 (Grammar III 326). About 60 times he has substituted de for kai, and although he has 93 instances of historic present, he often alters Mk's characteristic imperfect and historic present to more normal aorist (he retains only about 20 examples out of 150). Here again, however, caution is required. He retains 66 examples of *he says/ they say*, and so one should avoid exaggerating the extent to which Mt normalizes the style of Mk.

Sometimes the change of voice is towards a more conventional but less vivid Greek style, as when Mk 1^{12} *the Spirit drives him* becomes Mt 4^1 *he was led up by the Spirit*; Mk 1^{31} *he raised her up* becomes Mt 8^{15} *she arose*; and Mk 5^{40} *having put them all forth* becomes Mt 9^{25} *when the crowd was put forth*. On the other hand again, the very reverse process takes place from Mk 15^{46} *a tomb which had been hewn out of the rock* to Matthew's more vivid active voice, *which he had hewn in the rock* 27^{60}.

We must now look critically at the claim that Matthew avoids a compound verb followed by the same preposition (alleged by Allen, *Matthew* ICC). True, he does avoid it on a few occasions:

Mk 1^{16} *para-* . . . *para-* becomes Mt 4^{18} *peri-* . . . *para-*, Mk 1^{21} 2^1 3^1 5^{13} *eis-* . . . *eis* becomes either Mt 4^{13} 9^1 12^9—— *eis* or 8^{32} *ap-* . . . *eis*, Mk 5^{17} *apo-* . . . *apo* becomes Mt 8^{34} *meta-* . . . *apo*, and Mk 6^1 *ek-* . . . *ekeithen* becomes Mt 13^{53} *meta-* . . . *ek*.

This is not the whole truth, for Matthew retains Mark's *eis-* . . . *eis* on a number of occasions: 10^{11} $12^{4.29}$ $15^{11.17}$. He takes *ek-* . . . *ek* from Q ($15^{11.18}$) and from M (27^{53}). The avoidance is therefore a matter of chance and not a regular feature of style.

This is confirmed by the circumstance that in some other respects Mt is quite vernacular in style. He is indifferent to the distinction between definite and indeterminate relative pronouns, i.e. between *hos* and *hostis*. He has *hostis* on several occasions when *hos* would be less vernacular; and only one instance is taken from Mk (Mt 16^{28}), the rest being part of his special source M or of his editorial work 7^{15} 13^{52} 19^{12}bis 20^1 $21^{33.41}$ 25^1 $27^{55.62}$, or else they are peculiar to his Q material 7^{28} 22^2 23^{27}. Then again, in common with other NT authors (Mk, Lk-Ac, Jn) he attempts to use the gen. absol. but fails to use it properly, making it once agree with the subject (1^{18}M), and often using it in place of the ptc. in the dative: 1^{20} 9^{18} 8^{28} 18^{24} (M), 5^1 $8^{1.5}$ 21^{23} (Mt's Q), 9^{10} 27^{17} (Mt only). In textual transmission, atticizing scribes have often made the necessary correction.

b. More probable instances. It is difficult to decide how far Matthew's changes are intended to be improvements upon Mark, but there is no doubt that some of Matthew's changes make for smoother Greek: e.g. the substitution of *epi* for *eis* (e.g. Mt 3^{16} 24^{30}) and the replacing of vulgar and Semitic *pros* by a plain dative (8^{16} 9^2 17^{17} 22^{23} 27^{58}). Doubtless Matthew has improved the vernacular of Mark by avoiding his *hotan* with indicative (Mk 3^{11} $11^{19.25}$) and his *hopou an* with indicative (Mk 6^{56}) which also occur in Rev 14^4.

Avoidance of Redundancy. Matthew seeks to avoid Mark's repetition and prolixity of expression by some significant omissions.

Examples are as follows, the bracketed words being Mt's omissions : Mk 1^{15} (*the time is fulfilled and*) *the Kingdom of God has drawn near* ; *repent* (*and believe in the Gospel*), Mk 1^{32} *it being evening* (*when the sun had set*), Mk 1^{42} *and immediately the leprosy* (*went away from him and he*) *was cleansed*, Mk 2^{20} *then* (*in that day*), Mk 2^{25} *when they* (*had need and*) *were hungry*.

Matthew will avoid Mark's prolixity on occasion by removing a superfluous indirect object, whether introduced by plain dative or by *pros* (Sanders 158f).

First of all, after a verb of saying, the indirect object *to him/her/them/one another* is omitted by Mt (Mk 1^{40} = Mt 8^2, Mk 1^{41} = Mt 8^3, Mk 2^{17} = Mt 9^{12}, Mk 4^{11} = Mt 13^{11}, Mk 4^{35} = Mt 8^{18}, Mk 4^{41} = Mt 8^{27}, Mk 5^{34} = Mt 9^{22}, Mk 5^{39} = Mt 9^{23}, Mk 7^{18} = Mt 15^{16}, Mk 7^{28} = Mt 15^{27}, Mk 8^1 = Mt 15^{32}, Mk 8^{17} = Mt 16^8, Mk 8^{27} = Mt 16^{13}, Mk 8^{28} = Mt 16^{14}, Mk 8^{29} = Mt 16^{16}, Mk 9^{12} = Mt 17^{17}, Mk 9^{36} = Mt 18^3, Mk 10^{14} = Mt 19^{14}, Mk 10^{26} = Mt 19^{25}, Mk 10^{38} = Mt 20^{22}, Mk 10^{42} = Mt 20^{25}, Mk 11^{28} = Mt 21^{23}, Mk 12^{14} = Mt 22^{16}, Mk 12^{15} = Mt 22^{18}, Mk 12^{16} = Mt 22^{21}, Mk 14^{13} = Mt 26^{18}, Mk 14^{20} = Mt 26^{23}, Mk 15^2 = Mt 27^{11}, Mk 15^{14} = Mt 27^{23}). Then also after *command* Mk 6^{39} = Mt 14^{19}, *come* Mk 1^{40} = Mt 8^2, *mock* Mk 10^{34} = Mt 20^{19}, Mk 15^{31} = Mt 27^{41}, *bring* Mk 11^7 = Mt 21^7, *send* Mk 12^4 = Mt 21^{36}, *indignant* Mk 14^4 = Mt 26^8.

Matthew's intention, however, may be only apparent, else it is unaccountable why sometimes he makes a point of adding a superfluous indirect object to Mark.

Mt 19^3 *came up to him* (Mk 10^2), Mt 21^2 *bring him to me* (Mk 11^2), Mt 21^{33} *set a hedge to it* (Mk 12^1), Mt 21^{40} *do to those tenants* (Mk 12^9), Mt 22^{19} *brought to him* (Mk 12^{16}), Mt $26^{40.45}$ *comes to the disciples* (Mk $14^{37.41}$), Mt 26^{69} *came to him* (Mk 14^{66}), Mt 26^{68} *prophesy to us* (Mk 14^{65}). Mt adds the indirect object to Mk's verb of saying: Mt 21^6 = Mk 11^6, Mt 21^{25} = Mk 11^{31}, Mt 26^{10} = Mk 14^6, Mt 26^{64} = Mk 14^{62}, Mt 27^{14} = Mk 15^5.

Avoidance of the graphic. Matthew will often avoid the vividly and descriptively colourful in Mark, and will seek a more commonplace expression. Not that Matthew is less Semitic, but he certainly is less dramatically picturesque.

E.g. such phrases as *were opened* Mt 3^{16} in place of *split asunder* Mk 1^{10} ; *he was led up* Mt 4^1 in place of *he throws him out* Mk 1^{12} ; *throwing a casting-net* Mt 4^{18} in place of *casting around* Mk 1^{16} ; *bed* (a classical word) Mt 9^6 in place of *pallet* (a late loan-word) Mk 2^{11} ; *put on* Mt 9^{16} in place of *stitch on* (a very rare word) Mk 2^{21} ; *like the light* Mt 17^2 in place of *radiant* (a NT hapax) Mk 9^3 ; *eye* (classical) Mt 19^{24} in place of *hole* (in a needle) Mk 10^{25} ; *entrance* (ordinary Hellenistic word) Mt 26^{71} in place of *forecourt* (very rare) Mk 14^{68} ; *to persuade* Mt 27^{20} in place of *rouse the rabble* (late and rare) Mk 15^{11}.

Systematic arrangement of material. As a teacher Matthew favours certain didactic arrangements involving three, five, seven, and

14. Moreover, the midrashic element is prominent. Matthew betrays a scribal training in other ways too : by the portrait of Jesus which he presents, by his concern over the fulfilment of prophecy and by his conception of Christianity as a reformed Judaism. There are six large discourses containing the teaching of Jesus, each (except the fifth) ending with the formula, *and it happened when Jesus had finished* 7^{28} 11^1 13^{53} 19^1 26^1. 1. The Sermon on the Mount (5–7). 2. Apostolic Instructions (10). 3. Parabolic Discourse (13). 4. The Apostolate (18). 5. The Woes (23). 6. Eschatology (24–25). Perhaps 5 and 6 form one discourse, to make a five-fold division, like the Torah. Accordingly we presume that the author was a Jewish Christian who had undergone rabbinical training.

The Priority of Mark. Matthew's style then is less spectacular, without distinction, smoother than Mark's ; in this respect Matthew's Gospel may be said to be secondary to Mark's, and a development from it. It would be wrong however to conclude that the reduction of Semitisms is a sign of development. In an important chapter (" IV. Diminishing Semitism as a Possible Tendency of the Tradition," *op. cit.*), E. P. Sanders shows that although Mark is richer in certain Semitisms (e.g. parataxis, anacolutha), and although it " suited Mark's redactional style to write vernacular Greek more than it did the style of Matthew and Luke," yet on this evidence alone Mark is not the earliest gospel (Sanders 255). The Semitisms seem to me not to stem entirely from the speech of Jesus, but to belong to the style used by all the evangelists. How the Semitisms came into the language is a difficult question, but we doubt whether it was entirely through the translation of Aramaic or Hebrew documents. At any rate, although Mark is more Semitic in style it is not for that reason any closer to a primitive tradition.

§ 6. FURTHER STYLISTIC CHARACTERISTICS OF MATTHEW

Probably for mnemonic purposes, not clear to us, Matthew has the habit of repeating a phrase within the compass of a short passage, never to use it again. It seems no more than a curious habit.

Thus, within 2^{1-19} are three similar phrases : 1. *When Jesus was born* (gen. absol.) *behold.* 2. *When they departed* (gen. absol.) *behold.* 3. *When Herod was dead* (gen. absol.) *behold.* Within 3^{1-13} are two phrases : 1. *John comes.* 2. *Jesus comes.* Within 4^{12}-5^1 three phrases : 1. *And Jesus hearing.* 2. *And Jesus walking.* 3. *And he seeing.* Within 4^{20-22} *immediately leaving* (twice). Within 8^{23-28} two phrases : 1. *And having embarked* (dat.). 2. *And having come* (dat.). Within 9^{26-31} two phrases : 1. *Into all that land.* 2. *In all that land.* Within 11^{25}–12^1 : *And at that time* (twice). Within 13^{24-33} three phrases : 1. *He put forth another parable to them saying* (twice). 2. *Another parable he spoke to them*. Within 13[44-47] three phrases : 1. *Is like*. 2. *Again is like* (twice). Within 15[21-29] *And departing thence* (twice).

The Use of Prepositions. It is possible to some extent to determine the quality of Matthew's style from the kind of prepositions he uses and their relative frequence. From the evidence below Matthew would seem to be in a class with Hebrews, James, 1 Peter, and Luke-Acts.

Of all the NT authors it is Mt who comes nearest to Polybius in the use of cases with *epi* (Polybius gen : dat : accus : proportion of 1,5 : 1 : 3, Mt proportion of 1,6 : 1 : 3,3), in contrast to Jn (1,7 : 1 : 3,5) and the LXX (1,4 : 1 : 3,8) who are almost in the same category. However, in the relative frequence of *en* and *epi*, Mt is closest to Heb (1 : 0,41) ; and in the proportion of cases with *dia* he is closest to Jas (gen : accus :: 1 : 1). In the proportion of *en : eis* Mt is exactly in the category of Lk-Ac and 1 Pet (*en : eis* :: 1 : 0,8). Moreover, he is more careful than any NT author to preserve the distinction between *eis* and *en*, the nearest to him being Jn. In making a comparatively frequent use of *anti* (five times), Mt is comparable with Heb, Jas, and 1 Pet. Moreover, Mt and 1 Pet are the only NT authors to use *aneu* (Mt 10[29] 1 Pet 3[14] [9]). In the proportion of *apo : ek* Mt is once more in the class of Lk-Ac and Heb, as the following figures show :

Mt	1,2 : 1	Jas	0,4 : 1
Mk	0,6 : 1	1 Pet	0,6 : 1
Lk-Ac	1,2 : 1	2 Pet. Jude	0,6 : 1
Jn	0,2 : 1	Joh. Epp	0,6 : 1
Paul	0,5 : 1	Rev	0,3 : 1
Heb	1 : 1		

Mt's use of *pro* (once in 398 lines) is almost the same as Paul's (once in 366 lines) ; Mt's preference for *meta* c. gen as against *sun* is shared by the Joh. writings (including Rev) and Heb and to some extent Mk, viz.

Mt	15 : 1	Heb	14 : 0
Mk	9 : 1	Jas	0 : 1
Lk-Ac	1,2 : 1	Joh. Epp.	8 : 0
Jn	39 : 1	Rev	39 : 0
Paul	1,7 : 1		

Mt makes about the same use of *heneka* as Mk, and rather more than Lk-Ac or Paul, the only other NT users. The prepositional use of *heōs* by Mt (once in 104 lines) is nearest to that of Lk-Ac (once in 170) and Jas (once in 216), though Mk, Paul and Heb also have it to a less extent. Using *mechris*, Mt closely resembles Paul and Heb and to a less extent Mk and Lk-Ac. Mt uses *achri(s)* less frequently than Lk-Ac, Paul, Heb and Rev.

THE STYLE OF MATTHEW

The Use of Other Syntax. 1. *Number.* Zerwick (*Graecitas Biblica* § 4a) suggests that the use of *pluralis categoriae*, twice in Mt, should be rendered by the singular : 2^{23} *prophets* 27^{44} *robbers* (when only one prophet and robber is intended). But also : 14^9 (=Mk) 21^7 22^7 28^9. Moreover, *many crowds* 4^{25} $8^{1.18}$v.l. 13^2 15^{30} 19^2 is Mt's idiom for *a great crowd* and is not to be understood of separate groups. It may reflect late Greek usage (*Grammar* III 26).

2. *Tοῦ* c. infin. (in a final sense) belongs to the LXX and the higher Koine ; in the NT it is confined to the more " literary " books : Mt (six times), Lk–Ac (50), Paul (19), Heb (five), Jas (two), 1 Pet (two). The single instance in Rev is probably an independent imperative (cf. p. 152). The instances in Mt are usually his own work, but one is an agreement of Mt and Lk against Mk (13^3 *went out to sow*) while one is from Q (24^{45} *in order to give*), shared with Lk. Mt's own are 2^{13} *to kill him* (M), 3^{13} *to be baptized* (add. to Mk) 11^1 *departed to teach* (M), 21^{32} *repented in order to believe* (M).

Vocabulary. We can distinguish certain words as quite characteristic of Matthew. In total he has a vocabulary of some 1690 words, of which 112 are NT hapax. Among the latter, 26 occur in the LXX. Among Matthew's favourite words and phrases may be noted the following, which occur in all strata (Birth narrative, Markan sections, Q and L).

ὄχλος:	sing. and plur. 47 times (but Mk has 38).
πληρόω:	16 times.
δικαιοσύνη:	seven times.
ὑποκριτής:	ten times.
ἰδού:	45 times.
ἀναχωρέω:	ten times, borrowed from Mk at 12^{15}, but also in M.
προφέρω:	14 times.
προσέρχομαι:	52 times.
συνάγω:	24 times.
πλήν:	five times, as cp. with Mk one, Lk–Ac 19, Paul five ; Mt is especially fond of πλὴν λέγω ὑμῖν ($11^{22.24}$Q 18^7 $26^{39.64}$ adds. to Mk).
τότε:	about 90 times ; not only to mark a new paragraph, but also in narrative and parables.
ἐκεῖθεν:	12 times.
ὥσπερ:	ten times.
ὅπως:	17 times.

weeping and gnashing of teeth : seven times.
to outer darkness : 8^{12} 22^{13} 25^{30}.
to make fruit (a Semitism) : 3^{10} (Lk) 7^{12tt} (Lk) 13^{26} Rev 22^2.

ἕτερος: confined to Lk–Ac, Paul, and Mt, but it is not always correctly used (of duality). Mt uses it once correctly 6^{24} (Mt's and Lk's Q) 10^{23} *the next* (M) 11^3 (Mt's Q ; Lk alters to ἄλλον) 11^{16} (Mt's Q ; Lk alters to ἀλλήλοις) ; 15^{30} 16^{14} (add. to Mk). Thus Mt has it once in 249 lines. Lk–Ac once in 85 lines, Paul (including Pastorals) once in 156 lines, Heb once 120 lines. Mt comes very low on the list of " literary " writers in the NT, judging by vocabulary, as the following table will show ; it is arranged in descending order of richness of vocabulary.

	Total Vocabulary	Concentration
2 Pet–Jude	627	One new word in 0,19 lines
Jas	560	0,39
1 Pet	545	0,39
Pastorals	900	0,49
Heb	1038	0,6
Johann. Epp.	302	0,95
Lk–Ac	4093	1
Mark	1270	1
Mt	1690	1,2
Rev	916	1,4
Jn	1011	1,5
Paul	2170	1,8

Other Literature :

E. von Dobschütz, " Matthäus als Rabbi und Katechet," *ZNW* 27 (1928) 338–348.
T. W. Manson, " The Gospel according to St. Matthew," *BJRL* 29 (1946) 392ff.
M.-J. Lagrange, *Évangile selon S. Matthieu*[8], Paris 1947.
G. D. Kilpatrick, *The Origins of the Gospel according to Saint Matthew*[2], Oxford 1950.
F. V. Filson, " Broken Patterns in the Gospel of Matthew," *JBL* 75 (1956) 227ff.
J. C. Fenton, " Inclusio and Chiasmus in Matthew," *Studia Evangelica* I 1959, 174ff. (adds nothing to N. W. Lund, *Chiasmus in the New Testament*, N. Corolina 1942).
J. Jeremias, " Die Muttersprache des Evangelisten Matthäus," *ZNW* 50 (1959) 270ff.

CHAPTER FOUR

THE STYLE OF LUKE-ACTS

In assessing the Semitic style of Lukan Greek, it is essential to distinguish as far as possible the various strata of the Gospel and Acts, determining the peculiar contribution of the evangelist if we can. We must make a rough-and-ready division in some cases, as there is not unanimous agreement among literary critics, as to what is L and what is Q. In order to render investigation the more objective we have made samples of an equal number of lines (about 260 of Nestle) as follows :

The Infancy narrative : 1^5-2^{52} (269 lines).
Lk's version of Q (a sample of 277 lines) : $6^{20}-7^{10}$ 7^{18-35} $9^{57}-^{62}$ $10^{2-15,21-24}$ $11^{2-4,9-26,29-36}$.
Markan sections of Lk (a sample of 276 lines) : 8^4-9^{50}.
The special source L (a sample of 268 lines) : 15^1-16^{15} 16^{19-31} 17^{7-21} 18^{1-14} 19^{1-27}.
I Acts, i.e. 1–15 (a sample of 268 lines) : 3^1-5^{42}.
II Acts (a sample of 275 lines) : 17^1-19^{40}.
We sections : 16^{10-18} 20^{5-15} 21^{1-18} 27^1-28^{16} (253 lines).

§ 1. ARAMAIC INFLUENCE

Exclusive Aramaic influence, in the sense that it is not also Hebraic, is minimal, in our opinion. It may include more than the following, but other features seem to us questionable.

It is claimed that the influence of the Aramaic particle d^e has sometimes caused misunderstanding, resulting in Luke's abnormal use of *hoti*.

E.g. Ac 1^{17} *hoti* may be understood as a relative pronoun, as in Latin texts of Ac, through the ambiguity of d^e. Ac 7^{39}D *hoti* is read in the D-text instead of the relative in the B-text (Black[3] 74). Lk 8^{25} (=Mk 4^{41} Mt 8^{27}) *hoti* would be better understood as the dat. of relative pronoun (Black[3] 71f), the real meaning being *who is this whom* [not *because*] *the wind and the sea obey him.*

The use of *begin* in Luke-Acts is hardly superfluous enough to suggest the influence of *sharī*.

The use of *tote* is more significant (*Grammar* III 341), since it occurs in the LXX in the parts of Daniel and 2 Esdras which have Aramaic sources. Although the four instances in the We sections of Acts cannot point to translation (Ac 21^{18} $27^{21.32}$ 28^1) yet those in Luke's Q may do so (Lk 6^{42} $11^{24}B^{26}$ 13^{26} 16^{16}), for they are all in the words of Jesus, perhaps reflecting very primitive Aramaic sources behind the Greek Q. Even some of the instances in L (e.g. $14^{9.10.21}$), belonging to the words of Jesus, may reflect an Aramaic source. There are no instances in the Hebrew-sounding Infancy narrative.

Active impersonal plural (cf. p. 12) : Lk 4^{41} (add. to Mk) 8^2 (L) 12^{20} (L).

§ 2. Hebrew Influence

This is far more extensive, and is not confined to the Infancy narrative (which is believed in some quarters to be translated from Hebrew sources).

Sentence-construction. 1. The use of a partitive construction without article as subject or object of a verb occurs in both Matthew's and Luke's Q (Lk 11^{49} as object) ; it also occurs in Luke's own work (if it is the genuine text) when he is not following Mark or Q (8^{35}D ἐκ τῆς πόλεως as subject). Both of these might be taken from an underlying Hebrew source, a translation of a phrase with *min*, as in Gen 27^{28} : *May God give you* (some) *of the dew of heaven*. Cf. also the LXX 1 Kms 14^{45} 2 Kms 11^{17} 14^{11} 4 Kms 10^{23} 1 Mac 7^{33} 10^{37} etc. Nevertheless, an underlying Hebrew source is the more unlikely since the same construction is used by Luke in II Acts and even in the We sections, where we can safely rule out translation from any Hebrew text (Ac 19^{33} in the " Gentile " narrative at Ephesus ; 21^{16} in " diary " narrative). It looks as if the construction belongs to Biblical Greek, and as if the LXX idiom has entered the free-Greek books of Matthew, Luke-Acts, John, Revelation, and the *Shepherd* of Hermas.

2. Another construction, foreign to non-Biblical Greek, is ἐγένετο with a finite verb. H. St. J. Thackeray noted that the usual LXX construction follows the Hebrew literally (*wayᵉhî* followed by a second waw consecutive) : ἐγένετο καὶ ἦλθε. This is what the historical books prefer, whereas the earlier books, Pentateuch and Prophets, prefer it without καί (*Grammar of the Old Testament in Greek*, I Cambridge 1909, 50-52). Luke uses both constructions but consistently has the second in the Infancy narrative, and he prefers it

elsewhere (20 against 13). For this second construction there are no Koine parallels. True, the construction with the infinitive occurs, very rarely in non-Biblical authors, but the preponderance of the strictly Hebraic construction in Luke–Acts indicates that even when Luke sometimes uses the infinitive construction he is still writing Biblical Greek influenced by the LXX (II Acts 19^1; We 16^6 $21^{1.5}$ 27^{44} 28^8; also in I Acts).

3. The anarthrous participle as subject or object of the verb is Hebrew : LXX Isa 19^{20}. In Greek we expect some kind of pronoun, or similar word, to which it can stand in apposition. Lk 3^{14} (elsewhere in NT only in quotations) T Abr 109^{10}.

4. Prolepsis of the subject of a subordinate clause : Lk 24^7 *saying the Son of Man, that he must be betrayed* (add. to Mk), I Acts 3^{10} *they recognized him, that he was . . .*, II Acts 13^{32} 15^{36} *let us see the brethren . . . how they are*, 16^3 Textus receptus *they knew his father that he was a Greek*, 26^5 *knowing me that I have lived. . . .* (cf. pp. 12, 16, 33).

The Verb. 1. Characteristic of Luke is the construction *tou* with infinitive (epexegetical, consecutive, final), as in LXX a reflection of Hebrew *lᵉ*.

It occurs in II Acts (18^{10} $20^{3.20.27.30}$ $23^{15.20}$ 26^{18}bis) and even in We sections (21^{12} $27^{1.20}$) as well as widely elsewhere in Lk–Ac. It may be argued that, in Lk–Ac, Paul, Heb, Jas and Pet, the construction has atticistic affinities, and that sometimes it appears in the papyri (Mayser II 1, 321). But never, outside Biblical Greek is it found so persistently as in the LXX, the NT, and other books written in this kind of Greek, e.g. eight times in T Abr.

The same may be said of *en tō* with present infinitive to express time during which, and aorist to express time after which. This is a frequent Hebraism in all parts of Luke–Acts except Q and the We sections.

Once Lk retains Mk's *en tō* (Lk 8^5), but elsewhere he adds his own to the Markan sections (Lk 3^{21} $8^{40.42}$ $9^{18.29.33.34.36}$ 18^{35} 24^4); he uses it in the Infancy narrative ($1^{8.21}$ $2^{6.27.43}$), in L ($5^{1.12}$ 9^{51} $10^{35.38}$ $11^{1.27.37}$ 12^{15} 14^1 $17^{11.14}$ 19^{15} $24^{15.30.51}$), and in I Acts 2^1 3^{36} 4^{30} 8^6 9^3 11^{15}). The only instance in II Acts (19^1) is so clearly Septuagintal (ἐγένετο ἐν τῷ) that it renders it the more probable that all these instances are influenced by the LXX despite their occasional appearance in the papyri.

2. The literal translation of Hebrew infinitive absolute comes into Biblical Greek from the LXX, where the general method of rendering it is by means of the finite verb with a dative of the cognate noun or else by means of the finite with a participle (which appears in the NT only in quotations). The first method is widely used by Luke in the following phrases : Lk 2^9 (Infancy) *feared with great fear*, 22^{15} (L) *with desire I have desired*, Ac 4^{17} Byzantine text (the main authorities

omitting by homoeoteleuton) *with a warning let us warn them*, Ac 5²⁸ *with a charge we charged you*, Ac 23¹⁴ *with an oath we have taken an oath*. It occurs in other NT books, some of which are thought to be fairly "literary" : Mt 2¹⁰ Jn 3²⁹ *rejoiced with joy*, Jas 5¹⁷ *pray with prayer*, 1 Pet 3¹⁴ *fear their fear*, Rev. 16⁹ *scorched with great scorching*. This is not necessarily a sign of literal translating (cf. the classical Greek instance of *flee with flight*, and the instances in James and 1 Peter), but in the NT indirect Semitic influence seems to me very probable.

The Lukan method corresponds with that of the Pent. in the LXX, for which Thackeray gives these figures : dat. of cognate noun 108 times, participle 49 times. This is the reverse of the position in the later historical books, which employ participial construction almost exclusively. The free-Greek books of the LXX do not have the construction in either form. For classification of the LXX evidence, cf. Thackeray *Grammar* 47-50.

3. The use of the verb *add to*, meaning to do once more, is one of the most frequent Hebraisms in the LXX. Luke has three examples : one in Luke's own Q, one in an addition to a Markan section, and one in I Acts. We assume that Luke was consciously emulating the style of the LXX, rather than taking over source-material ; for although he is not followed by any other NT author, except in the D-text of Mk 14²⁵, yet the idiom belongs to the style of Clement of Rome (cf. Lightfoot's note, Part I, vol. II p. 49, line 18) and of Hermas *Mandate* 4.3.1. As Thackeray observed, the instance in Josephus bears a different meaning (*JTS* 30 [1929] 361ff).

The LXX has three methods of rendering the Heb. verb *ysp* (Thackeray, *Grammar* 52f) : a. By finite verb followed by infin. of the other verb (109 examples). b. Two finite verbs linked by *and* (only nine examples). c. The verb *added* becomes a participle, the other verb becoming finite ; this method, the nearest to normal Greek, is very rare in the LXX (Gen 25¹ Job 27¹ 29¹ 36¹ Est 8⁸). Luke has three examples of a : Lk 20¹¹ᶠbis *he added to send*, Ac 12³ *he added to arrest Peter* ; and only one example of c : Lk 19¹¹ *adding he spoke a parable*.

4. The imperatival infinitive may be derived from the Hebrew infinitive absolute (cf. p. 89) : Lk 22⁴²v.l. παρενέγκαι Ac 15²³ 23²⁶ (Jas 1¹).

Adjectival Genitive. The genitive of quality also occurs in non-Biblical Greek, but some phrases in Luke–Acts are peculiarly Hebraic. As they do not occur in what one can be quite sure was Luke's own composition, it must be left open whether this genitive derives from Semitic sources or from free Semitic Greek.

Lk 16⁸ *the steward of dishonesty*, 18⁶ *the judge of injustice* (both L). Similar to this is the expression of quality of character by the phrase *son of* (in pre-Biblical Greek confined to such phrases as *a son of Greece*, *Grammar* III

208) : Lk 5³⁴ (Markan) 7³⁴ (Lk's Q) 16⁸ (L) Ac 13¹⁰ (perhaps due to Paul's own language). These are Septuagintal phrases, as also is *man of* : Lk 10⁶ (Lk's Q) 20³⁶ (peculiar to Lk).

Physiognomical Expressions. Prepositional phrases with *face, hand*, and *mouth* abound in the LXX. Howard agreed that even the non-Biblical *before the face of* Lk 2³¹ Ac 3¹³ was suggested by OT idiom (*Grammar* II 466). He should have added Lk 10¹ Ac 13²⁴. Some of these phrases occur in the papyri, which may not themselves be free of Semitic influence. In the words of Radermacher (143), " da auch sie von semitischer Beeinflussung nicht frei sind." Moulton regarded prepositional phrases with *face* as " possible in native Greek " but he thought their extensive use was because they render exactly " a common Hebrew locution " (*Grammar* I 14, 81). Specially interesting is their occurrence in II Acts where the question of Semitic sources does not arise : 17²⁶ (Paul preaching obviously in Greek at Athens) 24⁷v.l. (Tertullus speaking, in Jewish [?] Greek, addressing procurator Felix). The preposition *enōpion* occurs twice in II Acts in non-Jewish narrative, concerning Paul in Ephesus, and once in the We sections 27³⁵ in the shipwreck narrative. It belongs to the Koine and medieval Greek, but also to the LXX (for *liphnê* and *le'ênê*). It was a " secondary " Hebraism according to Moulton, due to the " over-use " of a Hebrew phrase which at the same time is not impossible Greek (*Grammar* II 15). The large proportion of its occurrences are not in the Koine but in Biblical literature, and the papyri instances are relatively slight when compared line by line with the LXX, Testament of Abraham, Testaments of the Twelve Patriarchs, Greek Enoch, Psalms of Solomon, and other works of this kind. There are 34 instances in Luke-Acts, 31 in Revelation. In view of its place in Luke's own composition, it is not only a word of translation Greek but belongs to Jewish Greek.

Vocabulary. There are several characteristically Hebrew phrases, found often enough, and not always in the Infancy narrative, especially *rhēma* (= *matter*) Lk 1⁶⁵ 2¹⁵,¹⁹,⁵¹ which is a Septuagintism for *dābhār* Gen 15¹8¹⁴ 19²¹,²² etc. Moulton and Milligan had little to urge against its Hebrew origin, merely observing that *logos* in a similar sense has classical authority, and that *rhēma* in this sense was a Hebraism which may have been so used in vernacular Greek. There is no evidence for its use in vernacular Greek, so far as we know, and its use is confined to translated writings of the OT and those which may also perhaps have been translated (Lk 1 and 2), and also to the Testament of Abraham rec. A 96¹⁵ (probably not a translation), Testament of Solomon V³, V¹⁰ (*do not hide the matter from me*).

Concerning the original language of T Sol, McCown was inclined to favour Greek, with the possibility that the author used Semitic sources already in Greek. C. C. McCown, *The Testament of Solomon*, Leipzig 1922, 43.

But there is another Hebrew phrase not confined to the Infancy narrative: *he has made strength in his arm* 1^{51}, which has the LXX parallel (*Grammar* II 482f). *To make* (*magnify*) *mercy with* Lk 1$^{58.72}$ 10^{07} (L). This is also a Hebraism from the LXX: Gen 24^{12} 1 Kms 12^{24} 20^8 Ps 108 (109)^{21} v.l. It is uniquely Biblical, and in Luke is not due to translation, unless L is a translation from Hebrew. More likely, with Wilcox, we may suspect that " it belongs to the vocabulary of the early Church " (M. Wilcox, *The Semitisms of Acts*, Oxford 1965, 85).

To make with (without the word *mercy*) is entirely Lukan in the NT (Ac 14^{27} 15^4) due to the Hebrew '*im* or '*ēth*. Helbing 7, 324.

Magnify (=*glorify*) is a LXX Hebraism, though it is found sometimes in non-Biblical Greek, but not nearly to the same extent as in Biblical: Lk 1$^{46.58}$ (Infancy), Ac 5^{13} 10^{46} (I Acts), 19^{17} (II Acts).

κατοικέω ἐπί c. gen. is Biblical; elsewhere it is transitive or has ἐν or κατά Ac 17^{26} (II Acts), also Rev and Hermas S 1^6.

σπλαγχνίζομαι came later into non-Biblical Greek. To Bauer's references add T Abr rec. B 116$^{31.32}$. It is frequent in the Synoptic Gospels.

§ 3. Semitic Influence

This is vast, enabling the respective advocates of Aramaic and Hebraic sources to claim the features as Aramaic or Hebrew to suit their purpose.

Parataxis. This is not an incontrovertible Semitic feature, as it is shared with post-classical non-literary Greek. For what it is worth it may be tested by counting the number of main verbs per line and by noting the infrequence of aorist participles of precedent action and genitives absolute. There is no doubt about Luke's paratactic style, although it is much modified in Acts, especially in the We sections (which are well below classical standards in this respect, and much nearer to the non-literary Greek, as far as we examined it, with main verbs and subordinate verbs about equal, quite unlike the classical language which averages considerably more subordinate verbs than main verbs).

The Infancy narrative has 218 main verbs, samples of Lk's Q have 230, the Markan sections have 255, L has 267; but I Acts has much longer sentences with only 176 main verbs; II Acts has about the same with 168; the We sections have even longer sentences, i.e. 147 main verbs. These samples were all about the same length. We may tabulate and thus make a simple comparison of approximate figures as follows.

THE STYLE OF LUKE-ACTS 51

	Lines	Main Verbs	Subord. Verbs	Aor. Ptc.	Gen. Abs.	Subord. Total	Proportion Main : Sub.
Infancy narrative	269	218	52	9	3	64	1 : 0,3
Lk's Q (sample)	277	230	56	18	5	79	1 : 0,3
Markan sections (sample)	276	255	55	38	9	103	1 : 0,4
L (sample)	268	267	64	35	3	102	1 : 0,3
I Acts (sample)	268	176	57	24	6	87	1 : 0,4
II Acts (sample)	275	168	38	42	13	93	1 : 0,5
We	253	147	46	75	27	148	1 : 1
T Abr rec.A I–VII	256	210	30	34	8	72	1 : 0,3
Select papyri	306	200	108	12	19	139	1 : 0,7
Plato *Apolog.* II 1–94, Thucyd. II 1–4, Andocides 1–10	295	129	153	23	14	180	1 : 1,4

Select papyri comprised P. Petrie II xi (1); P. Paris 26; 51; P. Oxy. 294; 472; 533; 742–746; P. Brit. Museum 42.
Under subordinate verbs we have not included participial clauses. Under aorist participle we have not included the obvious Semitisms, *answering, rising, going*.

The Verb. 1. A feature which is alien to non-Biblical Greek is the use of the redundant participles, *rising, answering*, and the various constructions modelled on the Hebrew *wayyēlek*. In some instances it may be assumed that Luke is deliberately Septuagintal because the narrative suggested it, as when the Lord is addressing first Ananias and then Saul. Doubtless, Hebrew was appropriate for the Lord's words on these occasions, and so the earliest tradition was in that language. But Semitic sources cannot really account for the instance in the Sanhedrin scene, which may well have seemed to Luke a felicitous setting for a Septuagintism. Neither can a Semitic source hypothesis account for *answering said* (Hebrew *wayya'an w...*) in II Acts, and yet this particular form of the redundancy is never found outside of Biblical Greek. It is certain therefore that here is an undoubted Semitic feature which is not due to translation; it must belong to Semitic Greek.

Rising constructions do not occur in Lk's Q or the We sections, but are plentiful elsewhere: e.g. II Acts $22^{10,16}$ 23^9 26^{16}). *Answering said* permeates all parts except the We sections (but cf. 21^{13} as a variant), including II Acts (22^{28}D 25^9). Cf. also T Levi 19^2, T Sol II^2, T Abr $106^{4,11,18}$ 107^1B $108^{1,21,23}$ $110^{7,16,21}$ 111^{18} $112^{6,9}$ 113^9 114^6 118^{15}.

2. The otiose participle *saying* (*lēmōr*) occurs often in all strata of Luke-Acts, even in the We sections in such characteristically Greek material as the Lydia-story (16$^{15.17}$), the gaoler (16^{28}), and Paul on shipboard (27$^{10.24.33}$). True, the participle is never indeclinable, as in Revelation and in some books of the LXX, where it is due to direct rendering of the infinitive construct. It belongs essentially to Biblical Greek, although similar expressions occur elsewhere: ἔφη λέγων (Sophocles, Herodotus), ἔφασκε λέγων (Aristophanes), λέγων εἶπεν οὕτω (Demosthenes). It is however a marked feature of Jewish Greek books, e.g. Testament of Abraham rec.A (seven times) and rec.B (six times).

A few papyrus examples were quoted in *Grammar* III 155, but the conclusion reached there was that " such expressions when used on a large scale, as in Bibl. Greek, point away from the popular language to a specialized Semitic background."

3. The periphrastic verb *to be* with participle, as a substitute for imperfect is thought by some to be an Aramaic construction, but in the LXX it renders a Hebrew phrase which is more frequent in later than in earlier books. The periphrasis may be more characteristic of Aramaic, especially that of the OT and Palestinian Talmud, where the perfect $h^a wâ$ and a present participle expresses a continuous state in past time. Its feasibility as a Semitism is reduced by the fact that it is not unknown in non-Biblical Greek and by the doubt whether the periphrasis is not deliberate in Luke-Acts.

We should probably, however, not give the idiom its true periphrastic force in many instances, but regard it as a Semitism (*Grammar* III 87).

There are 33 examples in Lk and 27 in Ac. They do not indicate a Semitic source, for the idiom is found in the We sections 16^{12} 20^{13} 21^{3} and in the rest of II Acts 18^{25} 19^{32}. There is no reason why Semitic sources may not account for its use in Lk 1$^{7.10.21.22}$ 2$^{26.33.51}$ (Infancy narrative), 8$^{32.40}$ 9$^{32.45}$ (Markan) 5$^{1.24}$ (L), Ac 4^{31}, and yet it is more probably not a feature of translation Greek in view of the other references. In the LXX: 2 Esd 4^{24} 5^{11} (from Aramaic). In the periphrastic future which occurs at Ac 6^{4}D 11^{28} 24^{15} 27^{10} (and nowhere else in the NT) the periphrasis probably has genuine force.

Recitative *hoti*. Although this device may be urged as normal Greek, nevertheless either *kî* or *dî* recitative is likely to be the explanation in the large concentration of occurrences in all parts of Luke-Acts, excepting the We sections. Even in II Acts it is well attested, although there is sometimes nothing in person or tense to indicate whether *hoti* introduces direct speech, and not rather indirect (we follow Bruder here). It is prolific in the LXX, the Testament of Abraham and other books of Jewish Greek.

Infancy narrative $1^{25.61}$. Lk's Q 7^4. L 15^{27} 17^{10} 19^{42} 22^{61}. Add. to Mk: 20^5. (Taken from Mk: 4^{41} 5^{26} 8^{49}). I Acts: Ac 3^{22} $5^{23.25}$ 6^{11} 7^6 11^3 13^{34} 15^1. II Acts: 16^{36} 19^{21} 23^{20} 24^{21} 25^8. Xenophon *Anabasis* I, 6,8. Thucydides I 137,4. P. Oxy. I 119^{10}, BU 602^5, 624^{15}, P. Fay. 123^{15}. Herodotus II 115^4. Cf. also MM s.v. *hoti* 2.

Pronouns. There is confusion of personal and demonstrative pronouns in Luke-Acts which may well be due to a similar confusion in Hebrew and Aramaic. Dr. Black considers that *autos ho* may be due to the influence of the Aramaic proleptic pronoun and is therefore " evidence for a very primitive kind of translation or Semitic Greek " (Black³ 96–100). However, its distribution is widespread throughout Luke-Acts and is by no means confined to the words of Jesus or of anyone else who might have spoken Aramaic, especially Ac 16^{18}, and thus the second alternative of Dr. Black is the more probable.

Infancy narrative 1^{36} (Gabriel speaking) 2^{38} (narrative). Lk's Q: 7^{21}D (narrative) 10^7 (Jesus speaking)^{21} (narrative) 12^{12} (Jesus speaking). Additions to Markan sections: 4^{43}D (Jesus speaking) 20^{19} (narrative). L sections: 13^1 (narrative) ^{31} (narrative) 23^{12} (narrative) 24^{13} (narrative) 33 (narrative). I Acts: 7^{52}D (Stephen speaking) 11^{27}SB (narrative). II Acts: 22^{13} (Saul speaking). We sections: 16^{18} (narrative).

The incidence of resumptive pronoun after a relative occurs in Mark and Matthew, as we have seen (in John and Revelation too). It occurs in the D-text of Luke: 8^{12}D (add. to Mk) 12^{43}D (Q: *whom . . . the Lord will find him*).

Casus pendens followed by resumptive pronoun (cf. pp. 21, 34, 71 occurs 1^{36} $8^{14.15}$ $12^{10.48}$ 13^4 21^6 23^{50f} Ac 2^{22f} 3^6 4^{10} $7^{35.40}$ $10^{36.37}$ 13^{32} $17^{23.24}$.

Oblique cases of *autos* are characteristic of Semitic Greek when used in profusion. Of the Synoptic Gospels, Luke is the least addicted to this redundancy (cf. pp. 21, 35f, but he is high on the list when the NT is considered as a whole (cf. p. 72): one in 2½-lines (the papyri, one in 13 lines). But the occurrence in the various strata of Luke-Acts is considered below (p. 56).

And* (or *for*) *behold! An exclusively Biblical Septuagintal phrase, perhaps also from Aramaic, it is frequent in the LXX, and Luke and Paul probably obtained the expression from here. As it occurs in the possibly " free " Greek of the Testament of Solomon (seven times) and Testament of Abraham (ten times) it may be a feature of free Jewish Greek, derived perhaps from the translated books. It is scattered throughout Luke-Acts, even including II Acts $20^{22.25}$ and the We sections 27^{24}. It occurs in his own work in the Gospel, the Infancy narrative, L (12 times), and his additions to Mark.

Interrogative *ei*. This undoubted Semitism appears only in Biblical Greek. Doubtless it originated in the translated books of the LXX, rendering *'im*, and thence passed into the free Biblical Greek of 2 Maccabees, the Clementine Homilies, the Gospel of Thomas, and the Testament of Abraham. The idiom is Luke's own, not from sources, plain evidence that he is writing free Semitic Greek.

It is used in II Acts 19², 21³⁷, 22²⁵. The question of sources does not arise, but perhaps Paul's own language accurately reported from Aramaic, accounts for these occurrences. This is not likely, because in speech there would be no need for it, the inflexion of voice conveying the interrogative. The instance in Lk 13²³ appears to be added to Q, and 22⁴⁹ to be added to Mk. The instances in I Acts (1⁶ 7¹) may be from Semitic sources, but in view of the above evidence it is more likely that they too are part of Luke's own style. We do not include the following, which are bordering on the indirect question, for person and tense are not decisive, but they *may* be direct questions : Lk 6⁹ 22⁶⁷ 23⁶ Ac 4¹⁹ 5⁸ 10¹⁸ 26²³ᵇⁱˢ.

Pros **after verbs of speaking.** The use in non-Biblical Greek is so occasional as to be negligible, and its use here cannot be anything else than a Semitism. The very rare and eccentric examples in classical Greek are often poetic and probably intended to be emphatic. Its rare but increased use in the papyri is in line with the large use of prepositions in general, but it is still inconsiderable : in 300 lines which we examined we found but one instance as compared with eleven datives. In the higher Koine *it* is just as rare. Abel admitted it as a fact of the Koine but added, truly enough, that the construction would be favoured in Biblical Greek by the translation of *lᵉ* and *'el* (*Grammaire* § 50[l]). This is doubtless true, but it occurs relatively more often in rec.A than in rec.B of the Testament of Abraham, and that is the recension least likely to be a translation. Even in II Acts, likely to be translation-free, *pros* is more in evidence than the dative (4 : 3 in the B-text ; 5 : 3 in the D-text). As this use of *pros* is without doubt Semitic, then some parts at least of II Acts were composed in free Jewish Greek. Certainly, it scarcely appears in the We sections, which were probably a product of days before Luke had acquired the Biblical dialect. Later it became a conspicuous mannerism of his style.

Infancy narrative : 1¹³·¹⁸·¹⁹·³⁴·⁵⁵·⁶¹·⁷³ 2¹⁵·¹⁸·²⁰·³⁴·⁴⁸·⁴⁹ Markan sections (added to Mk) : 4³⁶·⁴³ 5²²·³⁰·³¹·³³·³⁴·³⁶ 6³·⁹·¹¹ 8²² 9³·¹³·¹⁴·²³·³³·⁴³·⁵⁰ 10²⁶ 18³¹ 19³³ 20²·³·⁹·²³·²⁵·⁴¹ 22⁵² 23²² 24⁵·¹⁰. L sections : 3¹²·¹³·¹⁴v.l. 4²¹·²³ 5⁴·¹⁰ 8²¹ 10²⁹ 11¹·⁵ 12¹·¹⁵·¹⁶ 13⁷ 14³·⁵·⁷·⁷·²³·²⁵ 15³·²² 16¹ 18⁹ 19⁵·⁸·⁹·³⁹ 22¹⁵·⁷⁰ 23⁴·¹⁴ 24¹⁷·¹⁸·²⁵·³²·⁴⁴. Lk's Q : 4⁴ 7²⁴·⁴⁰·⁵⁰ 9⁵⁷·⁵⁹·⁶² 10²·²³ 11³⁹ 12²²·⁴¹ 13²³ 17¹·²². The majority are in Lk's own work or his special source. I Acts : 1⁷ 2²⁹·³⁷·³⁸ 3¹²·²⁵ 4¹·⁸·¹⁹·²³·²⁴ 5⁸·⁹·³⁵ 7³ 8²⁰·²⁶ 9¹⁰·¹¹·¹⁵ 10²⁸ 11¹⁴·²⁰ 12⁸·¹⁵ 13¹⁵ 15⁷·³⁶. II Acts : 16³⁶·³⁷ 17¹⁵18⁶·¹⁴ 19²·²·³v.l.25D 21³⁷·³⁹ 22⁸·¹⁰·²¹·²⁵ 23³·³⁰v.l. 25¹⁶·²² 26¹·¹⁴·²⁸·³¹ 28²¹·²⁵. We : 28⁴.

Cardinal for ordinal : in a We section *one* for *first* 20⁷.

Word Order. The practice of joining the article and noun together as closely as possible reflects the Semitic necessity to unite them as one word. Nothing can appear between the article and the noun in Hebrew or Aramaic. This very often involved Jewish writers of Greek in placing any qualifying matter in a separate subsequent articular phrase, where normal Greek would insert it between the article and the noun. So in Luke-Acts it is fairly rare for anything to obtrude between the article and its noun. From a study of the details we may assume that Luke's language, except in the diary behind the We sections, which would have been written in the early days of his Christian life, was in this respect different from normal Greek. But neither is Luke's usage that of the translated books of the LXX, which almost never separate the article from its noun (even in Genesis and Exodus); Luke's practice is that of the " paraphrase " Greek of the Epistle of Jeremy. Should it be urged that it is the parts of Luke-Acts which depend on Aramaic sources which have this word-order, let it be said that the stories of the Lost Sheep and Prodigal Son, which surely owe much to Luke's literary artistry, have this idiom three times : $15^{6,23,27}$.

In the Infancy narrative only twice does qualifying matter obtrude between art. and noun 1^{70} 2^3, although there are a further six occasions when it might well do so. In material which appears to be from L, or is Luke's own editorial work, he has no special preference, but allows the Biblical word-order to influence him considerably. In Acts, except for the We sections, he has the subsequent articular phrase too often for normal Greek ($3^{1,2,11,16}$ $4^{2,14}$ $5^{3,32}$ 17^{12} $19^{6,12,13,15,16}$), but in the We sections there is little that is not normal in this respect, for on the only two occasions when he permits a subsequent articular phrase a special reason seems to apply, viz. the formal *God Most High* 16^{17} and the Christian term *the Spirit the Holy* 21^{11}. In papyrus texts of similar length there was no instance at all of the Jewish Greek word-order, although there were 35 instances where it might have been appropriate. The same amount of Philostratus yielded one instance of the subsequent phrase as against 27 occasions when it was avoided. There were no instances in a sample from Lucian, but nine opportunities for it ; Josephus yielded the same result.

§ 4. The Question of Sources

In spite of what has been argued above, there is no doubt that some of the Aramaisms, Hebraisms and Semitisms must be attributed to the use of sources, if not sources in Hebrew or Aramaic at least Greek sources which had been translated therefrom. It would be wise to follow Plummer here, for he derived the nature of Luke's Greek from several causes : the fact that he was a Gentile accounts for the literary nature of some of the Greek, he used sources, he knew the LXX, and he enjoyed a constant companionship with Paul. The last cause would account for his use of a Jewish kind of Greek (A. Plummer, *A Critical and Exegetical Commentary on the Gospel according to St. Luke*, ICC Edinburgh 1896, l).

There is no doubt that some of the Semitisms listed above occur most frequently in those parts of Luke-Acts where Semitic sources would be most likely, Luke 1 and 2, Acts 1-12. An instance would be the over-use of redundant personal pronouns, which is derived from the Hebrew and Aramaic use of the pronominal suffix.

The occurrence of non-adjectival *autos* in oblique cases, taken line by line, shows that the We sections (35 instances in 253 lines) resemble the papyri (24 in 306) and Philostratus (37 in 288). The rest of II Acts (56 in 275) resembles Josephus (46 in 257) ; whereas the Infancy narrative (109 in 269), L (83 in 268), the Markan sections (126 in 276), and I Acts (413 in 268) resemble the fairly literally translated books of the LXX : e.g. 4 Kms 1-4^6 (87 in 200).

Some have suggested that Luke 1 and 2 are so different in style from the rest of Luke's work that Luke used sources (most would think Hebrew) without polishing up the translation Greek. But Luke is a better handler of Greek than that ; he is quite capable of modifying his style, from the stylized classical Greek of the Preface and the Hellenistic style of the end of Acts, to the Jewish Greek of some parts of the Gospel and the early chapters of Acts. His conscious imitation of the LXX would adequately account for the Hebraisms of Luke 1 and 2, and Kümmel's verdict is about right : " Now the linguistic observations of Sparks, Benoit, and Turner show that the hypothesis of a translation of both chapters out of the Hebrew is hardly tenable " (W. G. Kümmel, *Introduction to the New Testament*, ET London 1966, 96). In the Appendix of the *Grammar*, vol. II, W. F. Howard quoted with approval Harnacks' view that Luke 1-2 show such intrinsic unity with the rest of Luke-Acts as to eliminate the probability of Luke's use of sources. That judgment still stands.

It has been represented that the Semitisms of Acts occur in " pools " or " nests," and that these accumulations indicate underlying sources. M. Wilcox, having reviewed the question of Semitisms in Acts, concludes that the " knots " of non-Septuagintal Semitisms in Ac 1-15 " do not permit us to argue in favour of translation of Aramaic or Hebrew sources by Luke." He does, however, allow that for some parts of Stephen's speech and Paul's in Acts 13 Luke " seems to be drawing on a source of some kind " (*Semitisms* 180-184).

Luke may well have had the skill to write what looks like a deliberate LXX style ; alternatively, his may have been part of the style of a Jewish kind of Greek. The language of the main body of Luke-Acts was perhaps Luke's natural speech which he was expert enough to elevate into something quite classical at times. One thing is certain, whatever his sources may have been, and however extensive, there is a linguistic unity throughout his two books, and the final editor has been able to impose his own style upon all his material. To us it seems doubtful whether such an artist would inadvertently leave any so-called " pools " of Semitisms, if his natural language were not Semitic Greek.

§ 5. The Literary Elements in Luke's Style

Moulton urged that the Septuagintal flavour of the early chapters of Luke and Acts accorded with the view that Luke was a proselyte, and Moulton was reminded of the style of Bunyan who also lived in the ethos of the Bible (*Grammar* II 8). Modern opinion prefers to see Luke as a Gentile (" this versatile Gentile who writes for Gentiles," Plummer, *Luke* ICC l), which if true would explain the lingering secularism in his style, for it would be less likely to be there if he were brought up within Judaism.

It is contended that Luke could write Greek that was free altogether of Semitic influence, as in some parts of Acts and particularly in Luke 15 and some other parables.

H. J. Cadbury found that Lk used classical expressions in a proportion comparable with good non-Biblical writers (*The Style and Literary Methods of Luke*, London 1927, 36–39). Cf. also J. M. Creed, *The Gospel according to St. Luke*, London 1930, lxxxi–lxxxiii ; *Grammar* II 6–8. True, Luke's style is more flowing, exchanging Mk's parataxis for a more periodic sentence by means of his more effective use of participles. He changes Mk's co-ordinate verbs for a ptc. on 33 occasions, whereas Mk changes Lk in the same direction on only one occasion. For detailed instances, cf. E. P. Sanders, 238–240. For effective use of participles in Acts, cf. 2^{36} 4^{35} $5^{11.19.25}$ 14^{27} 18^{22} etc. *Grammar* III 158.

Often Luke secularizes the style of Mark, eliminating the following words : *Cananaean* (replacing it with *Zealot* Lk 6^{15} Ac 1^{13}), *hosanna, abba, Golgotha, rabbi* (becoming *epistatēs* 9^{33}) and *rabbouni* (becoming *Kurie* 18^{41}) ; but he retains *Beezeboul, mammon, pascha, sabbath, satan, gehenna,* and he inserts *sikera* 1^{15}. Further, he retains *amen* on six occasions (4^{24} $12^{37.44}$ $18^{17.29}$ 21^{32}), although sometimes he gives it the translation *truly* or *of a truth*. Virtually, except for 8^{49}, he ignores Mark's historic present, and his more characteristically Greek *de* replaces Mark's connecting particle *kai*.

The figures for *de* : *kai* reveal that Ac and 4 Mac have an equal proportion and that all parts of Lk–Ac are near this figure, except the Infancy narrative (1 : 5). In reverse order of Semitic Greek, we may set out the following. (For Polybius, Plutarch, Epictetus, and Papyri, we rely on figures supplied by R. A. Martin, *NTS* 11 [1964] 41).

Polybius	1 : 0,07	Lk's Q	1 : 1,9
Plutarch	1 : 0,24	T Abr rec. A	1 : 2
Josephus, *Ant.* I		LXX : Exod 1–24	1 : 2,1
2–51 (Niese)	1 : 0,3	Genesis	1 : 2,4
Philostratus I i–x	1 : 0,4	T Abr rec. B	1 : 5
Didache	1 : 0,5	Mark	1 : 5
Acts : We sections	1 : 0,5	Lk's Infancy	1 : 5
Epictetus	1 : 0,6	LXX : Isa 40–66	1 : 8,3
II Acts (sample)	1 : 0,6	Isa 1–39	1 : 10,7
Paul (I Cor)	1 : 0,6	Exod 25–40	1 : 17
Lucian *Somnium*	1 : 0,6	Rev 1–3	1 : 17
Papyri	1 : 0,92	LXX : Min Proph	1 : 26
I Acts	1 : 1	Jer α	1 : 42
4 Mac	1 : 1	Ezek α	1 : 63
Lk, Markan sections	1 : 1,2	Rev 4–21	1 : 73
Ep. Barnabas	1 : 1,3	LXX : Judg. A	1 : 93
L	1 : 1,4	Ezek β	1 : 99
Matthew	1 : 1,5	Jer β	1 : 188

We may grant that in secular Greek, simple speech favours *kai*, but the above table reveals a progression from the free Greek to Biblical Greek, and thence to the more literally translated LXX books.

Other "improvements" on Mark. The superfluous pronoun as indirect object, which sounds none too elegant in Greek, *to/her/them/you*, is often removed by Luke in Markan passages.

Mk 1^{40} = Lk 5^{12}, Mk 1^{41} = Lk 5^{13}, Mk 4^{11} = Lk 8^{10}, Mk 5^9 = Lk 8^{30}, Mk 5^{19} = Lk 8^{39}, Mk 5^{39} = Lk 8^{52}, Mk 5^{41} = Lk 8^{54}, Mk 8^{27} = Lk 9^{18}, Mk 8^{28} = Lk 9^{19}, Mk 8^{29} = Lk 9^{20}, Mk 9^{19} = 9^{41}, Mk 9^{38} = Lk 9^{49}, Mk 10^{26} = Lk 18^{26}, Mk 11^6 = Lk 19^{34}, Mk 12^4 = Lk 20^{11}, Mk 12^{16} = Lk 20^{13}, Mk 12^{43} = Lk 21^3.
On the other hand, this works (less often) in the opposite direction :— Lk 5^{20} *your sins are forgiven to you* (Mk 2^5 om. *to you*), Lk 9^{50} *Jesus said to him* (Mk 9^{39} om. *to him*), Lk 22^6 *to hand over to them* (Mk 14^{11} om. *to them*), Lk 22^{11} *the Master says to you* (Mk 14^{14} om. *to you*).
Similarly Lk omits the gen. pronouns in Markan passages : Mk 1^{23} = Lk 4^{33}, Mk 1^{41} = Lk 5^{13}, Mk 3^{31} = Lk 8^{19}, Mk 10^{20} = Lk 18^{21}, Mk 11^1 = Lk 19^{29}, Mk 12^{44} = Lk 21^4. On the other hand, there is the reverse process again : Lk 6^8 *his hand* (Mk 3^1 om. *his*), Lk 22^{66} *their Sanhedrin* Mk 15^1 om. *their*). The matter is not really decisive. Indeed, as we have already seen (p. 56), certain strata of Luke-Acts resemble the fairly literally translated books of the LXX in this respect.

Vernacularisms removed by Luke from Mark are *krabbatos* (Mk 2^{11}) which becomes *klinidion* (Lk 5^{24}) ; *raphis* (Mk 10^{25}) which becomes *belonē* (Lk 18^{25}) ; *korasion* (Mk 5^{41f}) becoming *pais* (Lk $8^{51,54}$). Like Matthew, Luke tends to remove some of Mark's more vivid details : e.g. *the whole city was gathered at the door* (Mk 1^{33}), *they take him, as he was, in the boat*, etc. (Mk 4^{36-38}), and the detail concerning Legion in the tombs, night and day, cutting himself with stones (Mk 5^5).

Genitive Absolute. Nowhere in Luke–Acts is this mark of free Greek entirely absent. It seems to be characteristic of Lukan style without being alien to Biblical Greek.

In the Infancy narrative it occurs once in 43 verses, thus ranking it with the paraphrases in the LXX (Tob, Ep. Jeremy, Dan, 1 Esd), apart from the translated books. In Lk's Q it has about the same proportion as 4 Mac, which argues against Q having been written in anything but Greek (*Grammatical Insights* 178). In the We sections, the number exceeds anything in the LXX, and indeed in the NT, and is in this respect quite up to classical standards. In the samples of the rest of Lk–Ac the proportion is one in 17 verses, like the LXX free Greek books, much more frequent than the Pauline epistles (1 in 177 verses).

Men . . . de. This may also be cited, for there is nothing Semitic which provides an excuse for it. But before we claim it as something alien to Biblical Greek, we must note its occurrence in the free Greek books of the LXX.

There are no instances in the Infancy narrative. Lk's Q 3^{16} 10^2 11^{48}, L 3^{18} 13^9 $23^{33,41,56}$. Not surprisingly it occurs in II Acts (seven times), and We sections (twice). More unexpectedly, in I Acts, particularly in the story of Saul's conversion (Ac 9^7) where Semitic sources are most likely. However, it is doubtful whether there is a *de* to the *men* at 3^{22} 8^4 12^5 13^{36}, the subsequent *de* being independent, and 11^{16} owes its *men . . . de* to the passage (Lk 3^{16}) which it is paraphrasing; while Ac 14^4 (events in Galatia) is unlikely to depend in any case on a Semitic source. This leaves only Ac 1^5, and we must allow that *men . . . de* is possible in moderation within Jewish Greek, occurring fairly often in the free Greek books of the LXX.

The double particle *men . . . oun* may be adduced too as "literary," for Lk is fond of it in Ac (27 times, in all parts), if not in the Gospel (3^{18} only). However, it occurs in the LXX, mainly in the free Greek books: Gen once, Exod once, Wis twice, Dan LXX once, 2 Mac seven times, 3 Mac seven times, 4 Mac four times.

Relative attraction. It has been claimed that Luke's use of relative attraction "testifies to a relatively high standard of literary style" (Creed, *Luke*, lxxxi–lxxxiii), and yet (so the same author stated on the following page) this idiom is "by no means confined to the literary style in the later Greek." Indeed, the idiom was shared by Biblical Greek authors with others (*Grammar* III 324).

Other doubtful literary features. It is just as questionable to mention as "literary" the occurrence of the article with indirect interrogatives, since this is no more literary than our own quote marks; it occurs in the papyri (Mayser II 1, 80; II 3, 52f), and so does *tou* with infinitive, final and consecutive. However, there is more force in Creed's observation that *prin* with subjunctive (Lk 2^{26}) and with optative (Ac 25^{16}) "is correctly used to follow a negative" (lxxxii). To this we would add the suggestion that Luke has the literary ability to adapt the style of his speeches to the culture of the speaker (in the

60   A GRAMMAR OF NEW TESTAMENT GREEK

latter case the urbane Festus), and in the former case (Lk 2^{26}) the construction may be following the LXX (Sir 11^7).

We find it difficult to set much store by Creed's reasoning from Phrynichus, namely that " in a number of cases Luke's taste has led him to correct words and phrases in his sources which are found in Phrynichus's list of condemned vulgarisms " (Creed, *Luke* lxxxiii). Creed cited merely four instances, thereupon giving the conflicting evidence that Luke himself uses 33 times words which Phrynichus condemned or disapproved.

§ 6. SEMITISMS EVEN WHERE SOURCES ARE LEAST LIKELY

Moulton claimed that Luke 15 was entirely free of Semitic influence. We will confine our test of the truth of this to one part of the chapter, the parable of the Prodigal Son, which Moulton singled out as having nothing "which suggests translation from a Semitic original" (*Grammar* II 8). The truth is rather that the parable is full of Semitisms, all of which are features of Jewish Greek and which must either have come through the original Aramaic of the Lord's words or (we suggest) derive from the Lukan style itself.

They are the Aramaism *began* (15^{14}), superfluous *going* (15^{15}) and *rising* ($15^{18.20}$) and *answering* (15^{29}). There is $\gamma \epsilon \mu i \zeta \epsilon \iota \nu$ $\dot{\epsilon} \kappa$ (15^{16}) which is not a Septuagintism but which Luke shares uniquely with Rev 8^5. There is the peculiar phrase *came to himself* (15^{17}), which we can explain only by reference to the Hebrew *shûbh*, meaning *to repent*, the underlying idea in Hebrew being that of turning back and meeting with oneself (LXX 3 Kms 8^{47} Ezek 14^6 18^{30}). There are also the following : *eis* with *hamartanein* ($15^{18.21}$), which is due to LXX influence on account of the Hebrew l^e, rare indeed in non-Biblical Greek, for Bauer can cite but five examples and they mainly from classical Greek ; *enōpion* ($15^{18.21}$), *idou* (15^{29}), *esplagchnisthē* (15^{20}), *fell on his neck* (15^{20}, a Septuagintism : Gen 33^4 45^{14} 46^{29}), and *give a ring on (eis) his hand* (15^{22}). The use of *give* (=*place*) is Hebraic, as in Rev 3^8 ; and *give on (eis) his hand* (Esth 3^{10} LXX) is the same phrase as Lk 15^{22}).

Another significant factor in the parable of the Prodigal Son is the priority of the verb, the surest NT Semitism (Norden). The regular order in Hebrew verbal sentences is Verb—Prepositional phrase with suffix— Subject ; or else Verb—Subject—Preposition (if with noun) ; exceptions occurring when particular emphasis is sought. Kiecker's figures, as tabulated by Howard (*Grammar* II 418), show that in classical Greek the verb occupies more usually a middle position. The following figures give the percentage of verbs in the primary position, that is, the Hebrew position, and thus we obtain the reverse order of Hebraic influence, revealing that the parable of the Prodigal Son is in this respect the most Hebraic of all our samples and the furthest away from the classical Attic norm. (The verb has been considered only in relation to subject, object, or complement).

Polybius (Kieckers)	11%	T Abr. rec. A	36%
Attic (Kieckers)	17%	Infancy Narrative (Lk)	41%
We sections (Lk–Ac)	30%	Luke (Kieckers)	42%
Mark Kieckers)	31%	T Abr. rec. B	45
Matthew (Kieckers)	34%	Luke 15¹¹⁻³²	50%

There are indeed Semitisms throughout Luke-Acts, not even excepting the We sections, as we have seen. Luke's style varies somewhat, and the secular style of the We sections may be explained in either of two ways. 1. Luke may have been a proselyte, well acquainted with Jewish Greek, and may have secularized the language deliberately, when he felt the context demanded it, e.g. when describing Paul's journeys among Gentile cities. 2. Luke may not have been a proselyte but may have come as a raw Gentile to Christianity, and so we suppose that before arriving at Caesarea after Paul's third journey he had not quite succumbed to the full influence of Jewish Greek, as he did later. Thus we can account for the We sections with considerable display of " literary " or secular Greek, that is, of the Koine as used by Greek professional men, such as Luke.

Nevertheless, the hard line of division is not rigid, and his style is fairly homogeneous, for the LXX Hebraisms are widespread, occurring even in the most Gentile sections, where the possibility of translation-Greek is ruled out.

The closing chapters of Ac may be singled out as very Gentile in outlook and language, and yet even here (Ac 26²²) there is a peculiar construction which Lk shares with Rev 17⁸ and for which we find no non-Biblical parallel : viz. the use of an ensuing ptc. attracted to a previous relative pronoun. Ac 26²² οὐδὲν ... λέγων ὧν τε οἱ προφῆται ἐλάλησεν μελλόντων γίνεσθαι. Rev 17⁸ θαυμασθήσονται οἱ κατοικοῦντες ... ὧν οὐ τὸ ὄνομα ... βλεπόντων (we expect βλέποντες). The peculiarity, first noticed by W. H. Simcox (*The Language of the New Testament*, London 1889, 135), was explained by R. H. Charles as far as Rev was concerned as " a not unnatural rendering " of *birᵉ'ōtham*, by which he doubtless intended the Qal infin. with 3rd p. pl. suffix, though it is not easy to see why that would make attraction of case more natural in Greek. At any rate, the construction is more likely to be Hebraic than normal Greek (*A Critical and Exegetical Commentary on the Revelation of St. John the Divine*, ICC Edinburgh 1920, II 68).

In this part of Ac we have already noted the following : *tote*, the construction *it came to pass*, the independent non-articular infin., the dat. of the cognate noun in imitation of Heb. infin. absolute, Heb. physiognomical expressions, the Semitic *answering said*, the otiose Semitic ptc. *saying*, *autos ho, behold!* interrogative *ei, pros* after verbs of speaking, too close association of art. and noun for normal Greek, and we may have overlooked others. There is much here to commend the view of H. Grundman (*Das Evangelium nach Lukas*, Berlin 1959, 23) that Luke is writing " holy history ", as sacred as the OT itself.

§ 7. THE CHRISTIAN STYLE

There is the surest presumption that many or all of the Semitic features of style are incidentally part of the primitive Christian language, although probably Luke's own theology would tend to supplement their number. He conceived the Christian revelation as the fulfilment of the old Dispensation, and would in consequence tend by his language to emphasize the links between Old and New.

de Zwaan instanced the use of new Christian words, e.g. *way* for Christianity and the peculiar use of *believing* (*Beginnings of Christianity*, ed. Foakes Jackson and K. Lake, II London 1922, 63, 64). We may add *angel*, *scribe*, *devil*, *nations* (Gentiles), *evangelize*, *Kurios* (Jesus), *nomodidaskalos*, and *respecter of persons*. We may add that other words, belonging to Jewish Greek, seem to have been taken over by Luke and others to receive a special Christian sense : *agalliasis* (Christian joy), *alisgema* (weaker brother's pollution by contact with idols), *antapodoma* (the recompense of the Last Judgment), *lutrōtēs* (redeemer), and *false prophet*.

However, the unique character of Luke's language seems rather to rest on syntax, as for instance in his strong use of the optative mood, the language of devotion (*Grammar* III 118-133). The phrase *epi to auto*, familiar in the Greek Psalms, is thought by some to be virtually a technical term for Christian fellowship, since it occurs in Apostolic writings where it has been peculiarly Christianized (A. Vazakis, followed by M. Wilcox, *Semitisms* 93-100).

Referring to the optative, Moulton declared that Lk-Ac alone in the NT, along with 2 Pet and Heb, " show any consciousness of style," and he instanced the potential optative which made Lk " the only littérateur among the authors of NT books " (*Grammar* II 6ff). The optatives are widespread in Lk-Ac, and probably not always intended to be " literary," for Lk shares his love for the optative with the LXX. Volitive optatives : Infancy narrative 1^{38}, Lk's add. to Mk : 20^{16} (*God forbid !*), I Acts : 8^{20} (*may your money perish !*). Potential optatives : I Acts : 2^{12}E (*what could this be ?*), II Acts : 17^{18} (*what could he be wishing to say ?*) 26^{29}BAS^c (*I could wish*). Potential optative in indirect speech : (deliberative) : Infancy narrative : Lk 1^{29} (*what manner of salutation this might be*) 1^{62} (*what he might wish*), Lk's add. to Mk : 6^{11}B (*what they could do to Jesus*) 8^9v.l. (*what this parable might mean*) 9^{46} (*which could be greatest*) 18^{36} (*enquired what this might be*) 22^{23}v.l. (*which of them could be intending*), L document : 3^{15} (*whether he could be the Christ*) 15^{26} (*asked what this might be*), I Acts : 5^{24} (*what this might be*) 10^{17} (*what this dream could mean*), II Acts : 17^{11} (*to see if it could be thus*) 17^{20}v.l. (*to know what these things could mean*) 21^{33} (*asked who he might be*) 25^{20} (*whether he might like to go*). Conditional optative : II Acts : 24^{19}.

By now the optative was dead in popular speech, and yet Luke freely uses it. Many instances may be the corrections of atticizing scribes, but not all. Elsewhere it is suggested that the optative is part of Christian speech, expressing the Christian's devout aspiration, the language of devotion (*Grammar* III 118-133).

Other Literature :

W. K. Hobart, *The Medical Language of St. Luke*, Dublin 1882.
H. J. Cadbury, *The Style and Literary Method of Luke*, Harvard 1920.
M. Dibelius, " Stilkritisches zur Apg," in *Eucharisterion* II (1923) 27-49.
H. J. Cadbury, " Lexical Notes on Luke-Acts," *JBL* 45 (1926) 190ff.
H. J. Cadbury, *The Making of Luke-Acts*, New York 1927.
S. Antoniadis, *L'Évangile de Luc* ; *esquisse de Grammaire et de Style*, Paris 1930.
H. F. D. Sparks, " The Semitisms of St. Luke's Gospel," *JTS* 44(1943) 129ff.
E. Schweizer, " Eine hebraisierende Sonderquelle des Lukas ? " *Theologische Zeitschrift* 6 (1950) 161ff.
H. F. D. Sparks, " The Semitisms of Acts," *JTS* NS 1 (1950) 16-28.
A. W. Argyle, " The Theory of an Aramaic Source in Acts 2 : 14-40," *JTS* NS 3 (1952) 213f.
A. Vögeli, " Lukas und Euripides," *Theol. Zeitsch.* 9 (1953) 415-438.
P. Winter, " Some Observations on the Language in the Birth and Infancy Stories of the Third Gospel," *NTS* 1 (1954) 111ff.
" On Luke and Lucan Sources," *ZNW* 47 (1956) 217ff.
N. Turner, " The Relation of Luke I and II to Hebraic Sources and to the Rest of Luke-Acts," *NTS* 2 (1955) 100ff.
M. Dibelius, " Style Criticism of the Book of Acts," *Studies in the Acts of the Apostles*, ed. H. Greeven, London 1956.
P. Benoit, " L'Enfance de Jean-Baptiste selon Luc I," *NTS* 3 (1956) 169ff.
R. Mc. L. Wilson, " Some Recent Studies in the Lucan Infancy Narratives," *Studia Evangelica* 1959, 235ff.

CHAPTER FIVE

THE STYLE OF JOHN

1. The Main Sources

Although it is generally recognized that the style of the Gospel is fairly uniform throughout, two distinct written sources have been proposed, following R. Bultmann, *Das Evangelium des Johannes*, Göttingen 1941 : a speeches-source (*Redenquelle*) and a signs-source (*Semeiaquelle*). Dr. Black is of opinion that the distribution of Aramaisms, corresponding to Bultmann's sources, is such as to suggest that there was a sort of Johannine Q, an Aramaic document lying behind the Gospel, a sayings-source as distinct from the narrative part of the Gospel (the signs-source or miracles-stories collection), of the latter of which the Greek is normal and without " Aramaic colouring " (Black[3] 150). However, it must be borne in mind that Bultmann himself declared the language of the signs-source to be Semitic Greek without being translation-Greek (e.g. 9^{1-4}). He pointed to certain Semitisms : asyndeta, superfluous *autou*, and the tendency of the predicate to come as near as possible to the beginning of the clause. Bultmann was right : we cannot say that any part of John is free from " Aramaic colouring," nor Hebraic colouring either. Except for one critic, who has insisted on the normal character of the Greek, which he thought resembled the style of Epictetus, most scholars have found the style of the Fourth Gospel to be Semitic to some degree, without necessarily being a translation. The idiom is the very simplest and the vocabulary the poorest in the NT, relatively to the size of the book. Dodd, Bultmann, and Barrett in their respective works on the Fourth Gospel, tended to the view that the author thought in Aramaic but actually wrote in Greek. Bultmann suggested that the author lives in a bilingual environment and hence used a language which was full of Semitic idioms. John is more Semitic than the other gospels, without being a translation, for else some errors of rendering must appear in what he called the editorial sections. Bultmann would think it not impossible that one of his sources was in Aramaic.

The Sayings-source. Bultmann's *Redenquelle*, which may have an Aramaic original, included the Prologue $1^{1-5.9-12.14.16}$, which he held to be " a piece of cultic-liturgical poetry," half revelatory, half confession, in which each couplet has two short sentences, in synonymous or antithetic parallelism, like Semitic poetry. The poetry has, moreover, a chain-locking device which links the clauses together, e.g. *in him was LIFE : and the LIFE was the LIGHT of men. And the LIGHT in DARKNESS shined : and the DARKNESS did not comprehend it.* Subsequent links are *world, his own, glory,* and *full.* The same device appears in the epistle of James (cf. p. 116).

Moreover, there may be chiasmic patterns in the Johannine discourses : in 6^{36-40} R. E. Brown sees an ABCBA pattern (*The Gospel according to John,* New York 1966, 275f.
A. Seeing and not believing,
B. What the Father has given shall not be cast out,
C. From heaven,
B. What has been given shall not be lost,
A. Seeing and believing.

Léon-Dufour sees further examples of chiasmus : (1) 12^{23-32}
D. The hour has come ^{23}
A. Fall INTO the ground ^{24}
B. Hate one's life in this world ^{25}
C. The Father will honour him ^{26}
D. This present hour ^{27}
C. Father, glorify thy name ^{28}
B. Judgment of this world ^{31}
A. Raised FROM the ground ^{32}

(2) 5^{19-30} : this fails to convince by its complexity (X. Léon-Dufour, " Trois Chiasmes Johanniques," *NTS* 7 [1961] 249–255).

Other examples of the antithetical poetic style are 3^6 (*flesh, flesh : spirit, spirit*)$^{8.11-13.18.20f}$ 4^{13f} (*earthly water, thirst again : water from Christ, satisfied*) 7^{37f} and 1 John.

Characteristic of the Sayings-source is the use of the artic. ptc. : $6^{35.47}$ 8^{12} 11^{25} 12^{44} 15^5. Also the use of *pas* with the ptc. (*everyone who*) : $3^{8.20}$ 4^{13} 6^{45} 15^2 18^{37} 1 Jn 2^{29} $3^{4.6.9f}$al. But this construction occurs outside Bultmann's Sayings-source, too : $3^{15.16}$ 8^{34} 11^{26} 16^2 19^{12}.

The Signs-source. Bultmann's other main source consists of stories which have a Semitic tone throughout, including among its idiom the superfluous *autou,* the verb near the beginning of the clause, and nearly all the clauses short and asyndetic (unless with a simple particleat uch as *kai, oun, de*). Bultmann rejected translation, on the ground th, s the language was not impossible as Greek and that a translator would have corrected the asyndeta ; he claimed it as a specimen of Semitic Greek, written by a Greek-speaking Jew.

1^{35-50} (the Call of the Disciples) is probably the introduction to the Signs-source (omit *and* in $^{37.38}$ with S*^{a1}), which begins properly at 2^{1-12} (Cana) and includes $4^{5-9.16-18.28-30.40}$ (Samaritan Woman), 6^{1-26} (Feeding), 5^{1-18} (Lame Man), 9^{1-41} (Blind Man), 11^{1-44} (Lazarus).

The Evangelist's additions. The evangelist is held by Bultmann to have joined the Sayings-source and the Signs-source together and to have added his own work in a characteristic style which can be detected. It was very prosaic by contrast with the Sayings-source and modelled itself on OT style, sometimes borrowing rabbinic linguistic usage : e.g. to have the commandments 14^{21}, episunagōgos (m^{e}nûdhah 9^{22} 12^{42} 16^2).

Instances of the evangelist's work are 1$^{6-8,18-20}$ 3$^{22-26}$ 4$^{43-44}$ 7$^{1-13,45-52}$ 10$^{19-21,40-42}$ 11$^{55-57}$ 13$^{34-35}$ 16$^{25-33}$ etc. Bultmann suggested that a marked characteristic of the evangelist was the use of the pronoun to resume a subject or object in the rabbinical antithetic style : e.g. he who sent me to baptize in water HE said to me 1^{33}, the resumptive being either ekeinos (1^{33} 5^{11,43} 9^{37} 10^1 12^{48} 14^{21,26} 15^{26}) or houtos (3^{26,32} 5^{38} 6^{46} 7^{18} 8^{26} 15^5). Other characteristic phrases are the rabbinical but in order that, with a suitable ellipse, e.g. he was not the light BUT (was sent) IN ORDER THAT, for this evangelist loves to state the negative of a proposition : 1^{8,31} (I knew him not, but) 3^{17} 9^3 11^{52} 12^{9,47} 13^{18} 14^{31} 17^{15} 1 Jn 2^{19} (Mk 14^{49}, and there is an occasional example in Soph. Oed. Col. 156 ; Epictetus 1.12.17).

Another instance of the evangelist's own work is the phrase which he shares with the Johannine epistles : διὰ τοῦτο ... ὅτι for this cause ... because, which seems to be his substitute for διότι (H. Pernot, Études sur la Langue des Évangiles, Paris 1927, 5) : 5^{16,18} 7^{22} 8^{47} 10^{17} 12^{18,39} 1 Jn 3^1 (without ὅτι 6^{65} 9^{23} 12^{27} 13^{11} 15^{19} 16^{15} 19^{11} 1 Jn 4^5 3 Jn^{10}). Paul is fond of a similar phrase : 1 Cor 7^{37} 2 Cor 2^1 13^9 1 Tim 1^9.

The evangelist favours the transitional phrase after this 2^{12} 11^{7,11} 19^{28} and after these things 3^{22} 5^{1,14} 6^1 7^1 19^{38} 21^1, as well as the connecting particles hōs de and hōs oun : e.g. 2^{23}. He shares with 1 Jn the recurring phrases : not only ... but also 11^{52} 12^9 17^{20} 1 Jn 2^2 5^6, and I know (you) that 5^{32} 12^{50} 1 Jn 3^{5,15}. Indeed, hoti-clauses are typical of the evangelist 3^{18} 5^{38} 8^{20} 10^{13}al.

Conclusion. It would appear that Bultmann has failed to make a convincing case stylistically (theology apart) for the presence of detectable sources, inasmuch as the stylistic details to which he points are found everywhere, cutting across the divisions of alleged sources, e.g. the resumptive this and that (demonstrative) occur several times in the Signs-source. E. Ruckstuhl has shown how arbitrary it is to escape from this dilemma by supposing that such examples are the evangelist's own editing of his sources (Die literarische Einheit des Johannes Evangeliums, Freiburg 1951, 62 n.2). Moreover the stylistic rhythms which Bultmann claims for the Signs-source are easily shown to belong as much to what he ascribes to the evangelist (Ruckstuhl 43–54).

E. Schweizer had already examined the language of John and found it impossible to isolate any sources, for the Gospel is stylistically a unity, e.g. emos instead of the more regular NT mou occurs forty times throughout the Gospel in more than one " source " (Ego Eimi ..., Göttingen 1939, 82–112). Ruckstuhl extended Schweizer's thirty-three stylistic tests to fifty and conclusively showed that they cut right across Bultmann's stylistic divisions (180–219). We must leave the question open, concluding that if the evangelist used written sources, their

THE STYLE OF JOHN 67

distinctive character is not discernible through the finishing work which he or a subsequent editor accomplished on his material.

Schweizer had nevertheless apprehended that in some parts of John the characteristic features of style, which were the subject of his tests, were less in evidence, viz., some narrative sections, $2^{1-10.13-19}$ 4^{46-53} $7^{53}-8^{11}$ $12^{1-8.12-15}$. He noted that the style of 1 John agreed not with these, but with the speeches (Bultmann's *Redenquelle*). T. W. Manson, too, felt that the author of 1 John was the author of that part of the Gospel least influenced by Aramaic. Manson's divisions, however, which he takes from Burney, do not correspond even broadly with those of Schweizer (*BJRL* 30 [1946] 322). The only permissible course is to ignore these divisions and to comment on the style of the Gospel as a unity.

Exceptions will be the pericope de adultera, $7^{50}-8^{11}$, which is generally agreed on textual grounds to be an interpolation, linguistically distinct from the Gospel style and vocabulary. One word is Lukan NT hapax : *early morning* 8^2. Other words and phrases are mainly Lukan : *arrive* 8^2, *people (laos)* 8^2, *sitting down he taught them* 8^2.

The other exception may be ch. 21, where there are some linguistic differences from the rest of the Gospel : e.g. a different word for *to be able* 21^6, partitive and causative *apo* $21^{6.10}$ (in all the other gospels, but not Jn), ἐπιστραφείς, 21^{20} for στραφείς, but the great words (e.g. *verily verily, manifest*) appear both here and in 1–20, along with words of less significance too (e.g. ὁμοῦ, ὁ ἀπό, ὁ λεγόμενος, and the weakened οὖν which appears in every part of the Gospel). Although ch. 21 presents 28 words which do not otherwise occur in Jn, only a few of them matter very much, there being no call for most of them in 1–20. C. K. Barrett examined this evidence and concluded that a separate authorship was not proven : *The Gospel according to St. John*, London 1955, 479f.

§ 2. SEPTUAGINT INFLUENCE

At first it looks as if the evangelist was unacquainted with the Greek Bible, as Burney argued, for he uses αἴρειν τὴν ψυχήν in two quite different senses, neither of them that of the LXX, which is *lift up my soul* (Ps 24[25]¹, 85[86]⁴ 142[143]⁸). In Jn 10^{18} the phrase must mean *take back one's life after laying it down*, and in spite of some ambiguity in 10^{24} it there seems to mean *hold in suspence*. A Jewish expression, *to take the soul away*, may be in the author's mind, as in the Testament of Abraham rec.A ch. XX, where the same expression is used of *taking* Abraham's *soul* to heaven.

The Johannine writings are very sparing in the use of artic. infin. after a preposition, a LXX construction.

The expression behind τηρέω λόγον $8^{51.52.55}$ $14^{23.24}$ 15^{20} 17^6 1 Jn 2^5 Rev $3^{8.10}$ $22^{7.9}$ is an OT phrase (Dt 33^9 Pr 7^1), but only at 1 Kms 15^{11} do the LXX render it by John's verb, and then not if we follow the A-text. The Heb.

phrase, *full of grace and truth* 1^{14} is not rendered in quite the same way in the LXX : cp. Exod 34^4 where *full of grace = polueleos*. As to citations, it is not quite the LXX version of Isa 40^3 that is quoted at 1^{23}, nor that of Ps 68(69)^{10} at 2^{17}, nor that of Ps 77(78)^{24} or Exod 16^8 at 6^{31}. Moreover, the passage, *they shall look on him whom they pierced* 19^{38}, follows the Heb. of Zech 12^{10} rather than the LXX. The *Hosanna* quotation 12^{13} is not from LXX Ps 117(118)^{28}, and Zech 9^9 is not the LXX version. Isa 6^{9-10} is not from the LXX at 12^{40}, nor is Ps 41^{10} at 13^{18}.

On the other hand, some knowledge of the LXX must be assumed : Isa 53^1 at Jn 12^{38} and Ps 22^{19} at 19^{24} appear to be accurately quoted, and there is some connection between 15^{25} and the Psalms, for δωρεάν renders *without a cause*.

There is no doubt about the expression τί ἐμοὶ καὶ σοί ; 2^4, which is a Hebraism and Septuagintism : *mah llî wᵉlāk* 2 Sam 16^{10} ; cf. *Grammatical Insights* 43–47 for full discussion. There are many other Heb. phrases in the Gospel, some of which are given in the LXX wording : e.g. *to do the Truth* : *'āsâ 'ᵉmeth* Jn 3^{21} 1 Jn 1^6 = LXX Gen 32^{11} 47^{29} Isa 26^{10} Tob 4^6 13^6 T 12 P Reuben 6^9 Benjamin 10^3. Qumran 1 QS 1.5 ; 5.3 ; 8.2. (It was therefore an expression widely used in Judaism). Although the Heb. phrase *wayᵉhî 'îsh* is not certainly rendered in the LXX by the Johannine ἐγένετο ἄνθρωπος (it is a v.l. in 1 Kms 1^1, but we find ἐγένετο ἀνήρ in Jg 13^2A 17^1 19^1), yet in the same verse 1^6 the Hebraism ὄνομα αὐτῷ is undoubtedly LXX : Jg 13^2A 17^1 1 Kms 1^1 9^1al (as in Rev 6^8 9^{11}). The phrase *unrighteousness is not in him* 7^{18} is LXX, though with a different order of words, Ps 91(92)^{15}, and a very frequent phrase in the LXX Psalms is *many waters* Jn 3^{23} Ps 17(18)^{16} 31(32)^6 76(77)^{19} 92(93)^4 143(144)^7. *To give in(to) the hand* occurs twice in John and twice in the Greek OT, once with *en* (Jn 3^{35} Dan Th 2^{38}) and once with *eis* (Jn 13^3 Isa 47^6). It is remarkable that John shares with the LXX the unusual construction of *ek* after *tines* (e.g. Exod 16^{27}).

John may have made his own Greek translation from the Hebrew, but more probably he used a version something like our own LXX, possibly in the form of a collection of proof-texts, or he quoted Aramaic or Greek Targums.

§ 3. OTHER HEBRAISMS

There are other phrases which Bultmann (*Kommentar* in loc.) claimed as Hebraic, Semitic, or at least as " not Greek," viz. *to do the works* 5^{36} $7^{3.21}$ $8^{39.41}$ $10^{25.37}$ $14^{10.12}$ 15^{24} 3 Jn^{10}, *work the works* 6^{28} 9^4, *to come as (eis) a witness* (rabbinical) *bâ lᵉ'ēdhôth* 1^{6-8}, *receive the witness* $3^{11.32†}$, *qābhal 'ēdhúth, receive the words* 12^{48} 17^8, *have the commandments* (rabbinical) 14^{21}, *having 38 years in his weakness* 5^5, *on that day was a Sabbath* 5^9.

As an example of colloquial Semitic speech Bultmann cited τί ὑμῖν δοκεῖ ; 11^{56}. There is ἴδε $11^{3.36}$, which may be the Hebrew *behold* ; and *come and see* $1^{39.46}$ 11^{34}, which is a rabbinical idiom (S.-B. II 371), but

THE STYLE OF JOHN 69

probably also a paratactic condition : *if* you come, you will see. There is the Hebrew OT phrase, *send saying* 11³, using *apostellein* absolutely, which is not normal for Greek.

Glory (1¹⁴ and 16 times) is one of those terms which radically changed meaning through Hebrew influence : originally *doxa* was *good repute*, but it became also *visible splendour* because in the LXX it rendered *kābhōdh (honour, glory)* and such words as *hōdh (splendour)*.

By the same influence *erōtān* comes to mean *ask a request* 4³¹ 12²¹, and *peripatein* becomes moral *walk* ($=hālak$) : 8¹² 11⁹ 12³⁵ 1 Jn 1⁶·⁷ 2⁶·¹¹ 2 Jn ⁴·⁶ 3 Jn ³·⁴ Rev 21²⁴ LXX 4 Kms 20³ Pr 8²⁰. *To believe in (eis)* is quite characteristic of this Gospel (33 times), a term shared with 1 Jn 5¹⁰·¹³, derived from *he'ᵉmīn bᵉ* : also Mt 18⁶ Ac 10⁴³ 14²³ 19⁴ Rom 10¹⁴ Gal 2¹⁶ Phil 1²⁹ 1 Pet 1⁸.

The Noun. 1. The Hebrew idiom *son of* 17¹². 2. The Hebrew infinitive absolute *rejoice with joy* (dative) 3²⁹ is rare in normal Greek, where in any event the cognate noun usually has the accusative ; dative of the cognate noun belongs to Biblical Greek ; LXX Isa 66¹⁰ 1 Thes 3⁹. 3. The Hebrew noun, if indefinite, may stand alone without the numeral *one* or the adjunct *man* or other form of indefinite article, whereas in non-Biblical Greek the absence of an indefinite pronoun would be unusual : Bultmann notes that in Jn 3²⁵ μετὰ 'Ιουδαίου would be improved by the addition of τινός. 4. The influence of the construct state is sometimes seen in the omission of the article : 1⁴⁹ *thou art [the] king of Israel*, 4⁵ *there was there [the] well of Jacob*, 5²⁷ *[the] Son of Man*, 9⁵ *[the] Light of the world*.

Negation. The strong negative *ou mē* with aorist subjunctive or future indicative is found in the NT outside Revelation mainly in LXX quotations or in sayings of Jesus. There are papyri instances (although it is rare in literary Hellenistic : *Grammar* III 96), and they are sufficient to show that this negative occurred in popular speech ; but it was doubtless LXX or Hebrew influence which made it a very prominent feature in John and Revelation : Jn 4¹⁴·⁴⁸ 6³⁵·³⁷ 8¹²·⁵¹·⁵² 10⁵·²⁸ 11²⁶·⁵⁶ 13⁸ 18¹¹ 20²⁵.

Other syntax. 1. In a variety of forms, *answered and said (wayya'an wayyōmer)* 1²⁶·⁴⁹·⁵¹ 2¹⁸·¹⁹ 3³·⁹·¹⁰·²⁷ 4¹⁰·¹³·¹⁷ 5¹⁹ 6²⁶·²⁹·⁴³ 7¹⁶·²¹·⁵² 8¹⁴·³⁹·⁴⁸ 9²⁰·³⁰·³⁴·³⁶ 12²³·³⁰ 13⁷ 14²³ 18³⁰ 20²⁸. Jn rings the changes with *answered saying, answered and said* (aor. and impf.), and *answered*. 2. Under the influence of *waw*, καί seems sometimes to be adversative, as 1⁵ 17¹¹. 3. The Heb. *liphnē* probably extended the use of *enōpion* in our Greek : Jn 20³⁰ 1 Jn 3²² 3 Jn⁶ and Rev 34 times.

Sentence Construction. 1. Prolepsis of the subject of a subordinate clause occurs frequently in John (as in Mt 25²⁴, Mark, Luke-Acts, 1, 2 Cor, 1, 2 Thes, Rev ; cf. pp. 16, 33, 36, 93, 151) : e.g. *look on the fields that they are white already* 4³⁵ 5⁴² 7²⁷ 8⁵⁴ 11³¹, and this is due to the influence of a Hebrew idiom, e.g. Gen 1⁴. 2. In Hebrew, the anarthrous partitive expression (cf. pp. 15, 46) may stand alone as subject or object of a verb 7⁴⁰ 16¹⁴,¹⁵,¹⁷ (*ek*), 21¹⁰ (*apo*). 3. Commonly in the LXX, especially 1 Mac, is *eis* used predicatively : 16²⁰ *your grief shall be INTO joy* (so Rom 5¹⁸ 1 Jn 5⁸ Rev 8¹¹ 16¹⁹).

§ 4. ARAMAISMS

Although Dr. Beyer's estimate is that Hebraisms predominated over Aramaisms in the Fouth Gospel (*Syntax* 17f), we suspect that the Gospel may have had a large Aramaic element, perhaps because of the dominating influence of Jesus' own language.

Asyndeton. This is an important element in Johannine Greek: scores of verses are asyndetic, even when verbs of speaking are left out of the count. An Aramaic original is not to be assumed from the presence of this Aramaism, for " the construction is one which would tend to predominate in Jewish or Syrian Greek " (Black³ 56). Dr. Black instances the *Shepherd* of Hermas as the same kind of Greek, influenced by Jewish idiom and marked by an over-use of asyndeton, though to a less extent than John. Because the asyndetic *he says/they say* is particularly frequent in the teaching of Jesus, Black has modified Burney's theory, to the extent that only for the teaching of Jesus did John edit and rewrite Greek translations of Aramaic traditions (Black³ 61).

The Verb. 1. The passive voice is rare in Aramaic (in Hebrew too), and the impersonal plural takes its place : 15⁶ 20² (cf. p. 12). 2. It is undeniable that the use of the historic present and imperfect tenses characterizes good secular Greek and the vernacular, but it may be under the influence of the Aramaic participle that the historic present occurs as frequently as it does in Mark (151 times) and John (164), together with the imperfect : Mark (222 times), John (165).

The Pronoun. 1. The idiom *one . . . one*, for *one . . . another*, occurs in 20¹² and elsewhere in the Gospels, Acts, and Paul (1 Cor 4⁶ Gal 4²² 1 Thes 5¹¹) : *Grammar* III 187. 2. A redundant pronoun is used proleptically to strengthen a following noun in a well-known Aramaic idiom (Black³ 96) : 9¹⁸ *his parents, his that had received his sight,* ¹³ *they bring him to the Pharisees, him that once was blind* (cf. p. 12).

Conjunctions. 1. ὡς *when* is frequent in John (16 times) and Luke-Acts (19+29) and may correspond to the Aramaic *kadh* (Black³ 89f). Elsewhere it is rare : in the NT only in Paul and Mark (3 times each). 2. *When* is sometimes a not unreasonable meaning for ὅτι enlarging its sphere in imitation of *dᵉ* : 9⁸ *when he was a beggar,* 12⁴¹ *when he saw.* However, a loose temporal use in Greek, as in English, may be enough

THE STYLE OF JOHN 71

to account for the extension "without any appeal to Aramaic" (Black³ 79).
Vocabulary. 1. λαμβάνω, bearing the meaning of παραλαμβάνω, Jn 1¹² is not secular Greek (Bultmann 35 n.4) but is influenced by the Aramaic *qbl*. 2. A manifest Aramaic phrase is *everyone who does sin* Jn 8³⁴ 1 Jn 3⁴ (Black³ 171, where it is effectively rendered back into Aramaic). 3. πρός c. accusative meaning *with*, Jn 1¹ 1 Jn 1², is a Semitism and it may be due to the Aramaic *lewāth*. If used in this sense in the papyri, it has the dative : cf. pp. 13, 93, W. F. Howard, *The Fourth Gospel in Recent Criticism*, London 4th ed. 1955, 285l

§ 5. SEMITISMS

Parataxis. Brief clauses linked by *and* are common to Hebrew and Aramaic. Biblical Greek will often disguise the parataxis by making one of the verbs a participle, e.g. *answering said*, but John prefers the co-ordination (*answered and said*), avoiding some of the redundant participles appearing in Biblical Greek (e.g. *coming, rising*) and preferring *they came and saw* 1³⁹, *he rose and went out* 11³¹.

The ptc. λέγων may be an exception, but even here Jn more commonly co-ordinates : (1) ... *and said* 1²⁹·⁴⁵ 2¹⁰ 4²⁸ 5¹⁹ 7³¹ 10²⁴·⁴¹ 12²² 18³⁸ 19⁴ 20²². (2) ... *saying* 1¹⁵·²⁶·³² 7¹⁵·²⁸·³⁷ 8¹² 9² 11³ 12²¹.
Parataxis may be (a) conditional : 1³⁹ *if you come you will see*, 16²⁴ *if you ask you will receive*. (b) temporal : 2¹³ *when the Passover was near, Jesus went up* ..., 4³⁵ *when it is the fourth month the harvest comes*, 7³³ *when I have been with you a little while I go away*. (c) consecutive : 5¹⁰ *it is the Sabbath, so that it is not lawful*, 6⁵⁷ *I live by the Father, so that he who eateth me* ..., 11⁴⁸ *all will believe in him, so that the Romans will come*, 14¹⁶ *I will ask the Father, so that he will send another Paraclete*. There are many such examples.

Casus pendens. The construction is very frequent in John compared with the Synoptists (Burney, *Aramaic Origin*, 34, 64f). Matthew has eleven examples, Mark four, Luke six, but John has 28 (Black³ 52). The pendens construction, *as many as ... to them* and *every ... he*, was recognized by Lagrange as a Semitism (Black). Casus pendens occurs mainly in the speech of Jesus, at least six-sevenths of the time, always in direct speech, thus favouring, according to Black, a translation-hypothesis. Nevertheless, it occurs in 1 Jn 2²⁴ where words of Jesus are not in question : *what you have heard from the beginning, let it abide in you*. As it is found, moreover, in vernacular Greek, it may not necessarily be a sign of translation.

Word order. Dr. Black faces " the difficulty of determining what order is un-Greek." It is largely a matter of determining the frequency over a fairly large piece of writing ; it is indeed a question of style, whether the concentration has become " such that no native Greek writer, uninformed by Semitic sources or a Semitic language, would have written it " (Black³ 51). The place of the verb is important : in Luke and John it is so often in primary position that it is no longer secular Greek. W. F. Howard was prepared to concede that it was " remarkable " (*Grammar* II 418).

The Verb. 1. Co-ordination of a participle with a finite verb " is a common custom with Hebrew writers " (Driver, *Tenses* § 117) and it occurs in the Aramaic of Dan 4^{22}. Jn 1^{32} *the Spirit descending* . . . *and he abode*, 5^{44} *receiving glory from each other, and you do not seek,* . . . 2. Superfluous auxiliary verbs are Semitic : 9^7 *go wash!* 6^{11} $13^{4.25}$ $19^{1.6.23.40}$ 21^{13} *took and,* 12^{11} 15^{16} *went and.* 3. Semitic also is the periphrastic imperfect $1^{9.28}$ 2^6 3^{23} 10^{40} 11^1 13^{23} $18^{18.25.30}$ (cf. p. 20, *Grammar* II 451–452).

Comparison. 1. Ellipse occurs 5^{36} *I have a witness greater than [that of] John*, and it is Semitic (Black³ 118). 2. The cardinal numeral replaces the ordinal $20^{1.19}$ (=*first*). " There is no need to ransack the papyri to explain the Hebrew or Aramaic phrase. . . . It is Jewish Greek " (Black³ 124). This particular phrase is common also to Matthew, Luke–Acts and Paul.

Pronouns. 1. As in Mk, resumptive pers. pronoun is found after a relative (Aram. d^e, Heb. '^{a}*sher* . . . *lô*) $1^{27.33}$ $9^{36?}$ 13^{26} $18^{9?}$ (cf. pp. 21, 36). E.g. *of whom . . . his sandal*. That similar constructions occur in the secular Koine makes direct translation from Aramaic less likely. 2. Often the oblique cases of *autos* are unemphatic and superfluous, as widely through the NT, too widely to detail each example. The redundancy may be explained partly by the tendencies of popular speech. By this rough test the NT books are seen arranged in order of non-literary, or else Semitic, quality and compared with some other texts.

Mk Mt Jn	1/2	(= one in two lines)
Lk–Ac	1/2½	
LXX : Gen, T Abr	1/3	
Johann. Epp., Rev	1/3	
Heb	1/5	
Jas 2 Pet Jude	1/6	
Josephus	1/6	
1 Pet	1/8	
Philostratus	1/8	
Paul	1/9	
Pastorals	1/13	
Papyri	1/13	
Plato	1/19	

3. The indef. pronoun in John takes the form of the indef. pronoun in Semitic speech, viz. *heis* (Heb. '*aḥadh*, Aram. *ḥadh*) $6^{8.70}$ 12^2 $18^{22?26}$ 19^{34} 20^{24} or *anthrōpos* (Heb. '*ish*, Aram. *barnash*) 1^6 $3^{1.4.27}$ 4^{29} 5^5D $^{7.34}$ $7^{22.23.46.51}$ 8^{40}

THE STYLE OF JOHN 73

$9^{1,16}$ LXX Gen 41^{33} (Black[3] 106f). 4. *A man cannot* is Semitic for *no one can* 3^{27} (Bultmann, contra E. C. Colwell, *The Greek of the Fourth Gospel*, Chicago 1931, 74) and *never man* 7^{46} (Burney 99, but Colwell declared not, 74). Likewise, *not . . . all* and *all . . . not (lô . . . kol)* as equivalent of *none* 6^{39} 11^{26} 12^{46} 1 Jn 2^{21} (Mk 13^{20} = Mt 24^{22}, Lk 1^{37} Ac 10^{14} Eph 4^{29} 5^5 2 Pet 1^{20} Rev 7^{16} 18^{22} 21^{27} 22^3 Didache 2^7 : *Grammar* II 434).

Conjunctions. 1. *Poiein* with *hina* is the Semitic causative : 11^{37} (Col 4^{16} Rev 3^9 $13^{12,13,15f}$). 2. According to Bultmann, Burney's view that *hina* often literally translated Aram. *dᵉ (who)* is arbitrary, because Colwell had pointed out that it may = *who* also in normal Hellenistic Greek. It is, however, the frequence of the occurrence that affords it significance. As Black[3], 76, says, the excessive use of *hina* in Jn is unparalleled, and is not that of the Koine. (It is frequent in the LXX, and increasingly so in the Koine, until at last the infinitive disappears to make way for it. *Grammar* III 103f ; Pernot 53–69.) Within the Fourth Gospel there is a wide range of usage—epexegetic, ecbatic, completing the action of verbs of will, command, beseech, agree, allow, etc. 1^{27} 2^{25} $4^{34,47}$ 5^7 $6^{7,29,40}$ 8^{56} $9^{2,22}$ $11^{50,53,57}$ $12^{7,10,23}$ $13^{1,2,29,34}$ $15^{8,12,13,17}$ $16^{2,7,30,32}$ $17^{3,4,15,21,24}$ 18^{39}. Some of these may be imperatival *hina* : 13^{34} 15^{17} *(love one another)*, more doubtfully imperatival : 1^8 6^{39} 9^3 12^7 13^{18} 14^{31} 15^{25} $18^{9,32}$ 19^{24}. Dr. W. G. Morrice notes with approval the opinion in *Grammatical Insights* that the Fourth Gospel is less " fatalistic " if the imperatival *hina* is recognized (*Bible Translator* 23 [1972] 327). As time went on, the less " literary " writers tended not to resist the encroachments of this conjunction : thus we have a rough guide to the " literary " quality of the NT authors. (Besides the test in the following table, and that concerning *autou* above, we may test the frequence of the pure nominal phrase, both for Semitic influence and lack of literary standards : Mk and Jn resort more often to the copula than any NT author, cf. *Grammar* III 294–310).

Incidence of *hina* per number of lines of Nestle	
Johnn. Epp., Jn	1/12, 1/13 (one in twelve lines)
Eph, Pastorals	1/15
1 Pet	1/17
Phil–Col–Phm	1/21
Mk	1/23
1,2 Thes	1/24
Rom–Cor–Gal	1/24
Rev	1/31
Heb	1/46
Mt	1/60
Lk–Ac	1/87
⎧ Infancy	1/269
⎪ I Acts (sample)	1/268
⎨ II Acts (sample)	1/138
⎩ We	1/253
Jude–2 Pet–Jas	1/136

Thus, the Johannine writings in this respect are the least literary, or perhaps the most Semitic, of all NT books. The Semitic influence on Jn cannot be doubted, and yet Bultmann (on 5^7) has correctly observed that this need not imply an Aramaic translation ; so also E. Ullendorff, " A Mistranslation from Aramaic ? " *NTS* 2 (1955) 50–52. Already in Jewish forms of Greek, *hina* may have come to embrace the same diversity of meanings as d^e, $dî$, and in a few instances it will probably still have the final force (Jn uses *hopōs* for a final conjunction once only, at 11^{57}) : e.g. Jn 6^{30}, cf. Black³ 78, Pernot 55. That *hina* has also the temporal sense (that too included in d^e) seems probable from 12^{23} 13^{1} $16^{2.32}$ (*the hour comes WHEN*). However, Hebraic is as likely as Aramaic, as an examination of the LXX will reveal : Gen 18^{21} 44^{34} 47^{19} Num 11^{15} 21^{27} Deut 5^{14} Josh 22^{24} 1 Chr 21^{3} Tob B 8^{12} Ps 38^{5} Ezek 37^{23} 2 Mac 1^{9} Job 32^{13}. *Grammar* III 95 : "virtually a Semitism." There are also many LXX examples of non-final *hina* in the various other senses, *Grammar* III 104. In many LXX books, *hina* is as often non-final as final.

Vocabulary. The use of *city* (*polis*) where village is meant (Jn 4 of Sychar, Mt 2^{23} of Nazareth) is a Semitism deriving from the Palestinian use of '*ir* and *qiryâ* for a place of any size (Bultmann). So perhaps is *sea* for *lake*. Believe c. *eis* (over 30 times) reflects the Hebrew *he'emîn b^e* or Aramaic *hêmîn b^e*.

§ 6. Johannine Clause-order

One or two points are of interest in the order of clauses within the sentence.

(1) The *kathōs-clause* has both pre- and post-position. In the pre-position it is usually taken up in the second half by *kai* or *houtos* or *tauta* : 3^{14} 5^{30} 6^{57} 8^{28} 12^{50} $13^{15.34}$ $14^{27.31}$ $15^{4.9}$ 17^{18} 20^{21}. In post-position : 1^{23} 5^{23} 6^{58} $10^{15.26}$v.l. 13^{34} $15^{10.12}$ $17^{2.11.14.16.21.23}$ 19^{40} ; they include the two instances 6^{31} 12^{14} which introduce quotations, and that probably means that we must punctuate differently at 7^{38} and count the clause as post-position (*Grammar* III 320).

(2) The *hotan* clause usually has pre-position : 2^{10} 4^{25} 5^{7} $7^{27.31}$ $8^{28.44}$ 9^{5} 10^{4} 15^{26} $16^{4.13.21}$ 21^{18}. Occasionally post-position : 13^{19} 14^{29} 1 Jn 5^{2}.

(3) The *hōs* (*when*)-clause always has pre-position : $2^{9.23}$ $4^{1.40}$ $6^{12.16}$ 7^{10} $11^{6.20.29.32.33}$ 18^{6} 19^{33} 20^{11} 21^{9} (as also in Acts, and very nearly always in Luke). Pre- : Mt 28^{9}v.l. Post- : Mk 9^{21}v.l.

§ 7. Use of Particles

John makes no use of *ara* or *dio* ; only once uses *kaitoi ge* 4^{2} and *dē* only once as a variant 5^{4}. Other connectives which he uses very rarely are *homōs* 12^{42} (a NT hapax, except for Gal 3^{15} 1 Cor 14^{7}v.l.). Another particle which is almost a NT hapax is *mentoi* 4^{27} 7^{13} 12^{42} 20^{5} 21^{4} (elsewhere only 2 Tim 2^{19} Jas 2^{8} Jude 8). But most characteristic of John are *alla* (once in 15 lines of Nestle, along with 1 Peter and Paul the most frequent in the NT), and *oun* (one in seven, quite the most frequent in the NT, followed next by Mark, less than half as often). Fairly frequent is *de*, but it is more excessive in the other gospels and Acts, Paul and the General Epistles. In this respect, the Johannine Epistles differ, making much less use of the particle. Except for Revelation and the Johannine Epistles, which do not use it at all, John makes least use of *men* . . . *de* (one in 264 lines, less even than Mark). He uses *gar* with about the same frequence as Luke–Acts and 1 Peter (once in 24 lines). He shares *ti oun* with the other gospels, Acts and Paul: more frequently than Luke–Acts, but not so much as Matthew-Mark and Paul, $1^{21.25}$ 6^{30}. On the whole, his use of particles is not strong. Eliminating *kai*, there is only one connective particle for 3, 1 lines, compared with Matthew's 2, 5 and (even allowing for the longer sentences and therefore less need of connectives) Luke–Acts 2, 9.

§ 8. Use of Prepositions

John uses his full share of ordinary Greek prepositions, with all cases. Thus the use of *epi* corresponds closely with that of Polybius: gen. dat. accus. = 1, 5 : 1 : 3 (John's 1, 7 : 1 : 3,5), in line with Matthew and the LXX, but not with the NT as a whole. The proportion of *en* : *epi* in the Ptolemaic papyri is 1 : 0,45, in the whole NT is 1 : 0,32, but in John it is 1 : 0,18 (the same as James, Paul, and 1 Peter), which marks a considerable increase in the use of *en*. As Mayser observes (II 2, 461), the use of accusative with *huper* is very rare in the papyri (gen : accus = 20 : 1); Johannine practice bears this out, John 13 :0, Epistles 3 : 0. But Matthew is a notable exception in the NT (0,25 : 1). With *peri* accusative is very rare in the NT, much more so than in the papyri (Mayser II 2, 446), and John is here at great variance with the papyri (gen : accus = papyri 1,5 : 1, NT 7,6 : 1, John 67 : 1).

Another general departure from NT standards is marked by the use of the case with *dia*, where the meaning can be almost the same, *through* (gen) and *because of* (accus). The proportions are Matthew 1 : 1, Mark 0,61 : 1, Luke–Acts 1,7 : 1, Paul 2 : 1, Hebrews 2,3 : 1, 1 Peter 4 : 1. Against these figures, those for John (0,37 : 1) and Revelation (0,12 : 1) stand out conspicuously. In the Ptolemaic papyri *en* is the most frequent preposition, with *eis* next in order, which is broadly the position in the NT, including John (200 : 180), to which Mark and Hebrews are exceptions. But perhaps it is in the use of *para* with its cases that we find the widest cleavage between NT and secular use (*Grammar* III 272f), where there is enormous use of the genitive. We do not find this in John, though perhaps he is nearest to the papyri in this respect of any NT author. Like the LXX, the NT also differs from secular Greek in having completely renounced the dative case with *hupo*, now a two-case preposition. John and the NT authors have much the same proportion of gen : accus as the LXX, and nothing like the secular writers (NT gen : accus = 3,3 : 1, John = 3 : 1).

But John is more fond of *eggus* than any NT author (11 times), yet always probably as an adjective rather than a prepositional adverb, reflecting as in the LXX the Hebrew *qārôbh 'ēl* (gen) or *lᵉ* (dat) or pronominal suffix (gen).

The Christian use of en. This is a slight extension of the local and spatial sense of *in* in a special direction to denote *in the sphere of*, especially of God, Christ and the Gospel. This is the *en* of spiritual union, very common in Paul, and important in John, as when he refers to walking *in* the light, or *in* darkness. " I *in* you, and you *in* me," is the beginning of the doctrine of co-inherence.

§ 9. The Limited Vocabulary

The Gospel vocabulary is limited to 1011 different words, only 112 of which are NT hapax. Many of these words are repeated, so that the vocabulary is only $6\frac{1}{2}\%$ of total word-use, almost the lowest in the NT (cf. p. 44). God the Father is mainly *living*, *holy*, or *righteous*, and the characteristic words of revelation (*know*, *bear witness*, *glorify*, *manifest*) are much over-worked. Other characteristic words are *true*, *truly*, *Truth*, *life*, *light*, *love*, *abide*. Quite insignificant words are given theological overtones : *from above*, *whence*, *whither*, *now*, *not yet*. We have noticed the over-worked *hina*. *Pneuma* serves for *spirit* and *wind* ; *lifted up* means both exaltation and death ; *water* has a hidden meaning, so has *blindness*, *sleep*, *departure*, *crossing over*, and *resurrection*. Even at a more trivial level, terms occasionally bear stereotyped meanings : *go up* = go to Jerusalem, *go down* = go to Capernaum.

§ 10. Pointless Variety in Style

On the other hand, John will occasionally use a needless synonym ; there are two words each for *love*, *send*, *heal*, *ask*, *speak*, *do*, *feed sheep*, *know* (references in Howard, *Fourth Gospel*[5], 278f). There is no apparent point in these synonyms beyond the avoiding of monotony, however hard one looks for a subtle distinction. Very occasionally, doubtless, he can be subtle in his distinctions ; e.g. *hear a voice* (gen) seems to mean *obey* $5^{25.28}$ $10^{3.16}$, whereas *hear a voice* (accus) is confined to perception 3^8 5^{37}. But on the whole the distinctions are pointless. The author of 1 John has the same pointless variation in syntax ; e.g. *a sin not* (μή) *unto death* and *a sin not* (οὐ) *unto death* $5^{16\text{f}}$ can have no difference in meaning. (Similarly 1 Pet 1⁸.) John shows this characteristic in the use of prepositions : when Jesus sees Nathanael he is *hupo* the fig-tree 1⁴⁹, but *hupokatō* the fig-tree 1⁵⁰ (Revelation always has the latter), and Philip is *apo* Bethsaida but *ek* the city of Andrew 1⁴⁴. Lazarus was *apo* Bethany, but *ek* the village of Mary 11¹. For some reason John is conspicuous among NT authors as being four times more prone to use *ek* than *apo* and the Johannine epistles are nearly twice as prone. The NT authors range from Luke-Acts, Matthew and the author of Thessalonians, who prefer *apo*, to John and Revelation at the other extreme, with the remainder having no particular preference. The Johannine writings, together with Revelation and Hebrews, shun the preposition *sun* ; there are three examples in John, only one of which is not a variant reading. Acts definitely prefers *sun*, to *meta* with genitive, but Paul and Luke have no preference. Matthew avoids *sun* (which he uses four times compared with *meta* (5 : 45). There is yet another exception to John's tendency to variety in the use of similar words, and that is his use of the negative, for he only once uses *ou* with the participle (10¹²), but whenever he negatives the participle he uses *mē* ; this was a Hellenistic tendency, but here John has advanced further than Hellenistic usage would permit : 3^{18} 5^{23} 6^{64} $7^{15.49}$ 9^{39} 10^{1} 12^{48} 14^{24} 15^{2} 20^{29}.

Desire to avoid monotony explains John's varying the tense according to the particular verb, but he varies it often enough with the same verb, e.g. 11^{36f} *were saying* (imperfect) . . . *said* (aorist).

The perfect of *erchesthai* is a favourite tense with John : $3^{2.19}$ 5^{43} 6^{17} 7^{28} $8^{20.42}$ $11^{19.30}$ $12^{23.46}$ $16^{28.32}$ 17^{1} 18^{37}. What is the difference between *I HAVE* (perfect) *come into the world as light* 12^{46}, and *I DID* (aorist) *not come to judge the world* 12^{47} ? Why the perfect tense of *send* $5^{33.36}$ 20^{21} and the aorist everywhere else ? Why the perfect *have known* 5^{42} 6^{69} $8^{52.55}$ 14^{9} 17^{7}, alongside the regular aorists ? Perhaps something theological enters here : the stress on the abiding significance of the Christian revelation. If so, the evangelist has not made his theology consistent always with his syntax.

Eccentricity is remarkable again when the choice is between a normal and a periphrastic imperfect : each may occur within two verses, e.g. 3^{22f} *was baptizing* with no apparent significance in the choice. Is there any real difference between the periphrastic perfect 20^{30} and normal perfect 20^{31} *have been written* ? The author of 1 John has the same habit : 2^{5} normal perfect, 4^{12} periphrastic.

Conclusion

These instances of Hebraisms, Aramaisms and Semitisms occur not only nor even mainly in the words of Jesus, as is sometimes assumed.

We conclude that John's language throughout is characteristic of Jewish Greek, syntactically very simple, dignified but without the flexibility of the secular language, pointlessly varied in syntax and vocabulary, but without the solecisms and without the linguistic energy of Revelation. It moves within well-defined Semitic limits of style and vocabulary. Perhaps it was based on an underlying *Mischsprache* of Hebrew and Aramaic (Black[3] 16) ; certainly the Greek itself is a mingling of Hebrew and Aramaic constructions with other constructions that may be either Hebrew or Aramaic.

It cannot be, as some have urged, that the Semitic Greek is simply due to the earliest Christian preachers being Jews who were using a second language, without complete mastery over it. If that were so, this kind of Greek would be a more clumsy language, inclined to mistakes, instead of which, even in Revelation, it obeys rules of its own syntax and style. Semitic features lend it solemnity, and they are not makeshifts filling the gaps left by ignorance of Greek. Moreover, Jewish Greek is not in fact restricted to early Christian preachers, but is found on the pens of men well accomplished in Greek, able to use it effectively, such as the authors of James, Hebrews, and 1 Peter. It appears in some free-Greek books of the LXX (e.g. Tobit), and some Jewish works as far away in time as the Testament of Abraham and the Testament of Solomon, which cannot be shown to be translations of Semitic originals. Ignorance of Greek as a cause of Jewish Greek, is altogether less probable than the influence of the Greek Bible through widely scattered synagogues, forming a new community language.

Other Literature :

C. Lattey, " The Semitisms of the Fourth Gospel," *JTS* 20 (1919) 330ff.
C. C. Torrey, " The Aramaic Origin of the Gospel of John," *HTR* 16 (1923) 305ff.
C. F. Burney, *The Poetry of our Lord*, Oxford 1925.
N. W. Lund, " The Influence of Chiasmus upon the Structure of the Gospels," *ATR* 13 (1931) 27–48, 405–433.
T. W. Manson, " The Life of Jesus : a Survey of Available Materials : (5) The Fourth Gospel," *BJRL* 30 (1946) 322–329.
O. Cullmann, " Der johanneische Gebrauch doppeldeutiger Ausdrücke als Schlüssel zum Verständniss des vierten Evangeliums," *Theologische Zeitschrift* 4 (1948) 360–372.
J. Bonsirven, " Les aramaïsms de saint Jean l'évangéliste," *Biblica* 30 (1949) 405f.
E. Hirsch, " Stilkritik und Literaranalyse im vierten Evangelium," *ZNW* 43 (1950) 129ff.
B. Noack, *Zur johanneischen Tradition, Beiträge zur Kritik an der literakritischen Analyse des vierten Evangeliums*, Copenhagen 1954.
G. D. Kilpatrick, " The Religious Background of the Fourth Gospel," *Studies in the Fourth Gospel*, ed. F. L. Cross, London 1957, 36ff.

R. Schnackenburg, " Logos-Hymnus und johanneischer Prolog," *Bibl. Zeit.* 1 (1957) 69–109.
H. Clavier, " L'ironie dans le quatrième évangile," *Studia Evangelica* I, Berlin 1959, 261–276.
S. Brown, " From Burney to Black : the Fourth Gospel and the Aramaic Question," *CBQ* 26 (1964) 323–339.

CHAPTER SIX

THE STYLE OF PAUL

Modern scholarly opinion requires that, as far as possible, we consider the various groups separately: *group* (1) 1 and 2 Thessalonians; *group* (2) Galatians, 1 and 2 Corinthians, Romans; *group* (3) Philippians, Colossians, Philemon; *group* (4) Ephesians. We have excluded the Pastoral epistles, but have noted parallels there, for they probably contain genuine Pauline elements at least. Unfortunately, we cannot take into consideration the view, not generally held, that parts of Paul's epistles may be earlier Christian fragments (e.g. R. Bultmann, " Glossen in Römerbrief," *Theologische Literar-Zeitung* 72 [1947] 197–202), or that Paul did not write 1 Corinthians 13, etc. It may be so, but the question lies beyond the scope of this volume.

§ 1. THE LITERARY CHARACTER OF THE MAIN GROUP

Compared with the others, *group* (2) above is marked by energy and vivacity, sincerity and a controlled outflow of words, reaching a high peak of eloquence at times, spontaneous, without contrivance. For simplicity and clarity alone, the first group would be more notable, as it is also the least literary, but the second group achieves sometimes a rare literary quality. Romans is more tightly constructed than 1 Corinthians, and neither of them is as full of feeling and quick changes of mood as 2 Corinthians, Galatians and Philippians. In the latter epistle, change of mood is so marked that it looks as if there has been an insertion: thus, some have considered whether a separate letter does not begin at Phil 3^2, perhaps added later by Paul while composing the same letter, but others declare against it (e.g. J. Jewett, " The Epistolary Thanksgiving and Philippians," *Nov.T.* 12 [1950] 40–53). Changes of mood are especially evident in 2 Corinthians and they tend to mar its literary excellence, as compared with 1 Corinthians, although chapters 9–12 are powerful in style. The polishing function of an amanuensis does not seem so evident in 2 Corinthians.

It is true that the Paulines and Hebrews are not wholly spontaneous in style, inasmuch as they show some influence of the rules of rhythm current in Asian Hellenistic circles, especially the influence of Polybius. Sometimes Paul could rise to the heights of Plato and Cleanthes, as in the ending of Romans 8, and in 1 Corinthians 13. E. Norden's comments should be observed on this aspect of Paul's style (*Die antike Kunstprosa vom VI Jahrhundert v. Chr. bis in die Zeit der Renaissance*, Leipzig 1898, 509). In his education, some part was doubtless played by Hellenism, and the influence of that was progressive perhaps, for none of the philosophical terms in the second group (*knowledge, wisdom, understanding, conscience, form*) occur in the earlier group. Yet Paul is fairly innocent of artificial rhetoric: the conventional rhetorical word-order is often neglected, e.g. Rom 14^9 "Christ *died* and *lived*, so that *the dead and the living*," Eph 6^{12} *blood and flesh*, Col 3^{11} *Greek and Jew*. These might seem quite inelegant to a stylist. Paul's art is usually unstudied. The eloquence is spontaneous, barely touched by an amanuensis. Of Bultmann's view that Paul's style is that of the Stoic-Cynic diatribe or popular moralizing address, it may be apt to comment that Paul's training as a rabbi probably taught him the skilful use of question and answer (*Der Stil der paulinischen und die kynisch-stoische Diatribe*), *FRLANT* 13, Göttingen 1910). Moreover, Paul's style is too passionate for the diatribe. However, there is something to be said for Bultmann's view: the defensive language of 1 Thes 2$^{1-12}$ is close to Dio Chrysostom's concerning some Cynic preachers, and it would seem that each of these two writers, in much the same style, distinguishes himself as a true philosopher from the charlatans. A. J. Malherbe has made this point ("'Gentle as a nurse': The Cynic Background to I Thess ii," *Nov.T.* 12 [1970] 203-217). Yet the language proves no more than that Paul may have been acquainted with the phraseology of Hellenistic writers such as Dio. Certain passages should be noted, especially Rom 2, 3, 4$^{1-12}$, 9$^{14-11^{32}}$, Gal 2^{17f} 3$^{19-22}$ 1 Cor 6$^{12.13.18}$ 15$^{29-34}$, in which are some features of the diatribe: the short simple sentence, the ironical imperatives, parataxis, asyndeton, rhetorical questions (especially characteristic of Romans, e.g. 3^1 4^{10} 8^{31} and also 1 Cor 7^{18ff}, which recall the diatribe of Epictetus), and introduction of the opponent's case by *they say* or *someone will say* (e.g. 2 Cor 10^{10} *his letters, they say, are heavy and strong* . . .). The question is not so much whether Paul's style resembles the diatribe as shown at its height in the Latin Seneca and the Greek Arrian's dissertations of Epictetus, and other Hellenistic literary features, but how the resemblances came to be in his letters. There is some superficial resemblance between Paul's language and Seneca's and Paul seems to use some Stoic catch-phrases, without however caring for the real Stoic meaning: e.g. 1 Cor 3^{21} (*all things are yours*) 4^8 (being rich and reigning) 7^{20} Eph 4^1 (cp. with Epictetus i 29.46, H. Schenkl's editio minor, Leipzig 1848: *called by God*) 1 Cor 9^{25} (cp. with Seneca, *Ep. Mor.* 78.16: athletes receive blows all over the body to win glory), 1 Cor 7^{35} (cp. with Epictetus iii 22.69: ἀπερισπάστως) Eph 6$^{10-20}$ (cp. with

Seneca, *Ep. Mor.* 96, *ad Marc.* 24 : the Christian warfare). J. B. Lightfoot's full discussion of the Stoic parallels is impressive (*St. Paul's Epistle to the Philippians*[6], London 1881, 289f). Although possibly Seneca knew something of Christianity, Lightfoot thought that it was more likely that the linguistic coincidences were due to the common elements in Stoicism and Christianity, since both of them were established in the Near East (cf. Lightfoot's dissertation, " St. Paul and Seneca," *op. cit.* 270-328). Even more probably, however, these Stoic traits and other forms of literary affection were mediated to Paul by way of the Hellenistic synagogue. By this very means the influence of the diatribes of Seneca and Epictetus would have reached Philo. " Regardless of the avenue by which Paul was introduced to this mode of expression, he appropriated it in no artificial way. It became part of his own style " (Malherbe, " The Beasts at Ephesus," *JBL* [1968] 73, 79). Paul was no conscious stylist, but his eloquence was "der Rhetorik des Herzens " (Norden 502), embellished at times perhaps by an amanuensis. The clarity of expression, more Greek than Hebrew, which some commentators have marked in the letters, may be due to occasional revision. The notion of a regular amanuensis, however, is not easy to credit ; too many inelegances were allowed to go uncorrected, and in particular some instances of zeugma, which scribes loved to rectify, are left alone. In 1 Cor 3[2] only one of the nouns suits the verb and this is an excellent example of zeugma (*I gave to drink milk, not meat*) ; in 14[34] very early scribes have corrected the zeugma, *it is not lawful for them to speak but to be submissive* (meaning, it *is* lawful to be submissive), into *let them be submissive* (DKG 1739 Old Lat Harkl Syr). There is no variant at 1 Tim 4[3] (*forbidding to marry and to abstain from meats*). Cf. also 1 Tim 2[12].

Almost all the literary forms in the NT were in use among contemporary Greeks and Romans. The *gospel* indeed was a new form, but the *logia* of a master, which formed part of the structure of the *gospel*, had already been collected by the students of philosophers ; they corresponded to the private summaries, as opposed to published works, a distinction made by Aristotle. Secondly, the Hellenistic form, the *dialogue* may be present, e.g. in the discussions between Jesus and the disciples over such questions as the Christians' attitude to the Law. Thirdly, the *diatribe*, a dialogue transformed into a monologue, in which an imaginary opponent is refuted, seems to be shared by Paul with Bion, Epictetus, Seneca, Philo, followed later by Clement of Alexandria. Fourthly, the *address* (or *homily* or *dialexis*) which was less to refute an opponent than to convince an audience, is exemplified in Hebrews. Lastly, the epistle, not so much private correspondence as something in the manner of the epistles of Epicurus and Polemon of Ilion, are considered by some to be models for Paul's letters, but the question remains whether his letters are indeed so " literary " or formal as these epistles. They were written to give instruction and they were intended to be read aloud, but Paul did not observe points of style or obey the laws of rhythm so closely. His are rather private *letters* than formal epistles, a distinction made by Deissmann (*Bible Studies*, ET Edinburgh 1901, 4ff), which is perhaps rather too naïve (cf. W. G. Doty, " The Classification of Epistolary Literature," *CBQ* 31 [1969] 183-199). Paul's letters begin with an address, " A. to B. grace and peace," but in secular letters in place of the Pauline *grace and peace* was simply *chairein* ; Paul's greetings are less formal and were often expanded into prayers. Like the Pastorals, Hebrews, 1 Peter and 2, 3, John, the Paulines end with a salutation, usually of a type which is common in the secular papyri : " Greet your mother and your father " (P.Tebt.412), but once first person, as in Rom 16^{22}, " I send greetings to your father and all your household " (P.Tebt.415). Cf. the useful article by T. Y. Mullins, " Greetings as a New Testament Form," *JBL* 87 (1968) 418-426. Paul's letters more often than not end with a grace, and in Romans and Corinthians with a reference to the holy kiss, which makes them uniquely distinct from secular letters. Nevertheless, they contain some phrases typical of private letters. *I beseech you, (brethren)* is very prominent in the Paulines : Rom 12^{1f} 15^{30} 16^{17} 1 Cor 1^{10} 4^{16} 16^{15f} 2 Cor 10^{1f} 1 Thes 4^{10b-12} 5^{14} Eph 4^{1-3}. C. J. Bjerkelund establishes that this phrase is found not so much in rhetorical writings, as in official and private letters (*Parakalô : Form und Sinn der parakalô-Sätze in den paulinischen Briefen*, " Bibliotheca Theologica Norvegica," 1, Oslo 1967. Cf. also P. Schubert, *Form and Function of the Pauline Thanksgiving*, Berlin 1939, also based on Pauline form-criticism). Other phrases of secular letters are : *I would have you know, I would not have you ignorant, I rejoice, making mention of you* (in prayer) (G. Milligan, *St. Paul's Epistle to the Thessalonians*, London 1908, 55). Yet Paul's letters do not lack the eloquence of the formal epistle which belongs especially to Asia Minor : oratory of the first order occurs very often (Rom 6 7 8^{31-35} 9 10 11, 1 Cor 3 4 8 9 12 13 15, 2 Cor 2 3 4 5 8 10 11 13), as do several of the literary devices of the epistle : irony (1 Cor 4^8, 2 Cor 11^{19}), aposiopesis (Rom 7^{24} Phil 1^{22}, perhaps 2 Thes 2^{3f}), prodiorthosis and epidiorthosis (Rom 3^5 8^{34}, 2 Cor 7^3 $11^{1ff.16ff.21.23}$ 12^{11}, Gal 4^9), paralipsis (he pretends not to say something but nevertheless says it : Phm ^{19}), and the rhetorical question closely paralleled in the diatribes of Epictetus (Rom 3^1 4^{10}, 1 Cor 7^{18ff}). Other literary devices are the allegory, metaphor, ellipse and the parallelism. Indeed, Paul's letters seem to be intended to be read aloud, like formal lectures and literary epistles. Not that this renders them any less spontaneous, nor on the other hand does their undoubted rabbinic dialect.

§ 2. The Contrast between Pauline and Ephesian's Style

Ephesians has very long periods, especially 1^{3-14}, 2^{14-18}, 3^{14-19}, and lacks Paul's usual flexibility of expression. Probably some of the clearest Semitisms occur in this epistle, e.g. *son of* (2^2 3^5 5^6), *everyone ... not* = no one (4^{29} 5^5), and ἴστε γινώσκοντες the Hebrew infinitive absolute (5^5).

Jülicher long ago felt the difficulty of the stiffness of style, the heavy catenae of sentences, the numerous particles and relative pronouns (another Semitism). Dibelius rejected Pauline authorship. Dr. Mitton concluded that Ephesians was written c. 90 by a discerning student of Paul in order to summarize and spread his gospel (C. L. Mitton, *The Epistle to the Ephesians*, Oxford 1951, 9–11, 31f). It may possibly be an apostolic homily, intended like 1 Peter for baptismal services, a revised edition of Colossians for the purpose (R. R. Williams, "The Pauline Catechesis," *Studies in Ephesians*, ed. F. L. Cross, London 1956, 89-96). Another suggestion from a liturgical angle is that if the artificial epistolary material be removed, a *berakah* for public worship, a Christian covenant-renewal, is arrived at, the word *blessed* no doubt promoting the idea: 1^{3-14} 2 3^{14-21}. Everything in the style of Ephesians fits the pattern of Qumran's covenant-renewal service at Pentecost; there are links with the Pentecostal cycle of readings, assuming that they existed before A.D. 70, and with the rabbinic exegesis upon them: Eph 4^8 5^{22-33} 6^2. It is suggested that later on this constituent of Christian worship was made into a letter: cf. J. C. Kirby, *Ephesians, Baptism and Pentecost : An Inquiry into the Structure and Purpose of the Epistle to the Ephesians*, Montreal 1968, passim.

The difference in style between the Paulines and Ephesians may be accounted for in part by the employment of a different amanuensis, in part perhaps because the tone of Ephesians is that of prayer and meditation in place of reasoning elsewhere. As the end drew near, perhaps, Paul wrote more serenely, as J. N. Sanders suggested ("The Case for Pauline Authorship," *Studies in Ephesians* 16). However, several stylistic features are common to Ephesians and the other Paulines: antithesis (cf. below under parallelism), *men ... de* (Romans 12 times, Corinthians 20, Galatians two, Philippians four, Ephesians once, Pastorals three), a simple rhythm (cp. Rom 8 and Eph 3), paronomasiae (Rom $1^{29.31}$ 2^1 5^{16} 8^{23} 11^{17} 12^{15} 14^{23} 1 Cor 2^{13} 13^8 15^{39f} 2 Cor $1^{4.13f}$ 3^2 4^8 8^{22} 9^8 10^{12} Gal 5^7 Phil 1^4 Eph 3^6), his rich use of the genitive, both subjectively and objectively (everywhere in the Paulines, and also Eph 1^4 2^{14} 4^9), the Semitic circumlocution with *mouth* (Eph 4^{29} 6^{19} and Paulines), the Semitic redundant *elthōn* (1 Cor 2^1 al. Eph 2^{17}), a predilection for *ara oun* (Romans eight times, nowhere else except

THE STYLE OF PAUL 85

Galatians, 1, 2 Thessalonians and Ephesians), *dio* (Paulines 22 times, Ephesians five times), and the use of metaphor, usually urban metaphors or metaphors connected with architecture, games, finance and the army ; when Paul enters rural areas his metaphors are not so successful, e.g. grafting olive trees in Rom 11$^{16-24}$.

Besides these, there are some other recurrent matters of style which need further discussion : e.g. the use of ellipse, such as *faithful [is] God* (1 Cor 1^9 10^{13} Phil 4^5 2 Thes 3^2 Eph 1^{18} 4^4 5^{17}), *wives [must be subject] to their husbands* (Eph 5^{24}), cf. also Rom 11^{16} 1 Cor 11^1. There is also a play on words, where the meaning as well as the sound is similar : Rom 1^{20} 5^{19} Phil 3^{21} Eph 4^1, and the particularly fine example in Rom 12^3 (μὴ ὑπερηφρονεῖν παρ' ὃ δεῖ φρονεῖν, ἀλλὰ φρονεῖν εἰς τὸ σωφρονεῖν), almost too perfect for one who discounted this world's wisdom. This may be due the work of the amanuensis ; it scarcely seems like Renan's " une rapide conversation sténographié et reproduite sans corrections " (*Saint Paul*, Paris 1869, 231). Also common to Ephesians and the rest of the Paulines are the digressions on account of word-association, as T. K. Abbott points out, quoting Paley (*A Critical and Exegetical Commentary on the Epistle to the Ephesians and Colossians*, ICC Edinburgh 1887, xxif) : *salvation* Eph 2^6, *went up* 4$^{8-11}$ *light* 5$^{13-15}$, *aroma* 2 Cor 2^{14}, *epistle* 3^1, *veil* ^{13}. Paul's asyndeton is effective in all his letters, whether emphasizing a new section (Eph 1^3 3^1 5$^{6.22.25.32}$ 6$^{1.5.10}$ Rom 9^1 10^1 11^1 etc.), leading successively to a climax (Eph 4$^{5.6.12.13}$ 6^{12} 1 Cor 4^8 2 Cor 7^2 1 Thes 5^{14} Phil 3^5), marking contrast (Eph 2^8 1 Cor 15^{42f}), or otherwise making for stylistic liveliness (Eph 1^{10} 3^8 4$^{4.28.29.31}$ 6^{11} Rom 1^{29ff} 2^{19} 1 Cor 3^2 13$^{4-8}$ 14^{26} al.).

§ 3. Harshness of Style

Some characteristics of Paul's style are harsh, particularly parenthesis, e.g. Eph 2^5. In 2 Thes 2^7 there may be a harsh parenthesis or trajection depending on the position in which *he who now restrains* is to be understood ; it is usually taken, " the mystery of lawlessness already works ; only he who now restrains will do so until he be taken from the midst," whereas it makes better sense when understood, " the mystery of lawlessness already works only until he who now restrains be taken from the midst." Perhaps also there is a parenthesis in 1 Cor 10^{11} : *they are written for our learning* is parenthetical, and thus " the ends of the ages " were come upon " them," not " us." Just as harsh a feature is trajection, the removal of words from their logical order : Rom 11^3 1 Thes 2^{13}. In Rom 5^6 there is a misplaced ἔτι γάρ for which one variant substitutes εἴ γε, others εἰ δέ, εἰ γάρ, and εἰς τι γάρ. Another trajection is the misplaced ὅμως (*nevertheless*) in 1 Cor 14^7 Gal 3^{15}, unless it be accented ὁμῶς (*likewise*). There is a possible trajection of the negative in Rom 3⁹ (*Have we an advantage ? Not altogether*), and the order should perhaps be reversed to read πάντως οὐ (*certainly not*), as in 1 Cor 16¹², but probably the confusion comes through dictation. Perhaps Paul made a pause in the voice between the two words, " No ! Absolutely ! " It is likely that Paul was given to trajection, doubtless because of the turmoil of his thoughts, and that scribes consistently sought to correct this stylistic solecism.

Despite the rhythmic quality of some passages in his letters, it is unlikely that he attended a Hellenistic teacher of rhetoric, for his anacolutha and solecisms are too numerous. There is direct object in the nominative case (Rom 2⁸), the antecedent of *ho* (neuter) can be masculine (Eph 5⁵) or feminine (Col 3¹⁴). We find extraordinary grammar in 2 Cor 12¹⁷ and casus pendens in Rom 8³. Paul's periods are rarely finished off neatly, a fault which Abel ascribes to forgetfulness as to how the period began, rather than to disdain of grammatical rules ; Paul allows himself to be drawn along on the wings of his thought in sharp bursts, resulting in parentheses and discords, while particles and participles are brought in to weave over gaps in the diction (*Grammaire* § 80f). His sentences became so involved that at a certain point he would close them and begin again. Good examples are Gal 2⁶ 1 Tim 1³ᶠᶠ (where there is one addition after another). Scribes have attempted to smooth out the anacolutha, e.g. Rom 9²³B 16²⁷B Gal 2⁴ᶠD.

§ 4. Judaism or Hellenism in Paul ?

Stylistic features which can be paralleled in Hellenistic literary works cannot rule out the fact that Paul was at heart a Jew. Norden found Paul's style to be " on the whole, unhellenic." Paul was a writer " der wenigstens ich mir sehr schwer verstehe . . . ist auch sein Stil, als Ganzes betrachtet, unhellenisch " (*Die Antike Kunstprosa* 499). Paul's work was almost exclusively among his co-religionists, in the synagogues of the Greek world, very seldom among the non-proselyte Gentile Greeks and barbarians, and only for brief spaces when the Jews refused him a hearing (e.g. in the school of Tyrannus). It is argued that for his work in " the West," no other language was possible than Greek or Latin. But the variety of Greek should be distinguished and specified. To maintain that Paul " was not likely to import into it words and constructions that would have a foreign sound " (*Grammar* II 21) is to overlook the possibility that for Jews the Semitic constructions of the Greek Old Testament would not have a foreign sound.

Even the so-called " literary " parts of Paul's letters owe their style mainly to Hebrew or to the LXX. Thus, even the neuter adjectives with dependent genitive (e.g. *the impossible things of the Law*) (Rom 8³) which is not found in the papyri, but in the higher Koine of Strabo and Josephus, is a feature of the free Greek of the LXX (2-4 Maccabees) and of the Apostolic Fathers (*Grammar* III 13f). It is now being appreciated that there was in the first century A.D. a body of Jewish and Christian writings in Greek which had the style of a Jewish-Hellenistic homily, of which Hebrews is a good example, which made good use of the OT and yet were influenced by the secular diatribe (cf. H. Thyen, *Der Stil der Jüdisch-Hellenistischen Homilie*, FRLANT, NF 47, Göttingen 1955). N. W. Lund complained that rarely had the Hebraic element been acknowledged in Paul's literary style, which is too often described as exclusively Greek, only modified by his method of dictation and his clumsy, repetitious sentences, the marks of his own temperament. Lund considered that allowance should be made for Paul's rabbinical training, his methods of argument, OT quotation, and his extensive use of allegory (*Chiasmus in the New Testament. A Study in Formgeschichte*, N. Carolina 1942, 139).

Allegory indeed is quite characteristic of Paul's style, and this rhetorical device, which is something more than a series of metaphors, was used by the Jews no less than the Greeks. Philo is an example, compared with whom " St. Paul's allegorism was firmly anchored to history, and thereby preserved from extravagance " (K. J. Woolcombe, in *Essays on Typology*, ed. G. W. H. Lampe and K. J. Woolcombe, London 1957, 56). Instances of Paul's allegory are his use of Sarah and Hagar in Gal 4²¹⁻²⁷, of unleavened bread in 1 Cor 5⁶⁻⁸, of the Law's forbidding to muzzle the threshing ox in 9⁹ᶠ. Very close to allegory is Paul's use of typology, which some define as a development of allegory, wherein he sees Adam as a type of Christ (1 Cor 15²² Rom 5¹⁴) and the Exodus as a type of conversion (1 Cor 10¹⁻¹³).

Lund moreover suggested that Paul's style was liturgical, and since Lund's book there has also appeared an article by J. M. Robinson (" Die Hodajot-Formel in Gebet und Hymnus des Frühchristentums," in *Apophoreta*, ed. W. Eltester, Berlin 1964, 194-235), who argues that *I give thanks* and *Blessed* introduce liturgical elements, as also in Jas 1. " Since Paul's letters were written to be read often, he gave them a literary form suitable for reading in wider circles than the local church to which they were first addressed. Their character as public liturgical writings is accentuated by the fact that they were cast in the well-known Old Testament liturgical forms " (Lund, *Chiasmus* 224). Lund's is an important thesis, less convincing perhaps because his elaborate analyses may be overdone.

Since that period, *Gattung*-criticism has been applied to Paul's letters, affecting larger literary groups than form-criticism ; thus 1 Cor 1-3 is seen as a kind of Jewish haggadic homily (W. Wuellner, in *JBL* 89

[1970] 199–204), and an underlying homily-pattern is discerned in Gal 3^{6-29} and Rom 4^{1-22} corresponding to something in Philo (*Leg.all.* III 65–75a; 169–173; *Sacra* 76–87. Cf. P. Borgen, *Bread from Heaven*, Leiden 1965, 46–50). It is noted that "homily-genres" appear in Palestinian midrashim of NT times, at first as separate units, later to be inserted in larger compositions. These homily-patterns seem to have the same characteristics as the above-mentioned Cynic-Stoic diatribe, viz. quotations and paraphrases of key-words (Bultmann, *Der Stil* 94–96). The main theme of the Corinthian homily (1 Cor 1–3) is the judgment of God on human wisdom (1^{19}) and the advantage of regarding it as a homily-*Gattung* is that 2^{1-5} is no longer seen as a pointless digression but rather as a characteristic feature of halakic discussions, intervening between the second and third treatment of the homily theme (the first treatment being 1^{20-25}, the second 1^{26-31}, and the third 2^{6ff}). The climax of the homily, future judgment, occurs at 3^{10-15} which is thus no longer seen as a diatribal digression (as Bultmann thought, *Der Stil* 98). It may be that Paul derived this theme of judgment from sermons which he had heard in the synagogue.

In a parallel way, form-criticism has been applied to Paul's letters, and an underlying judgment-form has been discerned (e.g. Rom 1^{18-32} 1 Cor 5^{1-13} 10^{1-14} 11^{7-34} Gal 1^{6-9} 5^{18-26} 6^{7-10} 1 Thes 1^{5-12} 4^{3-8} 2 Thes $2^{1-8.9-15}$). Whether consciously or not, Paul appears to be following the prophetic form of the OT pre-exilic prophets, modifying it with the purpose of warning and rebuking the Church (C. Roetzel, " The Judgment Form in Paul's Letters," *JBL* 88 [1969] 305–312).

One other interesting development in the Semitic direction has come from Qumran studies. Dr. Stachowiak is of opinion that *paraenesis* is a stylistic literary form with definite characteristics of its own, which he maintains is similar to and barely distinguishable from *paraklesis*. He maintains that the paraenetic parts of Paul's letters are comparable with the paraenetic parts of the Manual of Discipline, both being mutually independent yet both depending upon a common basic tradition (L. R. Stachowiak, " Paraenesis Paulina et Instructio de duobus spiritibus in ' Regula ' Qumranensi," *Verbum Domini* 51 (1963) 245–250).

§ 5. PAUL'S BIBLICAL GREEK SYNTAX

" The grammar shows little Semitic influence," it has been alleged (A. T. Robertson, *A Grammar of the Greek New Testament*[3], London 1919, 129), but the search could not have been carried very far. The Semitisms may be " secondary " in Moulton's sense that their deviation from the secular language is due to the over-literal rendering of a

Semitic original "defensible as Greek and natural to a Greek ear" (*Grammar* II 21), and to their being derived from the LXX. We need not suppose that the Semitisms and Aramaisms are due to his thinking in Aramaic while writing in Greek, for he was probably brought up to speak Greek from childhood (*Grammatical Insights* 83–85). There is very strong evidence for LXX influence, despite Moulton's surprising opinion that it did not exert much influence on Paul's style, much less was its diction copied. Nägeli, Guillemard and others, on the contrary, saw the Pauline Hebraisms as entirely due to Paul's use of the LXX. Everywhere there are verbal similarities with it, and there can be little doubt that he used a Bible closely resembling our present LXX texts or, perhaps, because the quotations are elaborately composite, it was a collection of Greek OT proof-texts.

Syntax of the Verb. *1. Impersonal plural.* Certain texts of 1 Cor 10^{20} (BDG Old Lat Marcion) reflect this Septuagintism: *they sacrifice*, but scribes sought to remove the Hebraism by adding a subject. It has been claimed as an Aramaism, but it is not exclusively so.

2. Co-ordination of finite verb with Participle or Adjective (e.g. LXX Ps $17^{33\mathrm{ff}}$) is not characteristic of non-Biblical Greek but is frequent in Paul: 1 Cor 7^{13} (adj) 2 Cor 5^{12} 6^3 7^5 $8^{18\mathrm{ff}}$ $9^{11.13}$ $10^{4.15}$ 11^6 Col 1^{26} Eph 1^{20-22}.

3. Infinitive as substitute for imperative may be derived from the Hebrew infinitive absolute, a more probable hypothesis than to suppose that vestiges of Homeric usage or the very slight precedent to be found in prayers in poetical classical Attic have any significance: Rom 12^{15} Phil 3^{16} (also Luke–Acts).

4. Imperative participle, used as a main verb, may well be a Hebraism (*Grammatical Insights* 165–168), but more probably ἐστέ is in ellipse (especially Rom 12^9), so that it is simply an instance of periphrastic tenses (*Grammar* III 303) and thus another Semitism; it is not sufficient evidence for a Hebrew *Vorlage* to Rom 12.

Rom $5^{10.11}$ $12^{9\cdot13.16}$ 2 Cor 1^7 8^{24}v.l. $9^{11.13}$ 10^4 Phil $1^{29\mathrm{f}}$ Col 2^2 $3^{1\cdot6}$ Eph 3^{17} 4^2. Paul does use periphrastic tenses, although Moulton held that he always used them in the emphatic way of class. Greek (*Grammar* II 23). Without emphasis they are characteristic of latish Hebrew and Aramaic and abound in the LXX, although the periphrastic imperfect may have real emphasis, signifying duration or repetition. So in Paul: Gal $1^{22\mathrm{f}}$ (*they kept hearing ?*) 2 Cor 5^{19} (*God kept on reconciling*) Phil 2^{26} (*he kept on longing*). But not always: there is no emphatic force in Gal 4^{24} (*are spoken allegorically*) 1 Cor 8^5 (*are spoken of*) 2 Cor 3^3 9^{12} Col 1^6 2^{23} 3^1 (Common in Mk).

5. Redundant participles (*elthōn*, etc.). There is not as much call for these in didactic material as there is in the gospel narrative, but Eph 2^{17} seems to indicate that the author would have used this

Semitism, given the opportunity (*he came and preached*). Other possible instances are 1 Cor 2^1 2 Cor 12^{20} Phil 1^{27}.

6. *Articular infinitive*. The excessive use of infinitival construction after *tou* ($=l^e$), although paralleled in small degree in non-Biblical texts, is Septuagintal (Radermacher 189). Paul's use is too extensive to be secular.

Consecutive : Rom 1^{24} 6^6 7^3 8^{12}. Final : 1 Cor 10^{13} 2 Cor 7^{12} Phil 3^{10}. After other verbs : Rom $15^{22.23}$ 1 Cor 16^4 2 Cor 1^8. Other constructions : 1 Cor 9^{10} 2 Cor $8^{11 bis}$ Gal 2^{12} 3^{23} Phil 3^{21}.

This is true of *eis to*, which belongs to the LXX and to some extent to secular Greek and is frequent in all the Pauline groups except Eph and Past : *Group* (1) 1 Thes $2^{12.16}$ $3^{2.5.10.13}$ 4^9 2 Thes 1^5 $2^{2.6.10.11}$ 3^9. *Group* (2) Rom $1^{11.20}$ 3^{26} $4^{11bis.16.18}$ 6^{12} $7^{4.5}$ 8^{29} 11^{11} $12^{2.3}$ $15^{8.13.16}$ 1 Cor 8^{10} 9^{18} 10^6 $11^{22.23}$ 2 Cor 1^4 4^4 7^3 8^6 Gal 3^{17}. *Group* (3) Phil $1^{10.23}$ (*Grammar* III 143).

It is true of ἐν τῷ ($=b^e$), expressing time during which with the present infinitive as in the LXX, very rarely in the papyri : Rom 15^{13} *in believing* Gal 4^{18} *while I am present* 1 Cor 11^{21} *in eating*.

7. The difficult adverbial expression εἰς τὸ σωφρονεῖν Rom 12^3 is best explained on the basis of the LXX as an adverb formed by literally rendering l^e with noun (Jer 4^{30} 6^{29}) ; here Paul has made the infin. into a noun (also on the LXX model) by prefixing the article.

8. The Semitic phrase ποιεῖν ἵνα occurs at Col 4^{16} (Heb. causative hiphil, Aram. aphel), shared with Mk Jn Rev T Abr.

9. The way Paul heaps up participial clauses, concerning the nature of God, especially in Eph and Col, was characteristic of the synagogue's liturgical style (E. Percy, *Probleme der Kolosser- und Epheserbriefe*, Lund 1946, 38f).

Syntax of the Noun. 1. The phrase, *son of*, used qualitatively, is good Greek, according to Deissmann (*Bible Studies* 161), who nevertheless conceded its LXX origin for Paul : Eph 2^2 5^6 Col 3^6 v.l. (*sons of disobedience*) Col 1^{13} (*son of his love*) 1 Thes 5^5 (*sons of the light and sons of the day*) 2 Thes 2^3 (*sons of perdition*).

2. The correct interpretation of the Pauline genitive is controversial : we believe it to be the Hebrew genitive of quality. The LXX translators so often faced the problem of the construct state in its adjectival function (Thackeray, *Grammar* 23) that apparently the habit of using a genitive of quality had been caught by Paul, leading to ambiguity of interpretation, whether it is subjective or objective. It is not found in non-Biblical Greek to the same extent as in Paul : e.g. Rom 1^{26} 2^5 (*day of wrath*) LXX, a sure Hebraism) 6^6 7^{24} 8^{21} Phil 3^{21} Col 1^{22} 2^{11} Eph 1^{14}.

3. The phrase, *words taught by human wisdom*, διδακτοῖς with the genitive (1 Cor 2^{13}), betrays direct influence of LXX Isa 54^{13} (*limmûdhê Yahweh*=διδακτοὺς θεοῦ).

4. The dative, *to God*, may be dativus commodi but is more clearly an imitation of the LXX rendering of the Hebrew device to produce a

superlative by means of *lêlōhîm* : Jon 3^3 (*a great city to God = a very great city*). Thus 2 Cor 10^4 : *mighty to God = very mighty*.

5. It is a Semitic construction to append the personal or demonstrative pronoun to the noun in the genitive rather than to the noun to which it really belongs : Rom 7^{24} *the body of this death = this body of death* (= *this dead body*), Phil 3^{21} *the body of our low estate = our body of low estate*, Col 1^{13} *the son of his love = his son of love* (= *his beloved son*). *Grammar* III 214.

Syntax of the Article. Paul is the most consistent breaker of Colwell's and indeed of any other rule regarding the article (*Grammar* III 183f), and it is seldom clear how far any noun is intended to be definite. The ambiguity is characteristic of Biblical Greek, as we found in the gospels, and corresponds to the disappearance of any formal distinction between definite and indefinite in Aramaic (cf. p. 21).

Syntax of Number. 1. Contrary to non-Biblical Greek, Paul often has the singular to denote something shared by a group of people, as in the Semitic idiom, e.g. *heart* (Rom 1^{21} 2 Cor 3^{15} Phil 1^7 Col 3^{16} v.l. Eph 1^{18} 4^{18} 5^{19} 6^5) or *body* (Rom 8^{23} 1 Cor $6^{19.20}$ 2 Cor 4^{10}).

2. The Hebrew plural *'ôlāmîm* is probably behind Paul's use of plural *aiōnes* (*eternity*) : Gal 1^5 Eph 2^7 3^{11}, and behind the plural *ouranoi* which, on the analogy of Hebrew *shāmayîm*, means the Jewish seven heavens in 2 Cor 12^2 Eph 4^{10}.

3. *One* (cardinal) for *first* (ordinal) is Hebraic and is natural to Paul in 1 Cor 16^2, no less than to the evangelists. It is Septuagintal for *yôm 'eḥādh* (Gen 1^5).

Syntax of the Pronoun. Paul has the Biblical Greek *anthrōpos* for the indefinite pronoun : 1 Cor 4^1 7^{26} 11^{28}, but his subject-matter, not being narrative, does not call for the other prominent Biblical Greek feature concerning the pronoun, viz., the use of oblique cases of *autos*. Thus it is not found so often as in the gospels, but is frequent enough to place Paul's style in line with Biblical Greek, especially in Ephesians.

Groups (1) and (2) : the occurrence is one in ten lines. *Group* (3) : the occurrence is one in eight lines. In Ephesians, it is one in five lines, which is very Semitic. Whereas the papyri have one in 13 lines, the narrative books of the LXX have one in three lines (Gen 1–4), or one in two lines (4 Kms 1–4).

Syntax of Conjunctions. 1. The importance of Semitic influence for specific exegesis appears in Gal 2^{16}, where a great deal of theology is involved in the question whether or not Paul confuses *ei mē* and *alla*. If he has not confused them, then we should read, as in non-Biblical Greek : " A man is not justified by the works of the Law, *unless* it be by way of faith in Jesus Christ," which is scarcely Paul's soteriology (for man is *in no way* justified by the Law), but it becomes more characteristically Pauline if, in common with the LXX and Biblical Greek usage, he equates *ei mē* with *alla*, and thus we render, " A man is not justified by the works of the Law, *but* by faith in Jesus Christ." The confusion arises in Biblical Greek because *kî 'im* (= *ei mē*) is usually rendered by *alla* (e.g. Gen 32²⁹ 1 Kms 8¹⁹ Ps 1⁴). The equation of *ei mē* with *alla* is seen in Mark and Matthew (Mk 13³² = Mt 24³⁶, Mt 12⁴).

2. The interrogative *ei* is an undoubted Semitism (a Septuagintism for *hᵃ* or *'im*), and Moulton-Geden give 1 Cor 7¹⁶bis 2 Cor 13⁵ as direct interrogative.

3. The meaning of the idiom *ti gar moi* (1 Cor 5¹²) is best explained by Hebrew influence (*Grammatical Insights* 43–47, 102) : *how does it concern me ?*

4. The compressed use of ἤ (*than* for *rather than*) is a borrowing from the LXX, conscious or otherwise, the few non-Biblical parallels being less convincing than the LXX : 1 Cor 14¹⁹ LXX Num 22⁶ 2 Mac 14⁴² (*Grammar* III 32).

5. Imperatival *hina* : 1 Cor 5² Eph 5³³. Our views in *Grammatical Insights* 147 and *Grammar* III 95 are endorsed by W. G. Morrice, *Bible Translator* 23 (1972) 328f.

Syntax of the Adverb. 1. A distributive adverb might be expressed in Hebrew by duplication of a noun (e.g. *yôm wāyôm* = *daily*) and Paul has resorted to this duplication in 2 Cor 4¹⁶, which though not directly Septuagintal, follows the anology of several other distributive duplications there, and it has found its way into modern Greek.

2. Adverbial *loipon* (= *ceterum*) (1 Cor 1¹⁶ 4² 7²⁹ 2 Cor 13¹¹ Phil 3¹ 4⁸ 1 Thes 4¹ 2 Thes 3¹ Eph 6¹⁰D 2 Tim 4⁸) may have come in by way of Aramaic and then found its way into the post-Ptolemaic papyri (A.D. 41) ; it is doubtful whether it has this meaning in the Ptolemaic papyri (Mayser II 3,145). 3. Adverbial *polla* may also be Aramaic (*Grammar* II 446) : Rom 16⁶,¹² 1 Cor 16¹²,¹⁹.

Syntax of Prepositions. 1. *Physiognomical and similar expressions.* As in the LXX, Paul uses certain nouns as circumlocutions in the Hebrew fashion : *mouth* (Rom 3¹⁹ 10⁹,¹⁰ 15⁶ 2 Cor 6¹¹ Col 3⁸ Eph 4²⁹ 6¹⁹ 2 Tim 4¹⁷) and *hand* (2 Cor 11³³ *escaped their hands* Gal 3¹⁹ *by the hand of a mediator*).

Such expressions belong to Biblical Greek, in the LXX and elsewhere, and so do the compound prepositions of like nature : *katenanti* (Rom 4¹⁷ 2 Cor 2¹⁷ 12¹⁹), *enōpion* = *qᵉdām* (a favourite of Paul : Rom 3 times, 1 Cor 11 times, 2 Cor three, Gal once, 1 Tim six, 2 Tim two), *opisō* (Phil 3¹³ 1 Tim 5¹⁵), *emprosthen* (2 Cor 5¹⁰ Gal 2¹⁴ Phil 3¹³ 1 Thes 1³ 2¹⁹ 3⁹,¹³), and *kata prosōpon*, which the LXX frequently use to translate the physiognomical *liphnê* and *bᵉ'ênî* (*Grammar* I 42).

2. Paul is influenced by the LXX in the use of *en* (b^e, meaning *because of, for the sake of*) Rom $1^{21.24}$ 5^3 1 Cor 4^6 7^{14} 2 Cor $12^{5.9}$ Phil 1^{13}, in the use of *pros* with verbs of saying (Rom 10^{21} *to Isaac he says* 15^{30} *prayers to God* 1 Thes 2^2 *speak to you* : thus, without special emphasis), and in the use of *ek* which in its causal sense is not characteristic of non-Biblical Greek, where its occurrence is negligible compared with that of the LXX or Paul, recalling the LXX rendering of *min* by *apo* or *ek* when *hupo* or the simple dative would have been appropriate (Rom 1^4 1 Cor 1^{30} 2 Cor 2^2 7^9 13^4 Rev 2^{11}). The use of *pros* meaning *with* (1 Cor $16^{6.7}$ 2 Cor 5^8 11^9 Gal 1^{18} 2^5 $4^{18.20}$ 1 Thes 3^4 2 Thes 2^5 3^{10} Phil 1^{26} Phm ^{13}) was probably encouraged by the Aramaic *l^{e}wāth* (Burney, *Aramaic Origin* 29). The use of *pros* with accus., answering the question *where ?*, must be understood as a Semitism, as it has dat. only in the papyri in this sense (Bultmann, on Jn 1^{1-2}).

3. After *logisthēnai* (Rom 2^{26} 9^8) and *hamartanein* (1 Cor 16^{18} $8^{12 b 18}$), Paul retains the LXX *eis* (l^e), and *en* (b^e) after *pistis, pisteuein*, which constructions are extremely rare outside Biblical Greek. To be *well-pleased in* (*en*) is also from the LXX and is unparalleled in non-Biblical Greek (influence of *ḥpṣ b^e*) : 2 Cor 12^{10}, cf. Mk 1^{11}=Mt 3^{17}. The phrase *exousia epi* (for the Semitic, cf. below p. 157) occurs at 1 Cor 11^{10}. The phrase ᾄδειν ἐν is a Hebraism (b^e), as we see from Ps 137 (138)^5 *sing OF the ways of the Lord* not *IN the ways of the Lord*. Therefore, in Col 3^{16} it may be *sing OF grace in your hearts*, rather than *sing WITH grace*. . . .

4. Whenever a series of nouns presents the opportunity to repeat the preposition, Paul will accept it 58% of the time (Rom, 1 Cor), 37% (Eph) and only 17% (Pastorals), as compared with LXX Ezek (B-text) 84%, Rev 63%, Jn 53%, Mk 38%, Mt 31%. Paul is in line with the rest of the NT and somewhere between the literal translation Greek of the LXX and the almost complete absence of repetition in classical and contemporary non-Biblical Greek (*Grammar* III 275).

5. Biblical Greek favours compound prepositions, e.g. *en mesō* (1 Thes 2^7), *heōs ek mesou* (2 Thes 2^7), *ana meson* (1 Cor 6^5).

Sentence Construction. The prolepsis of the subject of a subordinate clause is a Biblical idiom (cf. pp. 16, 33, 36, 69, 151) : Gal 1^{11} *I make known the gospel . . . that it is not . . .* 1 Cor 3^{20} *the Lord knows the thoughts of the unwise, that they are . . .* 14^{37} 16^{15} 2 Cor 12^{31} 1 Thes 2^1 2 Thes 2^4.

§ 6. Biblical Greek Vocabulary

We give but a few examples. In Rom 7^3 " being " with a man (= marrying him) is reminiscent of the LXX rendering of *kî thihyê l^{e}ish* (Lev 22^{12} ; cp. Num 30^7 Jg 14^{20} Ezek 23^4), because merely living with another man is not Paul's point : he speaks of freedom to marry again. *Kai idou* and *idou gar* also occur as a Semitism (2 Cor 6^9 7^{11}) and so does *splangchna* (2 Cor 6^{12} 7^{15} Phil 1^8 2^1 Phm $^{7.12.20}$). In Rom 2^{25} the meaning of *ōphelei* (*is of value*) is confined to Josephus, and in Rom 4^{20} Phil 4^{13} Eph 6^{10} 1 Tim 1^{12} 2 Tim 2^1 4^{17} we find the Biblical word *endunamoun*, but it overflowed from the LXX or the NT into Poimandres (c. i–iii/ A.D.). The word *walk* (*peripatein*) is used, in Hebrew fashion, of moral behaviour, some thirty times.

§ 7. Biblical Greek Word-order

Although Paul observes a characteristically Biblical word-order on the whole, yet he makes frequent exceptions in the interests of rhetoric, in order to emphasize a prominent thought, as do the authors of Hebrews and James. Prominent words or thoughts affecting the word-order are: " you " (Rom 11^{13}), " revealed " (Rom 8^{18} Gal 3^{23}), " each " (Rom 12^3 1 Cor 3^5 7^{17}), " mundane matters " (1 Cor 6^4), " weaker " (1 Cor 12^{22}), " tongues " (1 Cor 13^1), " love " (2 Cor 2^4), final clause precedes for effect (2 Cor 12^7), " the poor " (Gal 2^{10}), " the Lord " (1 Thes 1^6), " the Devil " (1 Tim 3^6). Sometimes Paul brings closely connected words together: " he has *authority, the potter over the clay*, from the same lump to make " (Rom 9^{21}), " we were *children by nature* of wrath " (Eph 2^3). He brings forward the predicate in the interests of euphony: Rom 13^{11} Phil 2^{11} 3^{20}.

Paul's word-order within the sentence is remarkably flexible, but it goes beyond this to clause-order, and trajection of clauses seems to occur at 1 Cor 15^2 (" if you hold it fast " may be misplaced for emphasis, and scribes attempted to correct), 2 Cor 8^{10} (" not only to do but also to wish " is scarcely logical in view of the next verse, " so that your readiness to wish it may be matched by your completing it "), Phil 1^{16f} (KL correct the illogical order).

Position of the Verb. The primacy of the verb, next to parallelism of clauses, is the surest Semitism in the NT, especially when it occurs in a series (E. Norden, *Agnostos Theos: Untersuchungen zur Formengeschichte religiöser Rede*, 4th ed. Leipzig 1923, 365). Paul is not a whit behind the gospels in preferring this position, whereas in contemporary non-Biblical, as in the modern language, the predominant order is the middle position for the verb. In main declarative clauses, excluding the verbs *to be* and *speaking*, the verb usually comes right at the beginning of the clause, after the connecting particle, e.g. Rom $1^{11,13,16,18,21,22,24,26,28}$ 1 Cor $1^{4,10,11,16,17}$ Gal $1^{11,13}$. In the same stretch, the subject comes before the verb only at: Rom $1^{17,19,20}$ Gal 1^{12}. The object precedes the verb only at 1 Cor 1^{27}. Rhetoric upsets the primacy of the verb in Rom 11^{13} 1 Cor 13^1.

Position of the adjective. Paul places the adjective or adjectival phrase after the noun, with repeated article, far too often for there to be any resemblance with secular practice. In iii/B.C. papyri there are only ten instances in this position, as opposed to twenty between article and noun; in ii–i/B.C. papyri the difference from Paul is even more marked 5/140. The LXX has predominantly Paul's position (*Grammar* III 8). The kind of phrase in which Paul follows the secular order is διὰ τῆς ἐν ἀλλήλοις πίστεως (Rom $1^{12,15}$ Gal 1^{17}), ἡ ἀσύνετος αὐτῶν καρδία (Rom $1^{21,23,26}$ 12^1 Gal $2^{3,13}$), τὰς ἑαυτῶν ψυχάς (1 Thes $2^{7,8,12,14}$)—i.e. a prepositional phrase, a single adjective, and ἑαυτῶν, or ἰδίων. The phrases involving the Biblical practice of repeating the definite article are: τοῦ Υἱοῦ αὐτοῦ τοῦ γενομένου (Rom 1³ 12³·⁶ Gal 1⁴·¹¹ 2⁹ 1 Thes 1¹⁰ 2¹²·¹⁴), τὸ θέλημα τοῦ θεοῦ τὸ ἀγαθὸν καὶ εὐάρεστον καὶ τέλειον (Rom 12²), ἡ πίστις ὑμῶν ἡ πρὸς τὸν θεόν (1 Thes 1⁸), ταῖς ἐκκλησίαις τῆς Ἰουδαίας ταῖς ἐν χριστῷ (Gal 1²²)—participles, prepositions, and a chain of adjectives. The occurrence in seven chapters of Romans, Galatians, 1 Thessalonians was twelve, far higher than anything we have met in secular Greek. In the first two chapters of 1 Corinthians there were five; in two chapters of Philippians there were two; in the final chapter of Ephesians, two examples. Cf. pp. 23f.

Position of the demonstrative adjective (houtos, ekeinos). This invariably is post-positive in Biblical Greek and pre-positive in secular (only *houtos*, for *ekeinos* in the papyri has lost its attributive use: Mayser II 2, 80), and it is overwhelmingly post-positive in all Paul's letters, with the exception of the Pastorals.

Position of πᾶς. Mayser (II 2, 102) disclosed four possible positions in the Ptolemaic papyri: 1) πᾶς ἄνθρωπος, 2a) πᾶς ὁ ἄνθρωπος, 2b) ὁ ἄνθρωπος πᾶς, 3) ὁ πᾶς ἄνθρωπος, with the plurals of each type. The figures in *Grammar* III 202–205 included LXX quotations. Without the quotations, the figures are as follows:

	Type 1		Type 2a		Type 2b		Type 3	
	s.	pl.	s.	pl.	s.	pl.	s.	pl.
(1) 1 and 2 Thes	9	1	2	7	—	1	—	—
(2) Rom–Cor–Gal	39	9	17	15	—	9	1	2
(3) Phil–Col–Phm	27	1	6	5	—	1	—	—
Ephesians	19	1	3	6	—	1	—	—
Pastorals	21	5	1	7	—	2	—	—
Hebrews	13	1	2	7	—	—	—	—
Papyrus iii/BC	17	2	14	40	18	56	22	5
Papyrus ii–i/BC	23	11	11	20	5	90	19	3

The enormous number of type 1 stands out at once; it is a Semitic type. Whereas non-Biblical Greek favours types 2b and 3, Biblical Greek follows the Hebrew constructions represented by types 1 and 2a (further figures for the LXX appear in N. Turner, " The Unique Character of Biblical Greek," *Vetus Testamentum* 5 [1955] 208–213, and *Grammar* III 202–205).

Position of the attributive genitive. In Biblical Greek and increasingly in the papyri as time went on (cf. Mayser's figures in *Grammar* III 217), the attributive genitive followed its governing noun without repetition of the article, but Biblical Greek still sometimes retained the method of repeating the article : 1 Cor 1^{18} 2 Cor 4^{11} p^{46} Tit 2^{10}.

Position of heneka (-en). Paul follows the Biblical Greek way of placing it before its noun, in accordance with all LXX books, the very reverse of that of the Ptolemaic papyri and Polybius (*Vetus Testamentum* 210f).

Position of pronouns and particles. Hebrew has no second-position particles, and the tendency of Biblical Greek is either to ignore them or to place them first, as it does with *ara* (Rom 5^{18} 7$^{3.25}$ 1 Cor 15^{18} 2 Cor 5^{15} 7^{12} Gal 2^{21} 5^{11} 2 Thes 2^{15} Eph 2^{19} al. cf. Lk 11^{48}), *menounge* (Rom 9^{20} 10^{18}), which may have passed into the secular Koine by the time of Phrynichus (cf. M. Thrall, *Greek Particles in the New Testament*, Leiden 1962, 36), indefinite *tis* (1 Cor 8^7 Phil 1^{15} 1 Tim 5^{24}) although *tis* often has some stress when it is the first word, immediately following the word to which it belongs in sense. The position of *men* in 1 Cor 2^{15} seemed to scribes unnatural and it was omitted by p^{46} ACD* al. In Tit 1^{15} it comes after an irrelevant word and has been omitted by some, and altered to *gar* by others.

§ 8. Biblical Greek Style

Hebraic parallelism. This, including considerable chiasmus, occurs throughout Paul's style ; it is clearly derived from Hebrew, partly through the LXX, and need not be attributed absolutely to the influence of the Stoic diatribe. Some of the instances of parallelism cited here may well be fragments of early Christian hymns (especially Eph 5^{14}). Sometimes there is rhyme (1 Tim 3^{16}). As the Paulines were written to be read aloud, it is difficult to judge when Paul quotes a hymn and when he freely composes. The same problem arises at Jude ^{24f} and at possible hymns in Revelation (e.g. 5$^{12-14}$). Menander is quoted (1 Cor 15^{33}), and Epimenides of Crete (Tit 1^{12}). The only other example of a Greek metrical pattern seems to be in 1 Cor 10^{12} (an anapaest), but it is probably quite accidental and without significance.

In a world torn by violence, it is little wonder if authors took naturally to an antithetical style and contrasted heaven and earth, light and darkness, life in Christ and death in sin, spirit and flesh, faith and unbelief, love and hate, truth and error, reality and appearance, longing and fulfilment, past and present, present and future. But besides the contrasts which form an *antithetic* parallelism (e.g.

"put to death for our sins : raised for our justification," Rom 4^{25}; cf. also Rom 2^{7f} I Cor 1^{18} 4^{10ff} 2 Cor 6^{4ff} I Tim 3^{16}), there is *synonymous* parallelism (e.g. "when the corruptible shall put on incorruption : when this mortal shall put on immortality " I Cor 15^{54}) : cf. also Rom 9^2 ("sorrow is great ; unceasing is pain " : chiasmus), 11^{33} I Cor 15^{42f} ("sown in corruption : raised in incorruption. Sown in dishonour : raised in glory. Sown in weakness : raised in strength "), 2 Thes 2^8 Col 3^{16} Eph 5^{14}. There is *mixed* parallelism too : 2 Tim 2^{11f} (" if we suffer with him, we shall also reign with him. If we deny him, he will also deny us. If we are unfaithful, faithful he remains "). All these are after the Hebrew pattern.

Chiasmus. Lund maintained that the application of the chiasmic principle solved the problem why in many passages the style seemed to be " verbose and repetitious " ; rather, he thought, it was conformable to certain laws of its own and ought not to be judged by Greek stylistic canons (*Chiasmus in the New Testament* 142). The style was based on the Old Testament and was part of the creative activity of Christianity in the Apostolic Age (p. 144). However, it should be noted that Paul's Bible was usually the LXX, where the chiasmus of the original is often (but not always) ignored. Some examples (e.g. I Cor 4^{10}) are far-fetched, but a Semitic pattern of chiasmus does seem to be established in many instances (*Grammar* III 345ff) : e.g. Rom 1^{22} (ABBA) I Cor 5^{2-6} [AB (ABBA) C (ABBA) B (ABCCBA) A], I Cor 12^{1-31a} [A]^{31b}–13^{13} [B] 14 [A]. On this pattern, cf. J. Collins, " Chiasmus, the ' ABA ' Pattern and the Text of Paul," in *Studia Paulinorum Congressus Internationalis Catholicus*, Rome 1963, vol. II 575–584. Col 3^{3f} (ABCDDCBA), 3^{11} (ABBA) Phm^5 (love for, faith in : : Jesus, the saints), Phil 1^{15f} (ABCCBA) 3^{10f} (ABBA). Dr. Bligh (in *Galatians : A Discussion of St. Paul's Epistle* [Householder Commentaries 1] London 1969) maintains that Galatians is one large chiasmus, centred on a smaller one (4^{1-10}) : A. Prologue, B. Autobiography, C. Justification by faith, D. Scripture argument, E. Central chiasmus, D. Scripture argument, C. Justification by faith, B. Moral section, A. Epilogue. Philippians too is full of chiastic patterns, e.g. 2^{5-11} (ABCBA. ABCDCBA. ABCDDCBA. ABCDCBA). Dr. Bligh observes that Philippians " from beginning to end, is one long chain of chiastic patterns " (cf. his review in *Biblica* 49 [1968] 127–129). Thus Phil 2^{5-11}, for instance, may have an Aramaic original (as Lohmeyer), and the matter is well discussed by R. P. Martin, *Carmen Christi*, Cambridge 1967, 38–41. Although the theory of an Aramaic original is not generally acceptable, Matthew Black holds this section to be " the oldest piece of Aramaic tradition in the New Testament " (*Bulletin of the John Rylands Library*, 45 [1962] 314f), and indeed the verses would link together in a perfect chiasmic chain like this :

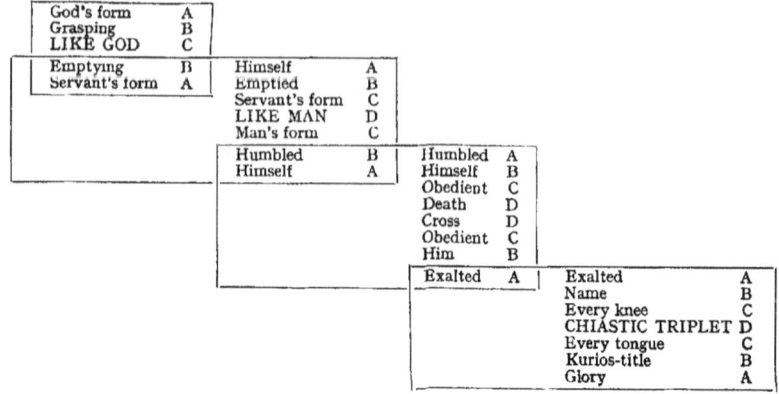

Moreover, Eph 2^{11-22} forms an elaborate triple chiasmus: (1) verses $^{11-13}$ (A. once, B. gentiles, C. flesh, D. uncircumcision, D. circumcision, C. flesh, B. strangers, A. now in Christ). (2) verses $^{13-17}$ (A. far-off: near, B. blood of Christ, C. both one, D. middle-wall, E. hostility, F. his flesh, G. Law, G. commandments, F. new man, E. peace, D. reconcile, C. one body, B. cross, A. far-off: near). (3) verses $^{18-22}$ (A. Spirit, B. Father, C. strangers, D. house of God, E. built, F. foundation, F. corner-stone, E. building, D. holy temple, C. built *together*, B. God, A. Spirit). Professor G. Giavini also sees a chiasm in the passage, but views it rather differently (" La Structure Litteraire d'Eph.II.11-22," *NTS* 16 [1970] 209-211).

It is said that Col 1^{15-20} may be a Christian hymn (E. P. Sanders, " Literary Dependence in Colossians," *JBL* 85 [1966] 36f, and the names cited there: Norden, Käsemann, J. M. Robinson). There is a deliberate allusion to the Day of Atonement, in Jewish fashion, and there is certainly a chiasmic pattern there but it starts at 1^{13}; G. Giavini starts it even earlier at verse ^{12} (" La struttura letteraria dell'inno cristologico di Col. 1," *Revista Biblica* XV [1967] 317-320. Cf. also N. Kehl, *Der Christushymnus im Kolosserbrief: Eine motivgeschichtliche Untersuchung zu Kol. 1, 12-20*, Stuttgarter Biblische Monographien 1, Stuttgart 1967). The chiasmus would run as follows:

We are brought from darkness into the Kingdom (13)	A
Redemption (14)	B
Image of God (15)	C
First-born (15)	D
Creation (16)	E
The heavenly hierarchy (16)	F
ALL IN CHRIST (17)	G
The Church below (18)	F
Beginning (Gen 1^1) (18)	E

First-born (18)	D
God dwelt in him (19)	C
Reconciliation (20)	B
Making peace by the cross (20)	A

Parataxis. If Rom 1–5^{11} be sampled (about 270 lines in Nestle) we find 117 main verbs and 80 subordinate verbs ; the sentences are much longer, and thus more " literary " than anything in Luke-Acts, even the We sections (which have as many as 147 main verbs in the same amount of text). The Pauline proportion is not like that of vernacular Greek, where the unliterary papyri have main and subordinate verbs in about equal proportion. Nevertheless, taking 1 Thes 1–2 Thes 2^{12} instead of Rom 1–5^{11}, there is little difference from the unliterary papyri texts (103 main : 117 subordinate). Earlier Greek, however, has many more subordinate than main verbs.

Genitive absolute. Excluding Ephesians and the Pastorals, Paul has one genitive absolute in 77 verses, the same proportion as the Fourth Gospel and the Epistle of Jeremy, very much less than most NT books, even non-narrative books, and in all but the translated books of the LXX (*Grammatical Insights* 178f). An ungrammatical genitive absolute in 2 Cor 12^{21} is corrected by scribes to the accusative, but not in 2 Cor 4^{18}.

§ 9. THE AMANUENSIS

In assessing the style of Paul, account must be taken of the possible part played by an amanuensis, for secretaries, besides being in general use (of which a great many instances are given by Norden, *Die Antike Kunstprosa*, 954ff), were employed by some NT authors, viz. Tertius in Rom 16^{22}, and Silvanus in 1 Pet 5^{12}. We need not go so far as to suppose that Luke was the amanuensis of the Pastorals. Paul could certainly speak Greek, for never is there mention of an interpreter in Acts, but he often hints that he did not regularly write it (1 Cor 16^{21} Gal 6^{11} Col 4^{18} 2 Thes 3^{17} Phm^{19}). The question is, how much help the secretary might have given to Paul. The secretary may have helped to choose the vocabulary, and would obviously modify the author's style if it were too eccentric. G. J. Bahr goes further : only the mind of Paul, and then only in part, is revealed by the main body of the letter, for the secretary composed it " on the basis of general guide-lines laid down by Paul." So only in the postscript (as Lightfoot had suspected) is either the language or thought exactly Paul's. This is what Bahr calls the " subscription," and he claims that in Romans the subscription begins at chapter 12, in Philippians at 3^{1}, in 1 Corinthians at 16^{15}, in 2 Corinthians at 10^{1}, etc. Although the detail is somewhat hypothetical, the thesis is probably correct in principle (" The Superscriptions in the Pauline Letters," *JBL* 87 [1968] 27-41).

On the other hand, J. N. Sevenster was more complacent. He argued that although some people for one reason or another could not write a letter at a certain moment and so gave instructions to a secretary who composed and wrote the letter, nevertheless there was no indication that this was a general practice (*Do You Know Greek ? How much Greek could the first Jewish Christians have known ?* Leiden 1968, 12). Josephus nevertheless admits to having " assistants," who helped him in Greek (*Contra Apion* I 50), and it seems probable that such men were the semi-professionals, or perhaps an educated friend (not necessarily a tachygrapher), who brushed up the Jewish Greek of Jews and Christians into the slightly atticizing efforts of James and 1 Peter.

Other Literature :

T. Nägeli, *Der Wortschatz des Apostles Paul*, Göttingen 1905.
C. E. Compton, *The Metaphors Used by the Apostle Paul in His Description of the Christian Life* (unpublished dissertation, Southern Baptist Seminary, 1948).
H. H. Rowley, *ET* 61 (1950) 154, review of J. Nélis, *Les Antithèses Littéraires dans les Épîtres de St. Paul.*
A. Roosen, " Le genre littéraire de l'Épître aux Romains," ed. F. L. Cross, etc., *Studia Evangelica* II, Berlin, 1964, 465-471.
J. D. H. Downing, " Possible Baptismal References in Galatians," ibid., 551-556.
R. Jewett, " The Form and Function of Homiletic Benediction," *Anglican Theological Review* 51 (1969) 18-34.
A. M. Harmon, " Aspects of Paul's Use of the Psalms," *Westminster Theological Journal* 32 (1969) 1-23.
A. W. Argyle, " M and the Pauline Epistles," *ET* 81 (1970) 340-342 (vocabulary-links between M and Paul).

CHAPTER SEVEN

THE STYLE OF THE PASTORAL EPISTLES

§ 1. Higher Koine Style

The style of the Pastorals is almost universally recognized to-day as distinct from the other ten Paulines in many important respects. P. N. Harrison, in his notable work, thus summarizes the genuine Pauline style with its irregularities and abruptness : " the tendencies to fly off at a tangent, the sudden turns and swift asides, the parentheses and anacolutha " (*The Problem of the Pastoral Epistles*, Oxford 1921, 41). The style of the Pastorals, on the other hand, is said to be " sober, didactic, static, conscientious, domesticated," lacking Paul's energy and impetus, intellectual power, and logic. Harrison admitted the use of Pauline prepositions but complained of the way they were used, loosely and vaguely. Moreover, he admitted the anacloutha which are characteristic of Paul (e.g. 1 Tim 1^3) as well as the parentheses, excepting some of these on the grounds that they came in genuine Pauline " fragments " (1 Tim 2^7 2 Tim 1^{18} 4^{7,14,16}). Harrison pointed out (42f, 44) that the Pastorals have no trace of the Pauline *oratio variata*, in which pairs of sentences run parallel without grammatical subordination : e.g. 1 Cor 7^{13} *the woman who has an unbelieving husband, and he is pleased to live with her, let her not leave her husband* (characteristic of Paul's Jewish Greek : cf. R. H. Charles's rendering of this phrase back into idiomatic Hebrew in *Studies in the Apocalypse*, Edinburgh 1913, 90 n.1).

The style of the Pastorals is largely exhortatory. The arguments are not sustained as long as they are in Paul, and in place of Paul's reasoned pleas comes assertion. Compared with Paul's, it is rather an ordinary style, lacking his energy and versatility ; it is slow, monotonous and colourless ; it is abstract with fewer concrete images. There are true Pauline echoes and a certain Pauline flavour about the Pastorals, and they have Pauline opening and closing formulae, but these are not enough in the opinion of some " to outweigh the impression made by the style as a whole " (Moffatt, *ILNT*^{3} 407).

However, Pauline parallelism is there, both synonymous and antithetic parallelism within the same verse : *If we suffer with him, we shall also reign with him. If we deny him he will also deny us. If we are faithful, faithful he remains* (2 Tim 2^{11f}. For antithetic parallelism, cf. 1 Tim 3^{16}).

The style of the Pastorals should not be compared with the more excitable and emotional parts of Paul's letters but rather with the parts which are most practical (Rom 10–15, 2 Cor 8–9). As W. Lock pointed out, there we shall find a similar adaptation of OT language and the use of rabbinical material, as well as quotations from Greek writers, a fondness for oxymoron (1 Tim 5⁶ *living she is dead*) and play on words (e.g. 1⁸ *nomos . . . nomimōs . . . anomois*, 1 Tim 1¹¹⁻¹⁶ *episteuthen, piston, apistia, pisteōs, pistos, pisteuein*, 1 Tim 6¹⁷,¹⁸ *plousios, ploutou, plousiōs, ploutein* (*A Critical and Exegetical Commentary on the Pastoral Epistles*, ICC Edinburgh 1924, xxviii).

The vocabulary of the Pastorals contain 901 words (of which 54 are proper names); 306 of them are not found elsewhere in Paul, and 335 are NT hapax which is a very high figure for Pauline letters. Thus, the vocabulary is richer than Paul's, but we are not convinced by the computerized methodology of measuring the average number of letters in a word. Of the NT hapax, most are fairly literary words, nearly all of them however in use before A.D. 50 (cf. F. R. M. Hitchcock, " Tests for the Pastorals," *JTS* 30 [1929] 278). The vocabulary, by and large, is not that of Paul. Indeed, the vocabulary of the Pastorals is nearer to Hellenistic literary writers, such as Epictetus, and especially to the Hellenistic-Jewish wisdom books. The Pastorals use LXX words to a less extent than Paul.

Characteristic words of Paul which never appear in the Past. are *eleutheros* and cognates, *akrobustia, apocalypse, testament, righteousness of God, body of Christ, to abound, to boast.* Moreover, characteristic words of the Past. are not found elsewhere in Paul : cognates of *sōphron-* (self-control), *euseb-* (piety), *semnos* (respectable), *hosios* (holy), *a good conscience, faithful is the saying, good deeds, epiphaneia* (for Paul's *parousia*), *charin echein* (for Paul's *eucharistein*). Often the Past. use a different word for the same Pauline idea : *parathēkē* for *paradosis, hupotupōsis* for *tupos, the now-age* for *this age, despotes* for *kurios.*

In vocabulary, it can be shown that the Pastorals have a family likeness one with another and a distinction from the other ten Paulines. Not everyone has felt happy with Harrison's statistical demonstrations, and some have urged that the difference with the earlier Paulines merely proves that Paul had changed his style somewhat. Perhaps the differences are too serious for that. That the Pastorals differ widely from the other Pauline epistles has been demonstrated by a sophisticated modern technique which tests the relation between vocabulary and length of text, and finally concludes that they cannot be Pauline because " the style is the man " (K. Grayston and G. Herdan, " The Authorship of the Pastorals in the Light of Statistical Linguistics," *NTS* 6 [1959] 1–15.

With regard to the hapax legomena, however, which are held to indicate a second-century date because some of them are not attested before the Apostolic Fathers, Apologists, and secular writers of that date, by the same method it would be legitimate to show that 1 Corinthians belonged also to the second century. As Lock observed, some of the hapax are " semi-quotations from faithful sayings, from liturgical doxologies and hymns, very possibly from existing manuals on the qualifications for various offices " (*op. cit.* xxix).

Turning to smaller, grammatical phrases, Harrison observed the absence of some characteristic features of Paul (38ff).

E.g. the absence of the Pauline *ho men . . . ho de*, of artic. infin. (125 instances in Paul), and of " the series of prepositions in a single sentence with reference to some one subject " : e.g. Rom 1^{17} *from faith to faith*, 11^{36} *from him and through him and unto him.* The nominative for vocative (of Paul) is avoided, and the article with adverbs is avoided.

Certain of Paul's prepositions are absent : *anti* (5 times in Paul), *emprosthen* (7), *sun* (39).

Small particles are rare in the Past., and some that Paul uses freely are entirely absent : *an* (Paul 20, excluding quotations), *ara* (27), *dio* (28), *eite* (38), *epeita* (11), *eti* (15), *mēpōs* (6), *nuni* (18), *hopōs* (6, excluding quotations), *ouketi* (13), *palin* (28).

The table below, showing the comparative frequence of particles (one per number of lines), puts the Past. in perspective with Paul and other NT authors.

	alla	*de*	*gar*	*oun*	*men . . . de*
Matthew	54	3	15	35	100
Mark	30	6	16	16	212
Luke-Acts	65	4	24	40	10
John	15	8	24	7	264
Paul	13	7	9	35	79
Pastorals	15	7	13	61	144
Hebrews	38	8	7	46	39
Jas. 2 Pet. Jude	31	6	13	204	Jude 23
1 Peter	13	7	21	31	43
Johann. Epistles	14	29	41	96	—
Revelation	99	185	72	216	—

In the case of *alla*, the frequence in Paul and Past. is closer than that between Paul's Roman-group (one in 12 lines) and his Captivity-group : Phil. Col. Phm (one in 25). The case with *de* is exactly the same in both (one in seven). There is a difference in the use of *gar*, but again nothing like the difference between the two genuine groups of Paulines, viz. Romans-group (one in seven) and Philippians-group (1 in 22). Admittedly, Paul uses *men . . . de* twice as often as the Past., but it is not used in 1 and 2 Thes, and barely used in Eph. In the case of *oun* also there is a greater use in Paul (mainly in the Rom-group).

The Past. make less use of conjunctions : *hōsper, hōste, ti oun, ouchi, te,* and *plēn* never occur in them (but 14, 39, 14, 17, 23, 5 times respectively in Paul).

In view of these striking differences in vocabulary and style, the question has been raised as to whether they are sufficient to rule out Pauline authorship. In defence of the unity of authorship, two considerations may be urged : 1. After staying at Rome for some time, may not the influence of Latin be seen in the enlarged and somewhat different vocabulary, particularly in the partiality for compound words, and in the smoother syntax, with less room for particles ? Latin may be reflected in the transliteration of *paenula, membrana* (2 Tim), use of *charin echein* (=gratiam habere) ; cf. E. K. Simpson, *The Pastoral Epistles*, London 1954, 20f. But not all the Latin parallels are very convincing. 2. May not Paul have used an amanuensis, e.g. Luke or Tychicus ? This is something for which there is little evidence in either direction, and 2 Tim 4^{11} is not decisive (*only Luke is with me*). However, there are 34 non-Pauline Lukan words in the Pastorals, e.g. *for which cause, the way in which, at a greater measure of, to make alive, to make an appearance, sōphrosunē, philanthrōpia,* and these may be significant. J. N. D. Kelly argues cogently for the amanuensis, urging that in the case of the Pastorals he may have been given a freer hand than he was with the Paulines, due to special circumstances, such as imprisonment which rendered the apostle less able to take any part himself in the writing ; even so, many true Pauline touches are apparent. Differences in style may be accounted for by the fact that it was a different amanuensis from that of the Paulines, no longer Timothy as perhaps in the earlier epistles. " This new secretary may have been a Hellenistic Jewish Christian, a man skilled in rabbinical lore and at the same time a master of the higher koine " (*The Pastoral Epistles*, London 1963, 26f).

§ 2. Relative Freedom from Semitism

The style of the Pastorals is not completely free from Semitisms but, compared with the rest of the NT, that element is fairly slight.

En after *pistis/pisteuein* (Heb. b^e) is shared with Paul (1 Tim 3^{13} 2 Tim 3^{15}). The use of *opisō* is shared with Paul (Phil 3^{13} 1 Tim 5^{15}), and so also is *enōpion* (Rom three times, 1 Cor eleven times, 2 Cor three, Gal once ; 1 Tim six times, 2 Tim twice). The Hebraic use of *mouth* with a preposition : Rom four times, 2 Cor once, Col once, Eph twice, 2 Tim 4^{17}. Adverbial *loipon* (which is in the Rom-group four times, the Phil-group twice, Thes twice, and Eph once) occurs also in 2 Tim 4^8.

The position of *pas* is exactly in accord with the rest of Paul (cf. p. 95) : type 1) is more prevalent than 2a) (the two Semitic positions) and there are only two instances of type 2b) (the position in non-Biblical Greek). The article is repeated with attributive genitive, in Semitic fashion, in Tit 2^{10}, and the indefinite *tis* is the first word in the sentence : 1 Tim 5^{24}. As to vocabulary, we observe the exclusively Jewish word *endunamoun* (Josephus, Paul) at 1 Tim 1^{12} 2 Tim 2^1 4^{17}. However, the Semitic repetition of the preposition with a succession of nouns or pronouns is indulged in much less often by the Past. than by Paul, and shows that the Past. is least Semitic in respect of this feature of style of all NT authors (repetition where there is opportunity to do so, is carried out in 58% of the opportunity in the Rom-group, 37% in Eph, but only 17% in the Past.

Beyer compares the ratio of Greek and Semitic conditional sentences and finds that the Past. have an overwhelming number of Grecisms as compared with Paul (Beyer 232, 295, 298).

We cannot say that the Greek style is the most elegant in the NT, but it is the least Semitic, most secular, and least exciting. It is commonplace.

Other Literature :

F. Torm, " Über die Sprache in den Pastoralbriefen," *ZNW* 18 (1917) 225-243.
F. R. M. Hitchcock, " Latinity in the Pastorals," *ET* 39 (1927) 347-352.
" Tests for the Pastorals," *JTS* 30 (1928) 272-279.
W. Michaelis, " Past. und Wortstatistik," *ZNW* 28 (1929) 69-76.
Die Pastoralbriefe und Gefangenschaftbriefe zur Echtheitsfrage der Pastoralbriefe, Göttingen, 1930.
F. R. M. Hitchcock, " Philo and the Pastorals," *Hermathena* 56 (1940) 113-135.
C. Spicq, *Les Épîtres Pastorales*, Paris 1947.
D. Guthrie, *The Pastoral Epistles*, London 1957.
B. M. Metzger, " A Reconsideration of Certain Arguments against the Pauline Authorship of the Pastoral Epistles," *ET* 70 (1958) 91ff.
C. F. D. Moule, " The Problem of the Pastoral Epistles ; a Reappraisal," *BJRL* 47 (1965).

CHAPTER EIGHT

THE STYLE OF THE EPISTLE TO THE HEBREWS

§ 1. LITERARY FEATURES

Moffatt gave full credit for the author's skilful oratory, sense of rhythm, and avoidance of monotony by the mingling of metres of varying kinds (*A Critical and Exegetical Commentary on the Epistle to the Hebrews*, ICC Edinburgh 1924, lvi–lxiv). Although there is a literary resemblance with the Book of Wisdom without its artificiality and striving for effect, and though the author is well acquainted with the Wisdom literature, yet he avoids the regular metrical verse patterns of Wisdom and maintains the free " prose " nature of his work. There is however a hexameter line 12^{13} if we read *poiēsate*, but *poieite* (breaking the rhythm) is read by p^{46} S* al. Moffat thought that the author was acquainted with the recommendations of Isocrates concerning prose rhythms, but that he adopted them in his own peculiar way, with favourite rhythms of his own, particularly the ∪ ∪ ∪ — with which he opens his book. He likes to begin a new sentence with the very same rhythm which closed the preceding one. He cares less for Aristotle's closing ∪ ∪ ∪ — than his own ∪ ∪ — —, and some others, such as the effective ∪ — ∪ — — — (*Rhet.* iii 8, 1409^9 18). However, all kinds of rhythms are mingled, as they should be in prose, according to Isocrates. It is possible that in some instances consideration of rhythm may affect the correct MS reading, but this author is not enslaved to set rhythms.

He avoids all roughness. Norden contrasted the style with that of Paul in this respect and testified, " wenigstens ich den sog. Hebräerbrief ... von Anfang bis Ende ohne jede Schwerigkeit durchlese " (*Antike Kunstprosa* II 499f). He avoids the hiatus of a word ending in a vowel and he loves parallelism of sound and sense (the *schemata* of Isocrates), though this could be a Jewish feature too. He uses the genitive absolute well, and varies the word-order considerably. He often inserts material between adjective and noun (e.g. 1^4 4^8 $10^{12.27}$), and between article and noun (e.g. 10^{11} 12^3); and his periods are often long and contrived (1^{1-4} $2^{2-4.14.15}$ 3^{12-15} $4^{12.13}$ $5^{1-3.7-10}$ etc), approaching the style of classical Greek, as with Luke-Acts. Indeed, his stylistic relationships are closest with Luke-Acts (as Clement of Alexandria observed), 1 Peter, and the Pastorals, but not perhaps sufficiently so to have significance for authorship. There are reminiscences of Paul, but no more than that. In the opinion of H. Thyen, the style resembles that of Stephen in Acts 7, and the Epistle of Barnabas (*Der Stil der jüdisch-hellenistischen*

Homilie, FRLANT NF 47, Göttingen 1956, 23). As Moffat recalls, this author can use even short sentences effectively (" Where there is remission of these, there is no more offering for sin " 10^{18} *ILNT* lx). The style of the opening four verses is less Pauline and Septuagintal than classical (J. Héring, *The Epistle to the Hebrews*, *ET* London, 1970, 129). Unique in the NT are the classical phrases ἦ μήν 6^{14}, δήπου 2^{16}, πού 2^6 4^4, πρὸς τὸν θεόν 2^{17} (accusative of respect), and the infinitive absolute (7^9), rare in the papyri but frequent in literary work (*Grammar* III 136). The vocabulary and style are " more vigorous than that of any other book of the New Testament " and the style is that of a practised scholar, exact and pregnant in expression (B. F. Westcott, *The Epistle to the Hebrews*, London 1889, xliv, xlvi). He has indeed a wide vocabulary and seems to have been familiar with philosophical Hellenistic writers as well as with the Jewish Wisdom literature : he borrows the following philosophical terms : *moral faculty, Demiurge, moderate one's feelings towards, bring to perfection, nemesis, model* (all from Philo), *will* (Stoics), *the final goal* (Epictetus, Philo). Moffat felt strongly, after a " prolonged study of Philo, that our author had probably read some of his works " (lxi). He is thoroughly literary in his love of the pure nominal phrase and avoidance of the copula, more so than Paul and John and the Pastorals. He has ellipse of the copula nearly twice as often as not (remarkable for Biblical Greek : *Grammar* III 299, 307). Perhaps the worst lapse towards vernacularism is his sharing of the Hellenistic indifference to nice distinctions between perfect and aorist (e.g. 7^6).

The author to the Hebrews has the instincts of an orator in other ways besides the feeling for rhythm. There are oratorical imperatives : *Take heed* 3^{12}, *Consider* 3^1 7^4 (borrowed from the diatribe), *Call to remembrance* 10^{32}. There are rhetorical questions, recalling the diatribe : *How shall we escape* 2^3, *To which of the angels said he*. . . ? 1$^{5.13}$, *Are they not all*. . . ? 1^{14}, *With whom was he grieved ?* . . *Did he not swear ?* 3$^{16-18}$, *How much more*. . . ? 9^{14} 10^{29} (cf. also 7^{11} 11^{32} 12$^{7.9}$). Thyen sees other echoes of the diatribe in the constant repetition of *by faith* in ch. 11 (Thyen 50, 58f). The author affects parentheses : not only short ones (*think you*), but long ones as in 7^{20t} (and cf. 7^{11}). Like an orator, he will repeat a phrase for the benefit of his hearers' attention : *He did not take on the nature of angels, but he did take on the seed of Abraham* 2^{16}. There are rhetorical flourishes : *What more shall I say ? The time will fail me if I tell.* . . ; parallels exist in classical authors and Philo. He has alliterations, a regular device in oratory where it specially concerns the letter p : e.g. 1^1 six times, 11^{28} five, 12^{11} four, 2^2 7^{25} 13^{19} three. It concerns other letters too : k 4^3 three times, p and k 9^{26} twice each. Play on words is often striking : 3^{13} παρακαλεῖτε . . . καλεῖται, 5^8 ἔμαθον . . . ἔπαθον 5^{14} καλοῦ τε καὶ κακοῦ 12^1 περικείμενον ἡμῖν . . . προκείμενον 13^2 ἐπιλανθάνεσθε . . . ἔλαθον. This was a Pauline characteristic. An unusual word-order seems often designed to arouse the readers' attention : *to whom Abraham gave a tithe of the spoils—the patriarch !* 7^4, *Jesus Christ, yesterday, and to-day the same—and for ever* 13^8 (cf. also 2^9 6^{19} 10$^{1.34}$ 12^{11}). A long chain of asyndeta is often effective: *they were stoned, they were sawn asunder, they were tempted, they were slain with the sword, they wandered* ... 11³⁷. Moreover, as Westcott noted (xlviii) the imagery is sometimes beautiful: the Word as a sword, hope as an anchor, the vision of a distant shore, coronation after suffering, healing the lame.

We conclude that, if the author was a Jew (a Hellenistic Jewish Christian, according to Thyen, *Der Stil* 17), he has at least succeeded in eliminating many of the characteristic features of Jewish Greek. We now examine the remaining ones.

§ 2. THE UNDERLYING TRACES OF JEWISH GREEK

Semitic Quality in General. It has been suggested that Hebrews is a Christian midrash formed on Jewish models, based in this case on certain synagogue lections, e.g. Pss 94, 109, 110, Gen 14–15 (Melchizedek), Exod 19 (Sinai), Num 18 (Aaron's rod). One writer ingeniously suggests that these Pentateuchal lections would occur at Pentecost each year in a three-year cycle, and that this has significance for Hebrews as " a piece of Christian didache " (A. Guilding, *The Fourth Gospel and Jewish Worship*, Oxford 1960, 72). All this work is discounted by W. G. Kümmel (*Introduction to the New Testament*, ET London, 1966, 279), who remarks, " The suggestion that this sermon is a homily on a specific passage of Scripture, such as Jer : 31 : 31–34, cannot be proved." Certainly, Hebrews describes itself as " a word of exhortation " 13²², i.e. a homily, a literary genre of which there were many Jewish examples : e.g. Philo's commentary on Genesis, 1 Clement, James, Epistle of Barnabas, *Shepherd* of Hermas, and parts of other books, e.g. the *Didache* and the part of the Zadokite Damascus Rule known as the Exhortation, *c.* 100 B.C. (C. Rabin, *The Zadokite Documents*, Oxford 1954). Like the Epistle of Barnabas, Hebrews is given to allegorizing. Its oratory therefore is probably Hellenistic or Palestinian rabbinical rather than secular Hellenistic, and its nearest parallel may be in Hellenistic synagogue addresses, such as 4 Maccabees. In Jewish Hellenistic homilies in particular, much use was made of the Pentateuch and Psalms, as here (Thyen, *Der Stil* 67). On the other hand, according to some critics, Hebrews may be Palestinian rather than Hellenistic. Cf. the one or two instances of this, listed by J. Swetnam, " On the Literary Genre of the ' Epistle ' to the Hebrews," *Nov.T.* 11 (1969) 261–269, especially 268f.

The Semitic bent of the author's mind is shown in several ways. His opening concept, " at the end of these days," is probably a reference to *this present age (hā'ōlām hazzê)* ; " sachlich ist damit die Zeit des Messia gemeint " (S.-B. III 671). Moreover, the impersonal *he says* 8⁵, *he has said* 4⁴ 13⁵ is " Jewish " phraseology, according to Winer-Moulton (656, 735), and we should note that in 13⁵ the pronoun " he " is added. Alford referred to Delitzsch's note that in post-Biblical Hebrew *hû* (=he) and *'ănî* (=I) are used as the mystical names of God. This impersonal use of " he says " is quite rabbinical and also Pauline (1 Cor 6^{16} 15^{27} 2 Cor 6^2 Gal 3^{16} Eph 4^8) ; numerous examples of rabbinical precedent are quoted by S.-B. III 365f, e.g. *wᵉ'ômēr* (Aboth 6,2.7.9.10.11).

The use of the argument *a minore ad maius*, a rhetorical figure (syncrisis), is held by some authorities to be the Jewish *a fortiori* argument (" light and heavy," as it was called), " so dear to the rabbis " (Héring 13 ; cf. also J. Bonsirven, *Exégèse rabbinque et exégèse paulinienne*, Paris 1939, 83ff). In Hebrews the argument takes the form of, *by so much better . . . as*, or *how much more* 1^4 2^3 3^3 8^6 9^{14} 10^{28-31} 12^4. There are parallels in Philo as well as the rabbis (C. Spicq, *L'Épître aux Hébreux*, I Paris 1952, 53).

Like Paul, this author is inclined to model his sentences on OT poetic sense-parallelism, e.g. *By faith Abraham, when he was tried, offered up Isaac : He that received the promises offered up his only-begotten Son* 11^{17} (cf. also $4^{15.16}$).

The careful straining after vocal impressiveness, by means of unconventional word-order, is not always quite successful and sometimes runs into ambiguity (e.g. 12^{23} where the free rhetorical order makes it impossible to tell whether the author means " God the judge of all," or " the Judge, the God of all "). Even the stilted classical affectation of antiptosis is paraded, reversing the natural (and indeed the LXX) word-order in the phrase *prosthesis artōn* 9^2, creating needless ambiguity again (" shewbread " or " setting forth of the loaves " ?).

Semitisms. Moffatt quoted with evident approval the opinion of Simcox that the whole language of the author is " formed on the LXX, not merely his actual quotations from it " (lxiv). Good use is made of the LXX, especially perhaps the A-text, but not certainly. G. Howard seems to disagree with this widely held opinion, and to think that the Qumran discoveries indicate that the author occasionally used the text of a Hebrew recension more ancient than the Massoretic text (" Hebrews and the Old Testament Quotations," *Nov.T.* 10 [1968] 208-216). It seems more likely that the recensions of the LXX were not standardized by the date of Hebrews. In Hebrews, the OT quotations may even be at second-hand from a liturgical source (S. Kistemaker, *The Psalm Citations in the Epistle to the Hebrews*, Amsterdam 1961, 59). Even so, the language is full of Septuagintisms. One of them is the articular infinitive, with *en tō* 3^{15} and *tou* 5^{12} 11^5. At 2^{15} the articular infinitive with an adjective qualifying is quite classical (cf. 2 Mac 7^9), but these many examples of articular infinitive are probably evidence of the author's desire to make a compromise between Jewish Greek (the language of the early Christians) and an imitation of pagan oratorical style, for this infinitive belongs to the higher Koine as well as to Jewish Greek (*Grammar* III 140 ; cf. p. 117). Other Septuagintisms are 1^1 ἐπ' ἐσχάτου (Gen 49^1 etc.), 3^{12} *heart of unbelief*="unbelieving heart" (Hebrew genitive of quality, cf. 9^5 *cherubim of glory*), 4^{16} *throne of grace* (cp. LXX *throne of glory*, and note Hebrew genitive of quality, and construct state), 5^7 δέησις τε καὶ ἱκετηρίας (Job $40^{22(27)}$ A). There are further Septuagintisms : the omission of the article thrice in 1^3 " is an imitation of the ' construct state ' of Hebrew syntax " (Héring 6), and *the word of power* is probably a Hebraism for *powerful word*. In 1^2 11^3 *aeon* is largely Biblical in its sense of *world* (Wis 13^9 14^6 18^4) ; the plural, corresponding to Hebrew 'ōlāmîm, Aramaic 'āl^emayyâ, may indicate the seven " worlds " in e.g. Enoch and Tob 13^{18}.

The author cannot always maintain his apparent literary style, and even with his deliberately eccentric word-order, he seems to relapse into Jewish Greek over the position of the genitive in relation to its noun, and other items of word-order. Authors like Thucydides, and even Philostratus, place the genitive before its noun at least as often as after it, yet Hebrews has only 16 instances at most of the preceding genitive (6^2 ?.^{5} $9^{8.13.15}$ 10^{36} $11^{1.7.25.36}$ $12^{2.9.17.27}$ 13^{11}), including those enclosed between article and noun, and it has 105 instances of the only possible Semitic order, that of the construct state (cf. Mark 0 : : 50). The position of *pas* has been examined for other NT authors and found to be quite Semitic. With this distinctively Biblical Greek word-order, Hebrews is quite in line (figures on p. 17).

The position of participial and adjectival phrases, qualifying an articular noun, is regularly between article and noun in non-Biblical Greek, unless there is special reason. However, in Jewish Greek the tendency is to place the adjectival phrase after the noun, as in Semitic languages, with the article repeated.

In Hebrews the usage is comparable to Luke's in his We sections.

	Between-position	After-position
Hebrews	$6^{4.7}$ 7^{27} $9^{6.11.12.15}$ 15 10^1 $11^{10.29}$ $12^{1.1.2}$ 13^{12} [15]	2^5 $6^{4.7}$ 8^2 $9^{2.4.8.9}$ 10^{15} 13^{20} [10]
We	Ac 16^{18} 27^{34} $28^{2.16}$ [4]	16^{17} 21^{11} $28^{2.9}$ [4]

Heb may seem to be in advance of other Jewish Greek in this respect (cf. pp. 23ff), but still it is far away from all secular Greek where the proportions are :

Contemporary papyri (selection)	35 : 0
Papyri (Mayser II 2, 54)	140 : 4
Philostratus (selection)	27 : 1
Lucian (selection)	9 : 0

Indeed, Heb and Lk–Ac stand much nearer to Mk's usage than to secular Greek, and Jas is nearer still (7 : 8).

It is true that the author of Hebrews makes wide use of particles : *gar* 91, *oun* 14, *men* 19, *te* 20, *dēpou* 1, *dio* 9, *alla* 16, *toigaroun* 1, *toinun* 1, *ara* 2. At the same time he is drawn by the Semitic tendency to seek only first-place particles or to place the others in first-place, as in Biblical Greek. So *toinun* 13^{13}, *toigaroun* 12^1, and *ara* 4^9 12^8 are placed first. *Toinun*, although occasionally first-place in poor secular Greek, is rarely so in good Greek (cf. Lk 20^{25}). Although his particles still occur in second place more than twice as often as in first place, the situation is not so literary as in some non-Biblical writers (Philostratus has second place *five* times as often), nor does it reach even the standard of II Acts or of Lucian (*three* times as often) but is about the same as in 2 Maccabees and the Testament of Abraham (rec.A), and the Ptolemaic papyri (cf. p. 119). All his particles are in use in the LXX.

In 9^{12} the aorist participle (*having obtained*) is used, although the action is not antecedent, the final salvation being not yet a fact but future (cf. Phil $2^{6\text{ff}}$). This use of aorist participle may be an Aramaism (Héring 77). In 2^{10} the point has some theological importance (*in bringing*, not "*having brought*"). The participle in 13^5 (reading plural, not singular with p^{46}) appears to stand on its own as an imperatival participle. I am not convinced that this indicates that a Hebrew "code" or *Vorlage* lies behind this passage, or behind Rom 12 or 1 Pet 2 ; nevertheless, the participle could well be an echo of Jewish Greek (*Grammatical Insights* 166f).

The Biblical *enōpion* 4^{13} 13^{21} is found occasionally in the Koine but it is more likely to be used here under the influence of *liphnê* (cf. pp. 49, 69, 92, 156). Moreover, to use *pros* with verbs of speaking ($1^{7,8,13}$ 5^5 7^{21} 11^{18}) is a rarity in the Koine and characteristic of Biblical Greek. Use of causal *apo* (= causal *min*) 5^7 is another Hebraism. In 1^1 *en* = *dia*, which is a Semitism often occurring in the LXX and NT, reflecting Hebrew *b^e* and Aramaic *d^e* (Héring 2).

There is a crux, which may be resolved on the ground that it is a Semitism, *kath' hēmeran* 7^{27}, for if this refers to the Day of Atonement, as seems obvious, the action took place *yearly*. The phrase then cannot mean *daily*. The suggestion is that it renders the Hebrew *yôm yôm* (Aramaic *yômā yômā*), understanding the Hebrew *day* in this context to signify "the Day [of Atonement]"; hence, *yôm yôm* would be *every Day of Atonement* and in 7^{27} we would render, "who needeth not on one Day each year, as those priests, to offer any sacrifice" (Héring 63, quoting J. H. R. Biesenthal, *Das Trostschreiben des Apostels Paulus an die Hebräer*, Leipzig 1878).

Finally, there is the question of the Hebrew circumstantial clause introduced by a waw, raised by Dr. Matthew Black at 11^{11} (reading the p^{46} text). The difficulty of exegesis would disappear if we could so take it: "By faith, even although Sarah was barren, [Abraham] received strength for procreation" (Black³ 87-89). I would not claim this particular case as strong evidence that the author of Hebrews wrote in Jewish Greek, but it may be a small pointer towards it. It occurs in Luke thus and provides a further link between the style of Hebrews and of Luke-Acts. Other instances in Hebrews, outside LXX quotations, are 2^{14} 4^{10} 5^2. It is very frequent in Revelation.

The influence of Hebrew over the meaning of words is possible in 12^7 εἰς παιδείαν ὑπομένετε (usually assumed to mean *endure with a view to discipline*), but the verb several times in the LXX translates *qāwāh* which has the meaning of *wait for, look eagerly for, endure*, and in Ps 129 $(130)^5$ and Jer 14^{19} the verb is followed by εἰς (for Heb. *lᵉ*). In the Psalm the meaning is: *my soul waited patiently for thy word*; in Jeremiah it is: *we looked eagerly for peace*. The verb with this particular preposition is thus a Hebraism in Hebrews, and might be correctly rendered: *wait patiently for discipline*, so indicating that the author used Biblical Greek (Helbing 104).

Then again, the phrase in 6^{18} *in which God cannot deceive*, contains a Hebraism (Helbing 106), i.e. *pseudesthai* with *en* of the matter of deception (cf. LXX of Lev 6^2 [5^{21}] when *bᵉ* is used three times of the matter). It is not a secular Greek phrase, as far as I can discover.

§ 3. Significance of Authorship

The question of authorship is relevant inasmuch as the author seems stylistically to have been a Jew or proselyte. Were he Luke, and were Luke a Gentile proselyte, the secularisms in Hebrews may be due, as in the "diary" (the We sections), to its being written in the early days of Luke's Christian life before he had acquired much Jewish Greek. Kümmel is unwarrantably dogmatic. "Hebrews . . . diverges so strikingly from Acts in style . . . that the author of Acts is not to be considered as the author of Hebrews" (*Introduction* 281). But there is no reason why the author should be anyone whose name is familiar, nor even a vague disciple of Stephen (W. Manson), nor even the Alexandrian Jew Apollos (Luther and many moderns). Supposing the author were Apollos, "who can say whether some Semitisms in this work may not be Coptisms?" (Héring 129). I would say that the NT period was too early for Coptisms, and it does not really matter in any case whether we refer to Coptic Greek or Jewish Greek for both probably owe their peculiarities in this respect to the same source. Moreover, Egyptian, the precursor of Coptic, was another Semitic language and had much of its syntax in common with Hebrew and Aramaic. For this point, close study of Egyptian is necessary, as R. McL. Wilson points out ("Coptisms in the Epistle to the Hebrews?" *Nov.T.* 1 [1956] 324).

As to the controversial chapter 13, which is a typical ending for a NT epistle, but a little strangely placed at the close of a work like Hebrews, which lacks a comparable opening, it has a unity of style with the rest of the epistle. The chapter is concerned with ethical and practical exhortation, and the whole book is an exhortation in letter-form, despite the absence of an epistolary opening. Dr. F. F. Bruce rightly censures the attempts of those who in various ingenious ways would detach this chapter (Wrede, Spicq, Badcock, etc.), and "their theories can be given no higher status than that of curiosities of literary criticism" (*Commentary on the Epistle to the Hebrews*, London 1965, 386f).

For all its oratory, Hebrews is no more than an epistle written in the exhortatory style, mingling theology and paraenesis in alternating sections, as distinct from Paul's method of keeping the theology and paraenesis apart. Nevertheless, Hebrews begins as a sermon and ends as an epistle.

Other Literature :

J. Cabantous, *Philon et l'Épître aux Hébreux*, Montauban 1895.
W. Wrede, *Das literarische Rätsel des Hebräerbriefs*, Göttingen 1906.
R. Perdelwitz, "Das literarische Problem des Hebräerbriefs," *ZNW* 11 (1910) 59ff.
J. Dickie, "The Literary Riddle of the Epistle to the Hebrews," *Expositor* VIII (1913) 371ff.
E. K. Simpson, "The Vocabulary of the Epistle to the Hebrews," *Evangelical Quarterly* 18 (1946) 38.
Y. Yadin, "The Dead Sea Scrolls and the Epistle to the Hebrews," *Scripta Hierosolymitana* IV (1958) 36ff.
J. Coppens, *Les Affinités Qumrâniennes de l'Épître aux Hébreux*, Paris-Bruges 1962.
"Les affinités qumrâniennes de l'Épître aux Hébreux," *Nouvelle Revue Théologique* 94 (1962) 128ff, 257ff.
A. Vanhoye, *La Structure Littéraire de l'Épître aux Hébreux*, Paris-Bruges 1963.

CHAPTER NINE

THE STYLE OF THE EPISTLE OF JAMES

§ 1. Authorship

Questions of authorship are relevant since it is widely felt that the style of Greek is too schooled for the Jerusalem James, the brother of Jesus. Many see the author of this brief epistle as a Hellenistic Jew, and one critic at least has urged that his use of *nomos* was not so much in accord with rabbinic Judaism as with wider Hellenistic ideas, arguing that a Greek would throughout his reading of this epistle be capable of understanding the conception apart from any thought of the *Torah* (C. H. Dodd, *The Bible and the Greeks*, London 1935, 39f). Although some will not accept a first-century date, e.g. K. Aland ("Der Herrenbruder Jakobus und Jakobusbrief," *TL* 69 [1944] 97–104), nevertheless others hold to the traditional authorship and to a date prior to the meeting of Paul and James described in Galatians (G. Kittel, "Der Geschichtliche Ort des Jakobusbriefes," *ZNW* 41 [1942] 71–105). Although the author seems well acquainted with the LXX and with Greek ideas and illustrations and Greek modes of preaching (e.g. J. H. Ropes, *A Critical and Exegetical Commentary on the Epistle of James*, ICC Edinburgh 1916, 50), yet the following scrutiny of the style of the epistle permits an early date and apostolic origin.

§ 2. Form-critical Analysis: a Diatribe?

Ropes argued that James has many characteristics of the Stoic-Cynic diatribe (ICC 10–18). The author begins with a paradox, in the diatribe fashion (joy: temptation). There are short questions and answers: *Who is a wise man? Let him show* . . . 3^{13}, *What is your life? It is even a vapour* 4^{14} *Is any man among you afflicted? Let him pray. Is any merry? Let him sing psalms. Is any sick among you? Let him call* . . . 5^{13f}. There are also rhetorical questions, with no answers: *Are you not become evil-thinking judges?* 2^4, *Hath not God chosen the poor* . . . ? 2^5, *What doth it profit* . . . ? 2^{14}, *Doth a fountain gush out sweet and bitter?* 3^{11}, *Can a fig-tree bear olives?* 3^{12}, *Know you not that the friendship of the world is enmity with God?* 4^4, *Do you think the Scripture says in vain* . . . ? 4^5. Other questions are ironical: *a man says he has faith, and yet he dismisses a destitute brother* 2^{14}, *Ye rich men, weep and howl* 5¹. Other shorter formulae are taken verbatim from the Hellenistic diatribe, e.g. *Do not err* 1¹⁶, *Ye know this* ¹⁹, *Wilt thou know?* 2²⁰, *What doth it profit?* 2¹⁴,¹⁶, *Seest thou?* ²² *Ye see then* ²⁴, *Behold!* 3⁴,⁵ 5⁴,⁷,⁹,¹¹, *Wherefore he saith* (before quotes) 4⁶, *Go to now!* 4¹³ 5¹ Some comparisons are shared with the diatribe : *rudder, bridle, forest fire,* and other natural phenomena ; and, in common with the diatribe, James quotes examples from lives of famous men. He quotes some verse : a hexameter line appears at 1¹⁷. Perhaps the most characteristic feature is the dialogue, whereby an imaginary objector (as in Romans) is introduced by the formula, *But someone will say* 2¹⁸, *he says,* etc., as in the Epistle of Barnabas 9 (*But thou shalt say*). Norden specially notices Jas 2¹⁸ (*Antike Kunstprosa* 556f).

On the other hand, Ropes conceded : " Of course, any one of these traits . . . could be paralleled from other types of literature. What is significant and conclusive is the combination in these few pages of James of so many. . . ." (14f). He noted that, by comparison with the diatribe, nothing in James is flippant, nothing bitterly humorous, merely gently ironical.

Most critics have observed the high literary character of this epistle. M. Dibelius noted the pleonasm of rhetorical style in the phrase, *is tamed and hath been tamed* 3⁷, and rhyme at 1⁶,¹⁴ 2¹² 4⁸, and the jingle that was perhaps not the work of our author in 3¹⁷ (*Der Brief des Jakobus*⁷, Göttingen 1921, 36).

According to J. B. Mayor, the author comes nearer to the classical standard than any NT author, except perhaps Hebrews, which has a larger variety of constructions (*The Epistle of James*³, London 1913, ccxliv). But that is an exaggeration. The author was an unimaginative, well-educated man, more devout than the diatribe writers ; alongside the genius of Paul he was " quiet, simple, and somewhat limited " (Ropes 15). Some of the vocabulary, it is true, belongs to the higher reaches of the literary Koine : *give birth to* (Plutarch, Lucian), *entice* (2 Peter, Josephus, Philo), *gloominess* (Plutarch, Philo). But there are limitations. He does not take the same care as Hebrews to avoid hiatus, which is found six times in one verse 1⁴ (Mayor ccvii). We may agree with Mayor that the rhythm is harmonious and sonorous (cclvif), but sometimes as in Hebrews the erratic word-order results in confusion : 3³,¹² 4¹³f. Indeed, we are led to ask whether an author with only moderate pretensions (or none) to classical Greek style may not have received some assistance. Kittel, in the article referred to above, suggested that the brother of Jesus might have had help from a Hellenistic Jewish member of the Jerusalem church, someone in Stephen's circle perhaps (*ZNW* 79f), and Mayor granted that the use of rare compounds is most easily explained by the employment of a " professional interpreter." " He may have availed himself of the assistance of a Hellenist 'brother' in revising his epistle " (cclxv). The help of a secretary need not necessarily be publicly acknowledged in the epistle, but it would need to have been a fairly extensive revision, as the literary features are widespread.

§ 3. Form-critical Analysis: an Epistle?

Form-critics further observe that, rather than a genuine formal epistle (for it has no epistolary ending), the epistle of James is an essay or a tract in the shape of an epistle, addressed to a wider circle of readers than a local community. It is a didactic composition, a collection of short discussions and proverbs and precepts (paraenesis), after the manner of the Wisdom literature, rather loosely connected. There are no clear instances of chiasmus, but there is certainly a "chain" of words proceeding throughout the book; always one word provides the link between two short discussions or sentences. Thus, right from the beginning, the chain is formed by the following links: *temptation, patience, perfection, lacking, asking, wavering* (1^{2-6}), *lust, sin, slowness, wrath, word, hearer, beholding, doer,* (1^{14-25}), and so throughout the book; details are given in Mayor ccl, and Dibelius 92f. These connecting-words seem to be designed for didactic purposes, to render the teaching easy to memorize. As a piece of Christian paraenesis, it belongs to the class of Hebrews, 1 Clement, Barnabas, the *Didache, Shepherd* of Hermas, but it has also strong parallels with 1 Peter (Jas $1^{2f} = 1$ Pet 1^{6f}; Jas $4^{1f} = 1$ Pet 2^{11}) with which it may share dependence on a common paraenesis.

§ 4. Jewish Affinities

However much it may resemble the Hellenistic diatribe in style, it much more resembles the Jewish Wisdom literature in subject-matter, and the Greek is not dissimilar, though James has more prosaic and varied rhythms than the Wisdom verse books. Like Paul and Hebrews, the author of James knows the LXX and quotes from it, and his vocabulary resembles that of other Jewish authors: Philo, 4 Maccabees, Clement of Rome, Hermas (who are Hellenistic), and the Testaments of the Twelve Patriarchs (Palestinian). So Ropes pointed out (20f), but Ropes felt that the language was not so literary as that of Hebrews and Philo; the grammar not so complex, nor his periods so long. Only two sentences are longer than four lines (2^{2-4} 4^{13-15}), whereas Hebrews has one sentence of ten lines, 1 Peter one of 12, Ephesians one of 20 (Mayor cclv). The author of James never strays far from Jewish Greek, for all his apparent education. The epistle is so generally Semitic that some critics have suggested that it is a thoroughly Jewish book, only made Christian by a few additions ($1^{18.21.25}$ 2^7 $5^{8.12}$). To A. Meyer it has appeared like a Hellenistic Jewish allegory, similar to Hebrews, based on Jacob's blessing of his sons (Gen 49) and later christianized (*Das Rätsel des Jakobus Brief*, Giessen 1930).

The epistle is unlikely to have a Semitic *Vorlage* (as some once suggested), for there are too many paronomasiae (1^{1f} $2^{4.20}$ 3^{17} 4^{14}), alliterations (on the sound p : $1^{2.3.11.17.22}$ 3^2, on m : 3^5, on d : $1^{1.6.21}$ 2^{16} 3^8, on d and p : 1^{21}, on l : 1^4 3^4, on k : 1^{26f} 2^3 4^8), and a parechesis (1^{24}). It is doubtful whether a translator would reproduce all these characteristically Greek devices.

§ 5. Aramaisms

Almost the only exclusive Aramaism, in the sense we have been using it in this book, is the use of asyndeton (Mayor ccliv) which is very frequent : $1^{16-18.19-27}$ 2^{13} $3^{8f.15.17}$ 4^{7-10} $5^{1-6.8-10}$. It may be a kind of didactic asyndeton, as in the Sermon on the Mount, the Fourth Gospel and 1 John : this seems to be so in Jas 1^{16-18}, but it is no less Semitic for all that. Or it may be a rhetorical asyndeton, merely the staccato of emphasis : $5^{3.6}$.

Another likely Aramaism is the adverbial *polla* (3^2) which appears in other NT writings (cf. pp. 13, 92). Moreover, some of the instances under Semitisms might in fact be due to Aramaic influence and Aramaic may well have had its formative influence upon the language of James, especially if he were the brother of Jesus. However, this circumstance cannot indicate an Aramaic *Vorlage*, for that is ruled out by the presence of so many exclusive Hebraisms too. Rather, it accords with the phenomenon of a Jewish Greek to which Aramaic and Hebrew have contributed.

§ 6. Hebraisms

The Verb. 1. The articular infinitive is much used : a. *Tou* with infinitive after *proseuchesthai* 5^{17} (*Grammar* III 142ff). In Luke-Acts and James, we must consider *tou* with infinitive as a Hebraism when it occurs after a verb which takes the simple infinitive in secular Greek. b. *Eis to* (LXX=l^e) $1^{18.19}$ 3^3. c. *Dia to* (LXX and papyri) 4^3. d. *Anti tou* 4^{15}. These are Septuagintal idioms.

2. The use of the anarthrous participle (4^{17}) used as a substitute for a nominal subject or object is characteristic of Biblical Greek, following the LXX, and foreign to secular Greek. It appears in the language of Mark, Matthew, Luke and Revelation (Mk 1^3 Mt 2^6 Lk 3^{14} Rev 3^{11f} v. l.).

The Noun. 1. There are indications of the influence of the construct state on the language of James, as often in the LXX, Paul and Hebrews: 1 Cor 1^1 2^{15} 6^9 10^{21} Heb $10^{28.39}$ 12^{22} Jas $1^{18.20}$ 2^{12}.

2. The Hebrew genitive of quality is again in evidence, as it is in Paul (p. 90) and Heb 1^8. Recognition of this fact would illuminate not a few dark places for commentators : the difficult phrase *shadow of turning* thus becomes a *changing* (or moving) *shadow* 1^{17} ; there is then no need for the emendation of Dibelius[7] *ad loc.*, and we need not adopt (with Ropes) the variant of BS*. *The face of his birth = his natural face* 1^{23}, *hearer of forgetfulness = forgetful hearer* 1^{25}, *our Lord Jesus Christ of glory = our glorious Lord Jesus Christ* 2^1, *judges of evil thoughts = evil-thinking judges* 2^4 (Bauer seeks to disperse the Hebraism by citing *thought* as a legal technical term for *decision*, cf. W. Bauer, *Wörterbuch*[4] 1952, col. 337). *World of injustice = unjust world* 3^6 v. l., *cycle of birth = natural cycle* 3^6, *meekness of wisdom = sober meekness* 3^{13}, *prayer of faith = faithful prayer* 5^{15}.

3. In view of this other evidence, we must probably understand *pray with prayer* 5^{17} as a Hebraism under the influence of the infinitive absolute (Mayor ccxlii), although Ropes (ICC 26) thought " probably not." Dibelius too regarded it as doubtful (" umstritten ") since similarly strengthened phrases occur outside Jewish Greek circles, citing Radermacher (Dibelius[7] 237). Cf. pp. 47f, 142f, and *Grammar* III 241f.

Word-order. Like the rest of the NT and LXX, James stands out from non-Biblical Greek in the position of *pas* (*Grammar* III 202–205).

§ 7. Semitisms

Parataxis. *Kai* is very frequent in the linking of sentences ($1^{11.24}$ 4^{7-11} $5^{2-3.4.14-15.17-18}$ etc., about 32 times). James makes small use of subordinating particles, " never doubles the relative, never uses genitive absolute, does not accumulate prepositions, or use the epexegetic infinitive—in a word, never allows his principal sentence to be lost in the rank luxuriance of the subordinate clauses " (Mayor cclvi gives the statistics : 140 sentences without finite subordinate verbs ; 42 sentences with single subordinate clause ; seven sentences only with two subordinate clauses ; three with more than two). It is characteristically Semitic.

Parallelism. Nearly every verse echoes the thought of the previous verse or of the following one.

The Verb. There are periphrastic tenses with the verb *to be* : *is coming down* (for *comes down*) 1^{17} 3^{15}, subjunctive *if he have committed* 5^{15}, where there is no special force ; and a periphrastic future with *mellein*, *intending to be judged* (meaning only *about to be judged*) 2^{12}.

THE STYLE OF THE EPISTLE OF JAMES   119

Noun.   1. As in the LXX, the article is dropped when a noun has the pronominal genitive 1^{26} 5^{20} (also Jude [14]).
  2. The nominative stands in apposition to an accusative (3^8), as often in Biblical Greek (p. 147).

Pronoun. Redundant oblique cases of *autos* occur at the rate of one in $8\frac{1}{2}$ lines of Nestle, about the same as Paul and 1 Peter, in distinct contrast with Mk and Jn, and Rev.

Preposition. The semitic *enōpion* 4^{10} and the instrumental *en* 3^9 both appear (*in* the tongue, must be *with* the tongue : $=b^e$).

Word-order.   1. The genitive tends to follow its noun, as in Biblical Greek, i.e. 50 after : 3 before.
  2. The position of attributive adjectives and participles relative to an articular noun tends in Jas to be nearer to Jewish Greek than even Heb and Lk–Ac (pp. 23f, 110f).

Between article and noun	New articular phrase
Jas $1^{5.14.21}$ $2^{7.15}$ 3^{13} 5^7 [7]	$1^{9.21}$ $2^{3.7}$ $3^{7.9}$ 4^1 5^4 [8]

  3. Particles connecting clauses in second place still tend to be rather more frequent than in first, to a proportion of 57 : 37. Second-place particles, with number of occurrences are : *de* 36, *gar* 51 (a Hebraism for *kî* ?), *oun* 5, *mentoi* 1. First-place : *kai* 32, *dio* 2, *age* 2, *alla* 1. In this respect, James is not so literary as Hebrews, nor does he even come up to the papyri, as the following table will show, giving approximate proportions in the reverse order of Semitic character :

	1st place	:	2nd place
Philostratus	1	:	5
Josephus	1	:	5
Lucian	1	:	3
Acts : We	1	:	3
II Acts	1	:	3
Hebrews	1	:	2 +
Papyri	1	:	2
T Abr : rec. A	1	:	2
2 Maccabees	1	:	2
James	1	:	1,6
I Acts	1	:	1
Markan sections of Lk	1	:	1
L	1	:	0,8
Lk's Q	1	:	0,76
Wisdom	1	:	0,66
Lk 1–2	1	:	0,25
Tobit B	1	:	0,18
Genesis	1	:	0,16
Revelation	1	:	0,05

§ 8. A Christian Biblical Vocabulary

As was the case with Luke-Acts, in James there are traces of the beginnings of a unique Christian style based on the LXX, or at least on the OT, and on Aramaic. It may have been a deliberate affectation, but these two writers in particular are not given to flamboyance of style; they have every appearance of sober and simple writers, educated but with no highly rhetorical pretensions. Since therefore a deliberate cult is out of the question, the following features were all constituents of the Biblical Greek dialect, especially as used by Christians.

$1^{8,11}$ *in (all) his ways,* ^{22} *doers of the Word,* 2^{23} *reckoned for righteousness* (LXX Gen 15^6: "Hebraistic," Mayor ccxlii), 2^9 *work sin,* 2^{13} *make mercy* (cf. Luke), 2^{16} *go in peace,* $2^{1,9}$ *accept the face,* 3^{18} *make peace* (cf. the compound *peacemaker* Mt 5^9, compound verbs Col 1^{20}, based on the Aramaic: Black³ 300), 4^{11} *doers of the Law,* 5^3 *for a witness,* and many other Biblical phrases, including the frequent *Behold!* (Semitic). Perhaps there should be included the pleonastic *man* at $1^{7f,12,19}$ 5^{17}, of which Black³ 106f gives examples from the gospels and Lk–Ac, and claims it as "almost certainly Aramaic." Perhaps also should be included the abrupt style of the imperative, *Submit* . . . *resist* . . . *draw nigh* . . . *cleanse* . . . *purify* . . . *be afflicted, mourn, weep* . . . *humble yourselves* . . . *speak not* . . . (4^{7ff}), as well as the accusations in 5^{5ff} (Dibelius⁷ 35).

Other Literature:

J. Chaine, *L'Épître de St. Jacques*, Paris 1927.
H. Songer, "The Literary Character of the Book of James," *The Review and Expositor* 66 (1969) 379–389.
F. O. Francis, "The Form and Function of the Opening and Closing Paragraphs of James and 1 John," *ZNW* 61 (1970) 110–126.

CHAPTER TEN

THE STYLE OF 1 PETER

§ 1. The Integrity of the Epistle

At first sight, this is the usual Jewish and Christian epistle, opening with address and salutation 1^{1-2} and closing with formal greetings 5^{12-14}. It appears to be an exhortatory letter addressed to several communities, especially resembling, according to C. Spicq, the " Epistle of Barnabas " in the Syriac *Apocalypse of Baruch* (*Les Épîtres de Saint Pierre*, Paris 1966, 13). It may incorporate a " catechesis," but so many NT epistles, as is observed not only by Spicq, but also by J. Coutts (" Ephesians I 3-4 and I Peter I 3-12," *NTS* 3 [1956] 115-127).

On closer study, the situation of the readers appears to change at 4^{11}: before that, these Christians are apparently awaiting persecution (1^6 2^{20} $3^{14,17}$), but in the second part of the epistle they have already tasted it ($4^{12,14,19}$ $5^{6,8}$).

This is argued, among others, by F. W. Beare, *The First Epistle of Peter*², Oxford 1958, 7. But it is questionable grammatically, as far as 4^{12ff} is concerned, for the present participle of *become* is a vivid present with future meaning, as often in the NT. It is, as the Authorized Version has it, *the fiery trial which is to try you*. Moreover, in the first part of the epistle, *present* suffering, not future, seems to be presupposed by the aorist participle in 1^6, and by the wording of 2^{12} 3^{16} 4^4, which implies present accusations.

On account of the sudden change of tone at 4^{11}, it is suggested that the first part of 1 Peter, which is not like an epistle, with its long and balanced sentences, is rather a (baptismal) sermon ending in " succinct general exhortations " and a doxology at 4^{11} (Beare 6). From that point onwards, however, it is said to resemble an epistle, addressed to a particular community in a definite situation, having a direct, simple style, without rhythm and antithesis, " the quick and nervous language of a letter written in haste " (Beare 7. Cf. the whole argument, Beare 6-9, and R. Perdelwitz, *Der Mysterienreligion und das Problem des I Petrusbriefes*, Giessen 1911, 26. But Perdelwitz and Beare, as I understand them, hold to unity of authorship). Thus, perhaps a *Taufrede*, a baptismal sermon because of the baptismal references in $1^{3,23}$ 2^2 3^{21}, and a *Mahnschrift*, an exhortatory epistle, have been combined : these form respectively 1^3–4^{11} and 4^{12}–5^{14}. The " epistle " is evidently designed to give rules of conduct to a church undergoing persecution. The " sermon " is not altogether about baptism, and it is suggested that pieces of paraenetic material have been inserted at 2^{18}–3^7 4^{7-11}.

Other critics suppose two sermons to have been combined in 1 Peter, one before the baptismal service perhaps, and one after (R. P. Martin, " The Composition of 1 Peter in Recent Study," *Vox Evangelica*, London 1962, 29ff). Others suppose that two epistles have been combined, one to those about to be, the other to those being, persecuted (C. F. D. Moule, " The Nature and Purpose of 1 Peter," *NTS* 3 [1956], 1ff). There is no lack of speculation. Thus, another guess is that a number of hymns, borrowed more or less literally, have been inserted (for some reason) into the epistle, for 1^{3-12} has a flowing rhythmical arrangement, and so perhaps to a lesser degree $2^{6-8.21-25}$ 3^{18-22} (M.-E. Boismard, *Quatre Hymnes baptismales dans la première Épître de Pierre*, Paris 1961).

H. Preisker held that the whole of 1 Peter was a liturgical composition forming a report of an assembly of the Roman church (*c*. A.D. 80), consisting of the various parts of a baptism service 1^3–4^{11}, the actual baptism not being mentioned because the rites were secret, taking place at 1^{21} ; the baptism service was followed by a service for the whole church 4^{12}–5^{11}, and the different occasion thus explains the different circumstances of the hearers (some about to face persecution, and the others having suffered). Preisker concludes this speculative analysis by suggesting that it was Silvanus, a Christian of the second or third generation, who drew up this liturgical report, made it into an epistle, and sent it to churches in Asia which Peter had once visited. Cf. the appendix in H. Windisch, *Die katholischen Briefe*[3], Tübingen 1951, 156ff., criticized by Beare 197-199.

W. Bornemann held that 1^3–5^{11} was a baptismal sermon by Silvanus, delivered in a city of Asia *c*. A.D. 90, based on Psalm 34, which was then given an epistolary framework. He held that the stylistic differences on each side of 4^{11} were not significant (" Der erste Petrusbriefe— eine Taufrede des Silvanus ? " *ZNW* 19 [1919] 143-165).

Also impressed by the baptism-motif were Cross and Strobel. Cross thought that 1 Peter was a liturgy (" the Celebrant's part for the Paschal Vigil ") based on instructions for the bishop's baptism during Passovertide, because of the repeated emphasis on *pasch*- (suffering), suggesting *Paschal*, and because of parallels with baptism, confirmation, and eucharistic rites in the *Apostolic Traditions* of Hippolytus (F. L. Cross, *I Peter. A Paschal Liturgy*, London 1954). Cross was answered by T. C. G. Thornton, " I Peter, a Paschal Liturgy ? " *JTS* NS 12 [1961] 14-26)' Strobel too was impressed by the connections with baptism and passover in 1 Peter, which was " Passafest-Rundbrief " (F. A. Strobel, " Zum Verständnis von Mat.XXV 1–13," *Nov.T.* 2 [1958] 210 n.1). M.-E. Boismard held that 1 Peter, Colossians, Titus, James and 1 John are all based on a baptismal liturgy. 1 Peter has the theme of " exile," made by a " redactor " to embrace all the various liturgical fragments (hymns and pieces of homilies) ; cf. " Une liturgie baptismale dans la Prima Petri," *Revue Biblique* 63 (1956) 182–208 ; 64 (1957) 161ff. So little of the epistle is concerned exclusively with baptism, for it just as much concerns suffering (in both parts) or general paraenesis. Lohse denied that it was a baptismal sermon, but saw the stylistic differences in many parts of the epistle as due to the employment of different sources (E. Lohse, " Paränese und Kerygma im 1 Petr.," *ZNW* 45 [1954] 68–69). Thus, it is a very widely-held opinion that the epistle is a composite work based on exhortatory and liturgical scraps. Beare, however, in his second edition, speaks not of direct use of liturgical fragments but of the free composition of a sermon with the liturgy in mind, with perhaps sometimes a quotation from a credal formula, and with the letters of Paul in the background of his memory (Beare 202). But we presume, from pp. 6f, that Beare is still referring only to part of the epistle, viz. 1^3–4^{11}.

§ 2. THE PART OF AN AMANUENSIS

So unsuitable is the type of Greek felt to be for the fisherman apostle, that the part of Silvanus in writing the epistle, or in revising it, with Peter perhaps concluding it himself (cf. $5^{12\text{ff}}$), has been seriously considered. How far did Silvanus, *through* whom the epistle purports to be written, have freedom to mould the apostle's thought, or was he merely represented as bearer of the letter to its destination ? The word *through* can designate the actual writer, as when 1 Clement is referred to as *written through Clement* (cited by C. Bigg, *A Critical and Exegetical Commentary on the Epistles of St. Peter and St. Jude*[2], ICC Edinburgh 1902, 5), and Selwyn supported this thesis by arguing that Silas, Paul's fellow-worker of Ac $15^{22,32}$, the Christian prophet, had the same role in writing to the Thessalonians, and that 1 Peter has links with those epistles. That would account for certain Pauline features in the doctrine of 1 Peter but there is not sufficient resemblance in style between it and Thessalonians. Beare (189) justifiably stigmatized Selwyn's views as " romantic " and found no grounds for supposing that this Silas was cultured enough to write 1 Peter. There was no indication that he was a Hellenist of the group of Stephen and Philip. Indeed, if Silas could have written 1 Peter, why not Peter himself ? In his commentary (*The First Epistle of St. Peter*[2], London 1947, 26f),

E. G. Selwyn had admitted that a classical Greek lexicon was more helpful than a Koine lexicon, and while there is no trace of "Atticistic affectation" the style is that of "a well-read Jew of good social standing" (Bigg 2f). The epistle, urged Beare (189), is far too literary to be written before the second or third Christian generation. But there seems to be no reason why an amanuensis *had* to belong to that particular generation, and he need not have been Silas. Beare was reasoning on the basis of his own assumptions about a post-Petrine date. However, if we must resort to the hypothesis of an amanuensis, his help might have been given at any time, and the following examination of the language makes it tenable that a Semitic style of Greek has been incompletely revised.

§ 3. Alleged Literary Style

The style of this epistle is generally felt to be less Semitic in colouring than Paul's, while it is less elegant than that of Hebrews or James. However, there are some strong Semitic features, and it will be observed that the style is too uniform throughout the epistle to support the view that 1 Peter has been compiled from two sermons or epistles by different authors or from various liturgical material, or that epistolary additions have been inserted at the beginning and end in a different hand. The kaleidoscope of subject-matter does not affect the style appreciably. Beare observes the attractive rhythm of the prose, and the "quiet warmth of feeling" which are not really consistent with the "patchwork" into which some critics (e.g. Preisker, Lohse) would slice the epistle (200).

Rhythm. 1 Peter shares with Hebrews and James a tendency to use rhythm and similar rhetorical devices. The relative clause prolonging the sentence is a conspicuous item of the rhythmic style. These extensions occur at $1^{6.8bis.10.12}$ter $2^{4.8bis.10.22.23.24}$ $3^{3.6.19.20.21.22}$ $4^{4.5.11}$ $5^{9.12}$. Sentences are correspondingly drawn out by means of the linking participle: $1^{3.5.9.11.18}$ $2^{12.16}$ 3^2 $5^{7.9}$. Such rhythmic devices are found on both sides of 4^{11}. The rhythm of the Psalms is present in 2^3:

> Who being reviled : reviled not again.
> Suffering : he threatened not.

4^{11} : If anyone speaks : as the oracles of God.
  If anyone ministers : as of the strength which God supplies.

The words *unto you* in 1^{10} are balanced by *unto Christ* in 1^{11}. There is chiasmus, too, reminiscent of the Psalms : 2^{21} *Christ died for you : to you he has left an example* . . . (ABBA). Bigg (4) noted the agreeable refinement at 1^{19}, citing Philo and Josephus as models, viz. the phrase with ὡς having the proper name at the close ; he found it elsewhere in

THE STYLE OF I PETER 125

the NT only at Heb 12^7, and he conceded that even the author of
I Peter failed to follow it up when there was another opportunity to
do so (cf. 2^{12}).

There is an oratorical jolt in the word-order of 1^{23}, reminiscent of
Hebrews : *through the Word of the living God—and the abiding*. In
3^{16} is a sensitive word-order in which the verbs *speak evil of you* and
may be put to shame are brought effectively together and in which
behaviour in Christ is emphatically placed at the end of the clause.
An orator appears to be speaking at 1^4 ἀμίαντον καὶ ἀμάραντον, 1^{19}
ὡς ἀμνοῦ ἀμώμου καὶ ἀσπίλου χριστοῦ. The epistle reads very well in
public, and the English Authorized Version has happily captured
many of its ringing cadences : 1^8 *whom having not seen, ye love*, 1^{11}
the sufferings of Christ and the glory that should follow, 1^{15} *so be ye holy
in all manner of conversation*. The antitheses are those of Hebrew
poetry, especially the Psalms, as well as of Greek rhetoric : 1^{18f} *ye were
NOT redeemed with corruptible things . . . but with the precious blood of
Christ*, 2^{16} *as free, and NOT using your liberty as a cloke of maliciousness*.
Such antitheses transcend the division of the epistle at 4^{11}, for they
appear again at 5^2 *taking the oversight, NOT as by constraint*, ^{3} *NOT
being lords, but being examples*. The rhythm of the opening ten verses
so much recalls Hebrew poetry (1^{3-12}) that the passage may be a
Christian hymn ; and yet the whole epistle is nearly at the same level :
1^3 *Blessed . . . abundant mercy*, ^{4} *inheritance . . . kept for you*, ^{6} *rejoice . . .
heaviness*, ^{8} *not seeing . . . believing*, etc. The author may have quoted
hymns and the LXX, and known Paul and James, but he blends
together beautifully all that he uses.

Phraseology. One reason for the attractive solemnity of style is, I
believe, that the author has studied the language of the Greek OT and
reproduced it to perfection, blending such LXX phrases as *Blessed be
God* (Ps 66^{20} 2 Mac 15^{34}), *taste that the Lord is gracious* (Ps 33 [34]^9),
elect and precious (Isa 28^{16}), *stone of stumbling and rock of offence*
(Isa 8^{14}), *a race elect, a royal priesthood, a holy nation, a people for his
possession* (Exod 19^6). Once he harnesses the phrase *gird up the loins*
(LXX Pr 31^{17}) with the new mental image : *gird up the loins of your
mind* 1^{13}. But this splendid use of the LXX is found not only in the
first part of the book (cf. especially 2^{1-10}), but all the way through :
e.g. 4^{17} *judgment shall begin from (apo) the house of God* (Ezek 9^6), 4^{18}
*if the righteous scarcely be saved, where shall the ungodly and the sinner
appear* ^{9} (Pr 11^{31}), 5^5 *God resists the proud and gives grace to the humble*
(Pr 3^{34}), 5^7 *casting all your care* (Ps 54 [55]^{23}), 5^8 *as a roaring lion*
(Ps 21 [22]^{14}). If these phrases were all inserted by a final redactor,
on varying material, then he was a very able craftsman.

Vocabulary : LXX influence. The vocabulary, as well as the phraseology, is based largely on the Greek OT, especially the Maccabees

books. Here are found 62 NT hapax, of which 33 are found in the LXX and five others in the other versions of the Greek OT.

Some are found fairly widely through the LXX :—*unrighteously* 2^{19} (in the Pss and Wis literature 20 times), *pass one's life* 4^2 (Wis literature and 4 Mac), *feminine* 3^7 (Pent, Tob, Jdt, Est), *enquire carefully* 1^{10} (Pent, Jg, 1 Kms, 1 Chr, Jdt, Est, Pss, Wis literature, Minor Prophets, 1 Mac), *remaining* 4^2 (Pent, Jg, 2 Kms, 1 Esd, Min Proph, Isa, Jer, Dan Th, 1, 3 Mac), *carousal* 4^3 (Pent, Jg, 1, 2, 3 Kms, Jdt, Est, Wis literature, Jer, Dan Th, 1, 3 Mac), *live with* 3^7 (Pent, Jdt A 1 Esd, Wis literature, Isa, 2 Mac). Some are LXX words, but much less extensive :—*an appeal* 3^{21} (Sir, Dan Th), *veil* 2^{16} (Pent, 2 Kms, Job), *well-doer* 2^{14} (Sir), *beget again* $1^{3.23}$ (Sir), *gird up* 1^{13} (Jdt B, Pr), *show honour to* 3^7 (Dt, 3 Mac), *a putting on* 3^3 (Est, Job), *proclaim* 2^9 (Pss, Wis literature), *priesthood* $2^{5.9}$ (Pent, 2 Mac), *credit* 2^{20} (Job), *wound* 2^{24} (Pent, Jdt, Pss, Sir, Isa), *terror* 3^6 (Wis literature, 1 Mac), *dirt* 3^{21} (Job, Isa), *sowing* 1^{23} (4 Kms, 1 Mac), *sympathetic* 3^8 (Job, 4 Mac), *perfectly* 1^{13} (Jdt, 2, 3 Mac), *pattern* 2^{21} (2 Mac), *loving the brethren* 3^8 (2, 4 Mac). The above are found only in the first part of the epistle ; the following only in the second part :—*unfading* 5^4 (Wis), *bear witness* 5^{12} (3 Kms, Neh, Sir, Min Proph, Jer, 1 Mac), *powerful* 5^6 (Pent, Josh, Jg, 1, 2, 3 Kms, 2 Chr, 2 Esd, Neh, Pss, Wis literature, Min Proph, Jer, Ezek, Dan Th), *Creator* 4^{19} (2 Kms, Jdt, Sir, 2, 4 Mac), *eagerly* 5^2 (2 Chr, Tob, 2, 4 Mac), *to roar* 5^8 (Jdt, Pss, Wis, Min Proph, Jer, Ezek). In both parts :—*brotherhood* 2^{17} 5^9 (1, 4 Mac). Then there are the two LXX words, NT hapax, which have a meaning unique to Biblical Greek :—*virtues* (plural) with the meaning of *praise* 2^9 (because it renders *hôdh* and *t^ehillâ* in Min Proph, Isa), and *humble* 3^8 (=*fainthearted* in non-Biblical literature) : Pr and early Christian literature. NT hapax which are found in Symmachus are :—*chief shepherd* 5^4, *observe* 2^{12} 3^2, *arm oneself* 4^1, *putting on* (περίθεσις) 3^3. In Theodotion :—*be dead* 2^{24} (ἀπογίνεσθαι).

It will be observed that the chief number of these NT hapax, which are drawn from the Greek OT, occur in 3^{6-8}, which I suppose to be a paraenetic section. But otherwise they occur consistently throughout the epistle and on both sides of 4^{11}.

In addition to the NT hapax there are other words, found elsewhere in the NT, which may be claimed as belonging exclusively to Biblical Greek : *spiritual inheritance* (LXX for *nah^alâ*), *to walk* in the sense of *behave* 4^3 gains its new meaning through the influence of the Hebrew *hālak* (which has both senses) ; *vessel* in the peculiar sense of rabbinical Hebrew (S.-B. III 632f) : *wife* 3^7. *Agitator* 4^{15} occurs nowhere else in literature, but it is derived from common enough words, meaning *an overseer of other people's affairs*, and it may be this author's own coinage ; *rejoice* religiously (*agallian*) is a Biblical Greek word, confined to the LXX, the Testaments of the Twelve Patriarchs, the Gospels, Acts and Church writers, but found in both parts of 1 Peter ($1^{6.8}$ 4^{13}). On this word, cf. R. Bultmann in *TWNT* I 18-20.

Vocabulary : Christian influence. In another way the vocabulary is typical of Biblical Greek ; not only is it strongly coloured by the

LXX but it embraces many words with a peculiarly Christian meaning, some of them entirely new words: *baptism, Christian, Devil, elect, faith, humble (tapeinos), love, preach the Gospel, predict* (1^{11}, a hapax, at least before the eighth century A.D., and probably Christian coinage), *presbyter, prognosis* (predestination), *sanctification, sharers of an inheritance, spirit, temptation, truth, wood* (= cross), *without respect of persons*, based on a Hebrew phrase *nāsâ pānîm*), an exclusively Christian word, " an instance of the creation of religious and moral vocabulary through the medium of the Septuagint " (Beare 75). Paul has a similar Christian vocabulary, not always coinciding with this, but at least he shares the phrase, *believe in (eis)* 1^8 (a Hebraism).

Choice of words. One of the stylistic weaknesses of this author is that he cannot always be said to be following any clear standard in his choice of words. He has within one verse two verbs for *seeing* 1^8, the one moreover negatived with *mē*, and the other with *ou*, pointlessly it would seem. Hort's plea that the change " is not capricious," I find unconvincing and almost meaningless (F. J. A. Hort, *The First Epistle of St. Peter, I–II 17*, London 1898, 45). Is the first negatived participle *although* and the second *because?* (Bigg 105). Neither Selwyn nor Beare are helpful. Indeed, I suspect that there is no rational answer.

NT writers almost universally favour *mē* with ptc. 1 Pet, Heb, Paul and Lk, Mt and Jn (once), are the only exceptions, and even there it is rare. The NT has gone much further than the Koine in the elimination of *ou* with ptc. (*Grammar* III 284f).

Further, the author of 1 Peter seems not to use *dokimion* in the normal literary sense of *testing* but in the sense of the vulgar Fayum papyri: *something tested (Grammatical Insights* 168f). Bigg had already suspected that the word was " incorrectly used " (3). The choice of the form *hupolimpanein* betrays eccentric and not very acceptable speech.

Lack of Synonyms. Alongside the use of a synonym pointlessly in 1^8 there must be set this author's monotonous habit of often failing to find any synonym at all. Certain key-words are repeated all through the epistle with careless iteration. Bigg found in this phenomenon some significance, for the same is true of 2 Peter, but I do not see his point about such a feature escaping the revision of an amanuensis, for an amanuensis could easily enough supply synonyms (Bigg 225–227).

The re-iterated words are: *faith* $1^{5.7.9.21}$ 5^9, *apocalypse* (and verb) $1^{5.7.12.13}$ 4^{13} 5^1, *rejoice* $1^{6.8}$ 4^{13}, *salvation* $1^{5.9.10}$ 2^2, *glory-glorify* $1^{7.8.11.21.24}$ 2^{12} $4^{11bis.13.14.16}$ $5^{1.4.10}$, *conduct* (and verb) $1^{15.17.18}$ 2^{12} $3^{1.2.16}$, *do(ing) good* $2^{14.15.20}$ $3^{6.17}$ 4^{19}, κόσμος 1^{30} 3^3 5^9 and five times in 2 Pet, *pasch-* (suffer) $2^{19.20.21.23}$ $3^{14.17.18}$ $4^{1bis.15.19}$ 5^{10}, *humble-humility* 3^8 $5^{5bis.6}$, *holy* $1^{12.15.16}$ $2^{5.9}$ 3^5 and five times in 2 Pet, *obedience* $1^{2.14.22}$, *evil-doer* $2^{12.14}$ 3^{17} 4^{15}, *be* subject $2^{13.18}$ $3^{1.5.22}$ 5^5, by the resurrection of Jesus Christ 1^3 3^{21}. Many of these instances cut across the epistle's dividing-line at 4^{11}, far too often for the theory of diverse authorship to be feasible.

Moods of the Verb. 1. The optative mood survives comparatively often in 1 Peter, perhaps as a literary feature.

In main clauses it occurs twice as a wish : 1^2 *may grace and peace be multiplied* (the phrase, " grace and peace," is Pauline, but the addition of the words, " be multiplied," is more characteristic of Jewish letters : Dan LXX 3^{98} 4^{34} ; cf. Beare 48). 5^{10}v.l. *may he renew, stablish, strengthen you.* This optative is used once in Heb and 2 Pet, twice in Jude, often in Paul, four times in Lk–Ac, and as a v.l. in Mk. This optative is characteristic of " the pompous and stereotyped jargon of devotion " in Biblical Greek (LXX references in *Grammar* III 120ff).

The other kind of optative is more literary : 3^{14} *even if you were to suffer,* ^{17} *should the will of God require it* (the fact that there are variant readings here and at 5^{10} may be due to scribal confusion of like-sounding word-endings). This kind of optative is not so frequent in the NT, being found in Ac and Paul only. Here it may be due to the writer's gentle tactfulness : persecution is present, but the writer says only, " if you *were to* suffer " (M. Zerwick, *Graecitas Biblica* § 228d). On the other hand, it may be due to the fact that this part of the epistle was indeed a solemn exhortation in rather archaic language. Before we ascribe the optatives to literary prowess we should heed Bigg's warning that the absence of *an* is enough to " show that the writer was not a Greek " (5). Rather, that he was not a Gentile Greek. " In neither LXX nor NT is there an instance of εἰ c. opt in the protasis and opt. c. ἄν in the apodosis " (*Grammar* III 127).

2. Good Greek would surely have avoided *ei* with present or future indicative on the first occasion in 2^{20}, for the Christians were *not* suffering through wrong-doing ; rather, the optative of the hypothetical condition is required. In 3^1, *ei* with indicative is not the classical construction.

3. 1 Peter prefers the aorist imperative to the present ; the aorist reflects conduct in specific instances, usually a command to begin some action or a prohibition against beginning it. However, in 2^{17} there is a puzzling change of tense : *start to honour all men* (aorist), *start to love the brotherhood* (aorist), *continue to fear God* (present), *continue to honour the King* (present). One cannot pretend to see any principle behind the choice of tenses, and the lack of it militates against the author's supposed literacy.

4. Another noteworthy feature concerning moods in 1 Peter is the use of a participle as an apparent substitute for imperative in $1^{14.22}$ 2^{18} $3^{1.7.8}$ 4^8. It is conceded that these examples occur in the first part, the part often alleged to be a " sermon ", although *knowing* 5^9 may be a further instance of participial imperative. The participle may, however, be part of a periphrastic construction, with *be* (imperative) in ellipse, or it may be a Hebraism in the author's Greek. That such a

feature reveals a Hebrew code of morals as a *Vorlage* of 1 Peter is most unlikely (discussion in *Grammatical Insights* 165-168).

The Impersonal verb. 1. A scribe has corrected the less acceptable Hellenistic impersonal construction in 2^6 (*it is written in Scripture*) to the better personal form (*scripture writes*), but the whole quotation may be understood as subject (*Grammar* III 52, 292). 2. The impersonal *it is preached to the dead* 4^6 is a Latinism rather than good Greek.

Ellipse of the Verb. The author is literary in that he tends towards the ellipse of the verb *to be*. Besides the imperatival ellipses just noted, there are many others. But the ellipse fails to be observed on several occasions, and these too are all in the first part: 1^{25} $2^{15.25}$ $3^{3.4.20.22}$.

Noun. 1. The Hebrew genitive of quality shows its influence several times: 1^{14} *children of obedience* = *obedient ones* is objective genitive, according to Beare, 71; but it is still a Hebraism ("children of"). 2^{12} *day of visitation* = *judgment day* (LXX), 4^{11}, 5^{11} *the ages of the ages* = *eternal ages* (the phrase occurs in both parts of the epistle); this plural (*ages*) is Semitic, cf. *Grammar* III 25. So also is the plural of *heaven* in 1^4, corrected by S to secular usage. 5^4 *crown of glory* = *glorious crown*.

2. The Hebrew infinitive absolute seems to appear in 1 Peter as in a great many NT authors: 3^6 *afraid ... with terror*, 3^{14} LXX 4^{13} *be glad with exceeding joy*.

Definite Article. 1. The usage on the whole is in accordance with good Greek, reminiscent in 3^8 of Thucydides, according to Bigg (4), separated often very far from its noun, with a genitive phrase in between: 1^{17} $3^{1.3.20}$ 4^{14} $5^{1bis.4}$. Thus the use of the article in this way does not differ on either side of 4^{11}.

2. However, there are occasions when a possible reviser (the amanuensis?) nodded and allowed what seems to be the original Jewish Greek to appear: especially in the omission of the article by influence of the Hebrew construct state $1^{2.3.7.9.25}$ 2^{12} (but a borrowed LXX phrase) ^{14} $3^{7.20.21}$ 4^{14ter} 5^{12}.

3. The omission of the article is not good Greek at $3^{19.20}$ when the participle follows a definite antecedent. There are times when no good reason is evident for the omission (Bigg 4).

Pronoun. 1. The relative *what kind of* has in the Koine come to mean no more than *what*, so that our author can for the sake of emphasis indulge in meaningless tautology: 1^{11} *enquiring at what or what kind of time*. 2. The redundant pronoun after a relative is a sure Semitism: *of whom by his stripes* 2^{24}S*LP.

Preposition. The pregnant construction 3^{20} is quite classical: *into which a few were saved* (i.e. *in which*, after entering *into*). But *into* is incorrect in 5^{12} *into which you stand*; it is part of the Hellenistic degeneration of prepositional usage. In 1^{25}, taken literally, the gospel is preached *into* you, a Semitic (perhaps Aramaic) construction. The dative is on its way out, and in later Greek as well as 1 Peter 1⁴ *eis* is an instance of non-classical usage (*for you*). The prepositions used with two verbs call for notice : (1) *elpizein* with *epi* (acc.) 1¹³ occurs frequently in LXX Psalms and early Christian writers ; it is an exclusive feature of Jewish and Christian Greek (including Philo). (2) Another Hebraism is *oneidizein en* 4¹⁴ which is due to the influence of *bᵉ*, e.g. 2 Kms 23⁹ (Helbing 22).

Conjunction and Particle. 1. The *hina* of 4⁶ seems only to be understood causally, as in later (2nd c. A.D.) Greek (*Grammar* III 102). In other places the use of *hina* is no more satisfactory : it is followed in 3¹ by the future indicative, and in other places by the subjunctive, whatever the sequence, not at all in keeping with good Greek (Bigg 4). 2. There is a paucity of connecting particles and too many asyndeta (on both sides of 4¹¹) for good Greek.

There are but ten connecting particles. A few occur in the first part (1³–4¹¹) alone : *alla* 1¹⁵ 2²⁰ 3¹⁴, *dio* 1¹³, *dioti* 1¹⁶.²⁴ 2⁶, *men* . . . *de* 1²⁰ 2⁴,⁽¹⁴⁾ 3¹⁸ 4⁶,⁽¹⁴⁾, and *hōste* in the second part alone (4¹⁹). The rest occur in both parts : *gar* 2¹⁹.²⁰.²¹.²⁵ 3⁵.¹⁰.¹⁷ 4³.⁶.¹⁵, *de* 1²⁵ 2⁷⁻⁹.¹⁰ᵇⁱˢ 3⁸.¹¹.¹⁴ᵇⁱˢ 4⁷.¹⁶.¹⁷⁽¹⁸⁾ 5⁵ᵇⁱˢ.¹⁰, *kai* 1¹⁷ 2⁵ 4¹⁸ 5⁴, *hoti* 2¹⁵ 3¹².¹⁸ 4¹⁷, *oun* 2¹.⁷ 4¹.⁷ 5⁽¹⁾.⁶.

3. *Kathōs* is an unfortunate choice for any author attempting good Greek, strongly disapproved as it is by Phrynichus and very largely confined to Jewish Greek.

Word-order (cf. p. 129). 1. In the secular Greek order, the adjectival or participial qualifying phrase, usually comes between the article and noun. In 1 Peter this happens at 1⁸.¹³ 2².⁹.¹¹.¹² 3¹.⁴.⁵ᵇⁱˢ,¹⁶ 4³ 5¹.⁴.⁶.¹⁰ (i.e. both sides of 4¹¹). The prepositional phrase in this position also occurs : 1¹⁰.¹¹ᵗᵉʳ.¹⁴.²¹ 3².¹⁵.¹⁹ 4⁸.¹² 5².¹³. The Semitic position (the article close to the noun) occurs at 1²⁵ (τὸ ῥῆμα τὸ εὐαγγελισθέν). 2. 1 Peter is in line with Biblical rather than secular Greek in the word-order with *pas*, i.e. a relatively large proportion (17%) of the type 2 (a) (*Grammar* III 194–205). 3. It is worth observing that the characteristic word-order involving the unemphatic pronoun in the middle position is found on both sides of 4¹¹ (1³ τὸ πολὺ αὐτοῦ ἔλεος, 5¹⁰ τὴν αἰώνιον αὐτοῦ δόξαν).

We must conclude that 1 Peter wears a veneer of good stylistic revision upon a basic draft of the same kind of Greek that is found elsewhere in the NT. It is tempting to ascribe the veneer to an amanuensis, not necessarily Silvanus.

Other Literature :

A. Stegmann, *Silvanus als Missionar und Hagiograph*, Rottenburg 1917 (he is the Silas of Acts).

L. Radermacher, " Der erste Petrusbrief und Silvanus," *ZNW* 25 (1926) 287–299.
B. H. Streeter, *The Primitive Church*, New York 1929, 123f.
R. Bultmann, " Bekenntnis—und Liedfragmente im ersten Petrusbrief," *Coniectanea Neotestamentica*, 1947, 1ff.
H. G. Meecham, " The Use of the Participle for the Imperative in the New Testament," *ET* 58 (1947) 207f.
C. L. Mitton, *The Epistle to the Ephesians*, Oxford 1951.
C. L. Mitton, " The Relationship between 1 Peter and Ephesians," *JTS* NS 1 (1950) 67–73.
J. Michl, *Die katholischen Briefe*, Ratisbonne 1953.
M.-E. Boismard, *Quatre Hymnes baptismales dans la première Épître de Pierre*, Paris 1961.
A. R. C. Leaney, " I Peter and the Passover : an Interpretation," *NTS* 10 (1964) 238–261.

CHAPTER ELEVEN

THE STYLE OF THE JOHANNINE EPISTLES

§ 1. Unity of Authorship

All three epistles come from the same hand, 2 and 3 John resembling each other in style and phraseology, and both resembling 1 John, e.g. in the following phrases : *a commandment from the beginning* 1 Jn 3[11] 2 Jn[6], *confess Jesus Christ coming in the flesh . . . this is Antichrist* 1 Jn 2[22] 2 Jn[7] etc. (Antichrist only in 1 and 2 Jn), *not a new commandment* (only in 1 and 2 Jn). In form, 2 and 3 John are Hellenistic private letters, except that they deal with themes rather more solemn.

§ 2. Unity of Authorship with Fourth Gospel

A. E. Brooke showed that the Epistles and Gospel were closely related in style and vocabulary (*A Critical and Exegetical Commentary on the Johannine Epistles*, ICC Edinburgh 1912, v–vii), as Moulton also thought (*Grammar* II 31). Dibelius, C. H. Dodd, and others differ, Dodd urging that 1 John has few prepositions, particles and conjunctions, and fewer verbal compounds than John, and noting that much of John's vocabulary is missing from 1 John (e.g. *oun* 194 in John, *gar* 63 in John, but only three in 1 John, *krinein* 19 in John, *doxa* 18 in John) : " The First Epistle of John and the Fourth Gospel," *BJRL* 21 (1937) 129–156. The Fourth Gospel, it was claimed, had an " intensity " and " inward glow " missing from 1 John, and the language of 1 John was not always lucid ; " it does not suggest the pen of a ready writer," but is in contrast with the " genuine power of style " of the Gospel despite the latter's small vocabulary and limited grammar (*The Johannine Epistles*, London 1946, xlix). The language of 1 John was said to be nearer to that of Hellenistic philosophy, but the difficult question of relative dates was not considered. The presence of some rhetorical questions in 1 John and the absence of them in the Gospel lacks significance, if it is considered that 1 John is an epistle, speaking to the readers more personally. In very careful critiques, W. F. Howard and W. G. Wilson showed that Dodd's arguments were inconclusive. Among other things, Howard pointed out that " the vastly wider range of subject-matter in historical narrative gives the Gospel unquestionably a richer vocabulary " (" The Common Authorship of the Johannine Gospel and Epistles," *JTS* 48 [1947] 12ff). Wilson demonstrated that undoubted Pauline epistles showed greater grammatical and lexical differences than any which Dodd alleged between John and 1 John ("An Examination of the Linguistic Evidence adduced against the Unity of Authorship of the First Epistle of John and the Fourth Gospel," *JTS* 49 [1948] 147-156). Kümmel could thus summarize the position : " Even if a certain linguistic difference between John and 1 John cannot be denied, it hardly goes further than is conceivable in the same writer at two different times sufficiently far apart " (*Intr.* 311).

The stylistic considerations in favour of unity are indeed overwhelming. The following phrases, though rather theological than stylistic, occur only in John and the Epistles : *to bear the sin, to have sin (life), to do the pleasing things, to do the Truth, lay down one's life* (Hebrew *sîm nephesh*), *to be of God (of the world), to abide in God (love), to walk in darkness (light), the only-begotten Son, the Saviour of the world, Paraclete* (NT hapax), *spirit of truth, born of God, children of God, from death into life, overcome the world, walk in darkness.* This is not to mention a host of words which they have in common, some of them used repeatedly : *abide, commandment, flesh, know, lie, life, light, love, manifest, murderer* (NT hapax), *witness.* Many of John's characteristic words, it is true, are absent from 1 John : *glory (glorify), the Holy Spirit* (cf. above). And some of 1 John's words are absent from John : e.g. *chrism, Antichrist, God's seal, koinonia, parousia, expiation, false prophet.* Nevertheless, the unity is remarkable, considering that both have a limited vocabulary, comparatively free from synonyms.

Moreover, they have common stylistic features ; repetition of the same grammatical construction, a paucity of particles, frequent asyndeton or connection mainly by means of *and, kai . . . ou* for *oude* (Jn 1⁵ 1 Jn 1⁵), *pas ho* with participle (Jn 3⁸·¹⁵·¹⁶ etc. 1 Jn 3⁴ 5⁴ etc.), *pan to* with participle (Jn 6³⁷·³⁹ 15² 1 Jn 5⁴), synonymous and antithetical parallelism (Hebraism), a practice of using the demonstrative pronoun (*in this* or *this*) to introduce a subordinate clause : that is to say, a conditional clause (Jn 13³⁵ 1 Jn 2³), a final clause (Jn 6²⁹ 15⁸·¹² 18³⁷ 1 Jn 3⁸·¹¹ 4¹⁷), and one introduced by *that* (Jn 3¹⁹ 5¹⁶ 9³⁰ 1 Jn 3¹ 4⁹ 5⁹). Moreover, they have in common the *kathōs . . . kai* construction (Jn 13¹⁵ 1 Jn 2¹⁸), the *ou kathōs* (Jn 6⁵⁸ 1 Jn 3¹²), the *all' hina* (Jn 1⁸ 9³ 1 Jn 2¹⁹), and *kai . . . de* (Jn 6⁵¹ 8¹⁶ 15²⁷ 1 Jn 1³.

It is a little remarkable that *para* c. accus. (comparatively flourishing in Biblical Greek) never occurs in the Johannine literature, including Rev, though there are 31 examples with gen. and ten with dat. Cf. the comparative table in *Grammar* III 272. Certain prepositions are absent from the Gospel and Epistles : *achri, mechri, heōs* (exc. Jn 8⁹S), not including the adv. *heōs arti.*

Brooke's list of over 50 phrases in common between John and 1 John, as Howard said, "overwhelms the examples of contrast" (Howard, *Fourth Gospel*[5], 287).

1 John is not likely to have been a linguistic imitation of John, for the last thing its author aims at is literary effect.

§ 3. Integrity of 1 John

Externally 1 John lacks the shape of a Hellenistic epistle, with no greetings or usual conclusion, and it is thought to be rather in the genre of the religious tract, like Jude, intended for the whole Church. In spite of lack of formal greetings, it still reads like an epistle addressed to certain groups of readers (cf. $2^{1.7f.12ff.18.21.26}$). The literary form of 1 John is unique. The other two Johannine epistles conform perfectly to the pattern of a Hellenistic private letter. Cf. R. W. Funk, "The Form and Structure of II and II John," *JBL* 86 (1967) 424–430.

Some critics have thought they could see a contrast between short solemn didactic sentences (1^{5-10} $2^{4.5.9-11.23.29}$ $3^{4.6-10.14.15.24}$ $4^{5.7.8.12.16}$ $5^{1.4.10.12}$) having pairs of parallel clauses, and other longer exhortatory paraenetic discussions (e.g. 2^{1f}). From this they assume that a non-Christian *Vorlage* has been revised and incorporated. In fact, all the sentences in 1 John have a stylistic unity and all are of the very simplest construction, except for the complex opening sentence which occupies eight lines of Nestle: 1^{1-3}. After that, the only sentences to extend over three lines are so rare as to lack any significance: 1^7 ($3\frac{1}{2}$ lines), 2^{15-16} (4 lines), 3^{17} ($3\frac{1}{4}$ lines), $^{19-20}$ (4 lines), 4^{10} ($3\frac{1}{4}$ lines), ^{17} ($3\frac{1}{4}$ lines). Most of the remainder vary from a line to two lines in length. As for complex sentence-structure, the sole methods of subordination, not including participles, are by *that* (*hoti*), *hina*, the relative, *if*, *hōs*, *kathōs*, *hotan*. It will be seen from the following table that these clauses occur regularly through the Epistles, not in certain sections only.

That (*hoti*)	1 Jn $1^{5.6.8.10}$ $2^{4.5.8.12.18}$bis.$^{22.29}$bis $3^{2.5.14.15.19.24}$ $4^{3.13.14.20}$ $5^{1.2.5.11.15}$bis.$^{18.19.20}$ 2 Jn^4 3 Jn^{12}
Relative	1 Jn 1^5 $2^{5.7}$bis.$^{8.25.27}$ $3^{2.11.17.22.24}$ $4^{2.3}$bis.$^{15.16.20}$bis $5^{10.14.15}$bis 2 Jn $^{1.5.8}$ 3 Jn$^{1.5.6}$bis.^{10}

If: *ei* *ean*	1 Jn $2^{19,22}$, 3^{13} $4^{1,11}$ $5^{5,9}$ 2 Jn^{10} 1 Jn $1^{6,7,8,9,10}$ $2^{1,3,15,24,28,29}$ $3^{2,20,21}$ $4^{12,20}$ $5^{14,15,16}$ 3 Jn^{10}
Hōs	1 Jn 1^7 2^{27} 2 Jn^5
Kathōs	1 Jn $2^{18,27}$ $3^{2,3,7,12,23}$ 2 Jn^{4,6} 3 Jn ^{2,3}
Hotan	1 Jn 5^2
Hina	1 Jn $1^{4,9}$ $2^{1,19,27,28}$ $3^{1,5,8,11,23}$ $4^{9,17,21}$ $5^{3,13,16,20}$ 2 Jn^{5,6}bis,^{8,12} 3 Jn^{4,8}

We conclude with Kümmel that the thesis of these critics is " improbable," and, " as for the differences in style, we may trace them back to the use of traditional material " (*Intr*. 309).

The style of the Epistles, together with that of the Gospel, is one of extreme simplicity all through, with some monotony of construction. No serious grammatical mistakes are made, but the author's sentences are very brief (except 1^{1-3}). Like the fourth evangelist, he is a cultured man but his Greek is elementary (*Grammar* II 33), and repetitive (e.g. the numerous *I write to you* . . . 2^{12f}), as if it were the style of an old man.

§ 4. HEBRAISTIC STYLE

Although 1 John has no OT quotations, there is evidence that the Greek is Jewish, without however being exclusively Aramaic or Hebrew.

To *do the Truth* (cf. above) is a Hebraism : '*āsâ* '*emeth, to show one's faithfulness*, then *to act uprightly*.

There are traces of the Hebrew infinitive absolute : *sinning a sin* 5^{16}, and of the Hebrew genitive of quality : *Word of life=living Word* 1^1, *the desire of the flesh=fleshly desire* 2^{16} (but perhaps an objective genitive : *desire for the flesh ?*). Besides, there is a good showing of the Hebrew construction (Davidson, *Hebrew Syntax* § 99) whereby the participle with article is used as a relative clause (*he who*) often in the gospels, including John (1^{29} etc.) and 1 Jn $2^{4.9.10.11}$ etc. The position of attributive *pas* is exactly that of Biblical Greek, in contrast to secular (*Grammar* III 205).

The imperatival *hina* (*they must be manifest* 2^{19} and possibly one or two others) is a Hebraism due to LXX influence (*Grammar* III 95) but the idiom would be in his Greek already, for the author of 1 John does not show many other signs of using the LXX. He does, however, use φυλάσσω ἑαυτόν ἀπό (as LXX uses the middle) in place of the accusative of secular Greek 5^{21} (Testament of Reuben 4^8), and shows further LXX influence by his exclusively Biblical expression αἰσχύνομαι ἀπό 2^{28} (=LXX Isa 1^{29}B Jer 12^{13}).

§ 5. Aramaic Style

Some influences are exclusively from Aramaic, and asyndeton is one that is prominent. Approximately 98/161 main clauses of 1 John are asyndetic (13/17 in 2 John, 11/19 in 3 John), and this strongly indicates Aramaic with its lack of connections, as it has also prompted scholars to ponder an Aramaic original to the Gospel (cf. pp. 70f). Connecting particles are not very profuse in the Epistles : *kai* is the most popular (41 in 1 John, two in 2 John, three in 3 John), followed by *de* (10 in 1 John, one in 3 John), and less often by *alla, gar, dia touto, hoti* (causative, *gar*), *hothen* and *oun*. The didactic asyndeton is much used by John and 1 John, to a less extent by James (cf p. 117).

Burney claimed that the excessive use of *hina* was due to Aramaic influence in John. Why not also in 1 John where it is just as prevalent, having 25 instances in 12 pages ? (cf. p. 73). T. W. Manson declared that a seminar in Manchester had found that Burney's Aramaisms were absent from 1 John (not mentioning *hina*) and that the most striking differences between 1 John and the Gospel were really between I John and the Aramaizing part of the Gospel. On such evidence he put forward the hypothesis that 1 John was by an author who composed freely, and that the Gospel was by the same author when his style was affected by his material (*BJRL* 30 [1946] 323f).

The presence of Aramaic influence, in Gospel and Epistles, raises the question whether the author was bilingual and whether his Aramaic were affecting his Greek. The supposition is a fair one, but it founders on the fact that some of the Semitic influence upon his Greek is exclusively Hebraic, and the only hypothesis which adequately explains the double influence of Hebrew and Aramaic is the use of a native Jewish Greek, formed from spoken Aramaic and perhaps spoken Hebrew and from the influence of the synagogue and Greek OT.

§ 6. Semitic Style

Some features may be due to Hebrew or Aramaic influence. Parataxis is conspicuous, as in John (1/12 lines of Nestle). In 1 John there are 160 main clauses in 240 lines of Nestle, and where they are not asyndetic they are usually connected by *and*.

Other Semitic features are periphrastic tenses: 1^4 4^{12} 2 John^{12} (cf. pp. 20f), partitive *ek* without article (*some of*) Jn 7^{40} $16^{14,15,17}$ 2 Jn^4 (Black³ 108; cf. below, pp. 15, 46, 151), participle co-ordinate with a main verb 2 Jn² : *the truth abiding in you and it shall be with you* (cf. pp. 72, 155), and casus pendens followed by resumptive pronoun (frequent in John) : 1 Jn 2^5 *whosoever . . . in him,* ^{24} *what you have heard . . . in you*.

In word-order, the position of the qualifying phrase is important.

1. The secular " compact " genitive (between article and noun) is never found in the Epistles, while the genitive following the articular noun, as in Jewish Greek, occurs quite often : 30 times in 1 John three times in 2 John. The nearest we come to the secular use is in one or two phrases : αὐτοῦ οἱ μαθηταί, δύο ἀνθρώπων ἡ μαρτυρία, which is not even then the " compact " construction.

2. Unlike the " compact " genitive, the " compact " adjective does occur, but is rare : 4^{18} 5^{20} 3 Jn^4, while the regular practice is that of Jewish Greek, viz. the adjective occurring in a following articular phrase : $1^{2,3}$ $2^{7,8,25}$ 4^9 5^4 2 Jn^{2,11,13}.

3. It is not true that there are no Semitisms in the Johannine Epistles ; there are both Hebraisms and Aramaisms, and a certain Christianization of language too.

There is a Christian use of *en* which we cannot properly ignore, a development of the spatial *en*, in a spiritual sense. This is the mystical doctrine of the Christian's life *in* Christ, inside a new sphere of experience. In the same way, Christ is *in* believers. It is a doctrine common to Paul and John, and it was probably important to all early Christians. *In* God is no darkness. Men walk *in the sphere of* (=*in*) darkness or of light, of truth or of lies, of love or of hate. His Word is *in* believers. His love is made perfect *in* them, if they abide *in* God and he abides *in* them. *With* is a possible translation of some of these instances, but on the whole it is inadequate. It is not the instrumental *en*, common to the Koine and to Semitic Greek (*Grammar* III 263).

Other Literature :

R. Bultmann, " Analyse des ersten Joh,." *Festgabe für A. Jülicher*, Tübingen 1927, 138, 158.

J. Braun, " Literar-Analyse und theologische Schichtung in 1 Joh.," *Zeitschrift für Theologie und Kirche*, 48 (1951) 262–292.

A. P. Salon, "Some Aspects of the Grammatical Style of 1 John," *JBL* 74 (1955) 96–102.
J. Héring, " Y-a-t-il des aramäisms dans la Première Épître Johannique ? " *Revue d'Histoire et de Philosophie religieuses* 36 (1956) 113ff.
W. Nauck, *Die Tradition und der Charakter des ersten Johannesbriefes*, Tübingen 1957.
E. Haenchen, " Neuere Literatur zu den Johannesbriefen," *Theologische Rundschau* NF 26 (1960) 1–13.
A. J. B. Higgins, " The Words of Jesus according to St. John," *BJRL* 49 (1967) 363–386.

CHAPTER TWELVE

THE STYLE OF JUDE AND 2 PETER

§ 1. LITERARY CHARACTER OF JUDE

C. Bigg, 311, described Jude's language as "strong, dignified, and sonorous." Jude is not epistolary in form, though it has an address at the beginning, but is rather a tract or manifesto, closing with a liturgical form of words.

Vocabulary. Jude has thirteen words found nowhere else in the NT, three of them found also in the Greek OT : *without stumbling (aptaistos)* [24] (3 Mac), grumbler *(goggustēs)* [16] (Symmachus and Theodotion : Prov), *to convict (elegxai)* [15] (Wisdom literature, Minor Prophets, Isa, 4 Mac) : Bigg 310. Of the remaining ten words, four appear in classical Greek and a further three in Aristotle. The most popular sources for the Hellenistic words are Plutarch (five words), Philo (four words), Josephus (three words). There are no words exclusive to Jude, as there are in 2 Peter. Though he was probably a *Jewish* Christian, he has a distinctly Hellenistic style. Nevertheless, the unique character of Biblical Greek is illustrated in Jude : *hagios*[3] = a Christian (unlike 1 and 2 Peter, but as in Paul), *psuchikos (carnal)* [19] is an unusual, perhaps a Gnostic-Christian term (also in James and 1 Corinthians), *klētos* [1] a Christian (as in Paul).

Rhythm. J. B. Mayor instanced fine rhythm in Jude[20,21] and he noted the rhyme in [8,10,11] *(The Epistle of St. Jude and the Second Epistle of St. Peter,* London 1907, lix). Another peculiar literary feature noted by Mayor (lvi) was Jude's fondness for triplets : *mercy, peace, love*[2], *ungodly, turning . . ., denying*[4], three punishments[3-7], *defile . . ., despise . . ., speak evil . . .,*[8] *Cain . . ., Balaam . . ., Korah,*[11] etc. He compares Jas 1[14,19] 2[23] etc.

Word-order. Three times ([1,12,23]) Jude allows the prepositional phrase in good Greek fashion, to obtrude between article and noun ; he allows an adjective between article and noun six times ([3bis,7,10,20,23]), but he does have the Jewish Greek method of repeated article once ([17]). Twice he allows a genitive to obtrude between the article and its noun ([4,9]), but he places the genitive phrase after the articular noun at 11ter,[13,17,21].

Redundancy of style. In good Greek *to you* would be superfluous at [3], so would *you*[5], and *men* added to *some*[4].

139

§ 2. Jewish Character of Jude

Jude is well acquainted with the LXX (*katenōpion*^{24} occurs in the LXX seven times) and with the Jewish haggadah and apocalyptic (the *Assumption of Moses* and *Apocalypse of Enoch*). Even so, his Greek is relatively un-Biblical and the Semitisms, though real, are merely occasional. Bigg thought that Chase was overstating the case when he said that the writer was steeped in LXX language (311), as the words which may be thought Septuangintal are probably from the *Assumption of Moses*. G. H. Boobyer argues, not very convincingly, that the verb, *to go in the way*^{11}, means " go to death," but the LXX references only mean " go to death " because of the obvious context (as we say, " He is gone ! ") Lk 13^{33} is very doubtful, as Boobyer admits (" The Verbs in Jude 11," *NTS* 5 [1959] 47). Even so, it would be a Hebraism, but it is more natural to take it as a Hebraism for *behave*. *Woe unto*^{11} is obviously Jewish ; the occasional references in Epictetus and the papyri are not significant.

The influence of the Construct State. The article before a genitive, even though required by secular Greek standards, is omitted at ^{6} (*the*) *judgment of* (*the*) *great Day*, ^{21} *in* (*the*) *love of God*, but it is more frequently omitted in 2 Peter.

Parataxis and Asyndeton. Though Jude uses a connecting particle 17 times, there are 27 main sentences, and his connection is almost limited to *de* (eight times), *kai* (four times), *gar* once, *mentoi* once, *men* . . . *de* (three times). Verse ^{11} is an example of parataxis.

§ 3. Literary Character of 2 Peter

Rhythm. Mayor instanced examples of fine rhythm 1$^{16.17}$, where there is also alliteration in m and p, 1$^{19-21}$ with alliteration in p and l, and 2$^{4-9}$ 3^{13} ; he also observed iambic fragments in 1^{19} 2$^{4.8.22}$ (lix). Bigg (227) noticed that 2 Peter tends to use an iambic rhythm in 2$^{1.3.4}$, and pointed out that some Jewish writers in Alexandria imitated the classical Attic tragedians and then passed their work off as classical fragments. " Such extracts were collected in anthologies, and were probably widely known among educated Christians at a very early date." Thus, Paul knew a verse of Menander. Bigg suspected that 2 Pet 2^{22} comes from a Jewish setting of Proverbs in iambic verse (Pr 26^{11}), combined with a secular proverb, but he could not rule out the possibility that our author took both proverbs from an Alexandrine Jewish collection of proverbs, Biblical and secular (228, 288). However, there is a Jewish parallel here too (S.-B. III 773). We find the synonymous (2^{3}) and antithetic parallelism (4^{6}) of Greek and Jewish rhetoric.

Word-order. In good secular fashion, the prepositional phrase is allowed to obtrude between the article and noun (usually very close together in Jewish Greek, as we have seen throughout the NT) : 1^4 τῆς ἐν τῷ κόσμῳ ἐν ἐπιθυμίᾳ φθορᾶς. Other instances occur at $2^{13.18}$ 3^{10} (they are relatively more frequent in Jude). Whereas the genitive phrase comes between article and noun eight times ($1^{8.16}$ $2^{7.16}$ $3^{5.12.15.17}$), in nine instances it follows the articular noun ($1^{3.11.14}$ $2^{2.15.17.20.21}$ 3^4) as in Jewish Greek. But it is true that the qualifying adjective or participle is always compact between the article and noun ($1^{3.11.12.17.18.19}$ $2^{1.21}$ $3^{1.2}$bis.^{15}bis.^{16}). In this way, " the style of 2 P. is more classical than that of most of the books of the N.T." (Mayor lix). Genitive absolute occurs three times, about the same as Hebrews.

Hellenistic religious terms abound in 2 Peter, especially in the first chapter : *theia dunamis* " belongs rather to Hellenism than to the Bible " (Biggs 255). Others are *eusebeia, epignōsis*, partakers of *theia phusis, egkrateia, epoptai, phthora, philadelphia*, and *aretē*. But 2 Peter's phrase, *doxa kai aretē*, may well be an echo of LXX Isa 42^8, thus reducing the force of the argument that Plutarch happens to use the two words together. All the above words doubtless have a new Christian meaning and are not used with their pagan connotations. In view of so much evidence, however, they too would seem to reflect literary pretensions.

Weakness of Style. 1. 2 Peter is even less lavish than 1 Peter in his use of co-ordinating particles, depending like Jude on *de* (21 times) and unlike Jude on *gar* (14 times), but also on *kai* (11 times), and to a smaller extent on *oun* (3^{17}) and *hopou* (2^{11}), *alla* (1^{21} 3^9) and *dio* ($1^{10.12}$ 3^{14}); *men* is not used at all. What we observed under 1 Peter concerning the use of *kathōs* applies here too (1^{14} 3^{15}). There is a good deal of parataxis in 2 Peter, alongside the use of some long cumbersome periods. 2. In these periods, the unusual and often pointless order of words as in Hebrews (cf. above), makes for ambiguity : e.g. in 2^{18} *of the flesh* is difficult to fit into the sentence ; it may be *the lusts of the flesh* or *through the licentiousness of the flesh*. Other passages, singled out as ambiguous by Mayor, a not unsympathetic critic, are 2^{10-13} $3^{5.7}$ (lxvi). 3. There is a meagre use of prepositions : it is enigmatic that, in 1^2 2^{20} the author writes *in knowledge*, but *through knowledge* in 1^3, and *unto knowledge* in 1^8 (Mayor lxv). There is, moreover, the tiresome iteration of four phrases introduced by *dia* in 1^{3f}. 4. There is vagueness and ambiguity in the use of pronouns : it is not clear to what *to whom* refers in 1^4, and in 2^{11} *against them* was felt to be so vague that versions altered the rendering to *against themselves*. *In their corruption* 2^{12} is just as vague. The pronoun is superfluous on at least two occasions : we do not need *their* after *their own* $3^{3.16}$. 5. Moreover, in spite of echoing literary models, the author has rather a poor command of vocabulary, e.g. *oligōs* 2^{18}AB *scarcely* (only elsewhere Strato, ii/A.D., and Aquila's Isaiah) is "characteristic of the writer's bookish style—Aquila and the Anthology appear to be its only supporters" (*Grammar* II 163). Much of his vocabulary is drawn from Hellenistic literary authors and, as in the case of Jude, Aristotle apparently is the quarry for many of his words (of the 28 words which do not appear elsewhere in the NT and Greek OT, twelve are classical, and all of them are literary Hellenistic : Philo (ten words), Josephus (nine words), Plutarch (eight words) ; twelve occur in the papyri. But of these words, some are not found elsewhere, although they are of easy formation : *mocking* (*empaigmonē*), *insanity* (*paraphronia*), *false teacher* (*pseudodidaskalos*), and one is an exclusively Christian word : *be shortsighted* (*muōpazein*). Always there is a striving after the pompous phrase. As Bigg remarked (225), " The vocabulary of 1 Peter is dignified, that of 2 Peter inclines to the grandiose." He instanced *vomit, initiates, roaringly, to Tartarize, cover with ashes* . . . But all is not pompous, as the delightful metaphors of 1^{19} show : *until the Day dawn and the Daystar arise in your hearts.* Nevertheless, the author has this in common with 1 Peter, that he is lazy in his search for a synonym and prefers to let the same word stand, often in more than two places. Here Jude has supplied synonyms wherever possible, for he has a greater sense of style and seeks to avoid meaningless repetition (Bigg 226). Among the iterations are : *his own* $1^{3.20}$ $2^{16.22}$ $3^{3.16.17}$, *escape* 1^4 $2^{18.20}$, *supply* $1^{5.11}$, *sure* $1^{10.19}$, *diligence* $1^{10.15}$ 3^{14}, *remembrance* $1^{12.13.15}$ 3^1, *reward of unrighteousness* $2^{13.15}$, *imminent* 1^{14} 2^1, *follow* 1^{16} $2^{2.15}$, *parousia* 1^{16} $3^{4.12}$, *prophecy* $1^{20.21}$, *knowing this first* 1^{20} 3^3, *damnation* $2^{1.3}$ $3^{7.16}$, *way* $2^{2.15.21}$, *long ago* 2^3 3^5, *spare* $2^{4.5}$, *reserve* $2^{4.9.17}$ 3^7, *gloom* $2^{4.17}$, *unprincipled* 2^7 3^{17}, *railing accusation* $2^{10.11.12}$, *entice* $2^{14.18}$, *speak bombastically* $2^{16.18}$, *commandment* 2^{21} 3^2, *elements melting with fervent heat* $3^{10.12}$, *look for* $3^{12.13.14}$.

6. There is anacoluthon at 2^4, for the protasis, *if God spared not angels*, has no apodosis, which would have come in 2^8. There is another anacoluthon at 3^{1-3}, where the nominative, *ginōskontes*, appears for the more grammatical accusative.

§ 4. JEWISH CHARACTER OF 2 PETER

Again we have the phenomenon of a Hellenistic vocabulary and certain literary constructions alongside assured Hebraisms.

The most conspicuous Hebraism is the genitive of quality, which has been identified as normative in all NT authors. *Heresies of destruction = destructive heresies* 2^1, *desire of corruption = corrupting desire* 2^{10}, *children of cursing = accursed children* 2^{14}, *way of righteousness = righteous behaviour* 2^{21}. Next is the use of a reinforcing cognate noun, which abounds in Biblical Greek by the analogy of the Hebrew infinite absolute : *destroyed with destruction* 2^{12}, *scoffers shall come with scoffing* 3^3 ; both these Hebraisms are avoided in the parallels in Jude, which suggests either that Bigg was right and that Jude depends on 2 Peter, correcting him, or that in spite of his model's more secular idiom, the author of 2 Peter lapses into his more familiar Jewish Greek. The phrase, *going after the desire of corruption* 2^{10}, has a double Hebraism ; in secular Greek it would be worded, *behaving according to corrupted desire.*

Usually the article is correctly used, according to secular standards, in both Jude and 2 Peter, but the author of 2 Peter falls back into Jewish Greek by his occasional neglect of the article with a definite noun before a genitive, reflecting the Hebrew construct state : 2^9 3^7 *(the) day of judgment*, 1^1 *in (the) righteousness of our God*, 1^2 *in (the) knowledge of God*, 2^5 *(the) world of ungodly men*, 2^6 *(the) cities of Sodom*, 2^{10} *(the) desire of corruption*. The expression in 1^2 *(the [knowledge] of God)* is written in the regular Greek way at $1^{3.8}$ 3^{12} ; presumably a redactor has revised the initial Jewish Greek composition (cp. 1 Pet 4^2 *by (the) will of God*, and often in Paul). The use of *pas . . . ou* for *oudeis* 1^{20}, and of *ou . . . pote* for *oupote* 1^{21} is infallibly a Hebraism, and so is the phrase *shall they be found* 3^{10}, for the passive of the verb *to find* is in Hebrew the equivalent of the verb *to be* (cf. Rev 16^{20}, Ps 36^{10} Pr 20^6). The avoidance of the divine name by the use of Magnificent Glory 1^{17} is ingenerate Jewish style, rather than a Hebraism of syntax.

LXX influence. Twenty-four of 2 Peter's 55 NT hapax derive from the Greek Bible (Bigg 224). Of these the following occur in the Wisdom literature : *apopheugein* (escape) $2^{18.20}$, *elegxis* (rebuke) 2^{16}, *exakolouthein* (follow) 1^{16} $2^{2.15}$, *tachinē* (imminent) 1^{14} 2^1, *tartaroun* 2^4, *mōmos* (blemish) 2^{13}, *homichlē* (mist) 2^{17}, *hus* (sow) 2^{22}, *katakluzein* (to flood) 3^6. The following are in the books of Maccabees : *epoptēs* (eye-witness) 1^{16}, *megaloprepēs* (magnificent) 1^{17}, *toiosde* (such as this) 1^{17}, *athesmos* (unprincipled) 2^7 3^{17}, *miasma* (corruption) 2^{20}, *strebloun* (distort) 3^{16}. The following occur both in the Wisdom literature and in the books of Maccabees, the author's favourite sources : *lēthē* (forgetfulness) 1^9, *mnēmē* (memory) 1^{15}, *argein* (be idle) 2^3, *entruphān* (revel) 2^{13}, *miasmos* (corruption) 2^{10}, *tēkesthai* (dissolve) 3^{12}. The pseudonym he adopts, Sumeōn, is the LXX version of Hebrew *Sim'ōn.*

Thus the author is more influenced by the Greek OT than is the author of Jude, but in Jude too the Wisdom literature and 3,4 Maccabees (i.e. Hellenistic Judaism) call for notice, indicating the impact of Hellenized Jewish writers on both Jude and 2 Peter.

Literary genre. It is sometimes claimed, in view of 1^{12-15}, that 2 Peter belongs to a type of " will " literature, professing to be a last will and testament, which was in vogue among Jews and Christians ; books of this kind, like the Testaments of the Twelve Patriarchs, sometimes threatened penalties against immoralities in the "last days", in the same manner as 2 Peter.

§ 5. LANGUAGE OF 2 PETER AND JUDE COMPARED

As 19 out of 25 verses of Jude are also in 2 Peter and because of dependence of subject-matter, we conclude that 2 Peter depends on Jude. Jude ^{2,3,5,17t} are especially significant for literary relationship.

Stylistic relationship with 2 Pet is shown as follows: Jude^2 optative (2 Pet 1^2), Jude^3 *all zeal* (2 Pet 1^5), *beloved* (2 Pet 3^{1,8,14,17}), Jude^5 *put you in remembrance . . . though you knew* (2 Pet 1^{12}), Jude ^{17t} *but beloved, remember the words which were spoken before of the apostles of the Lord. . . . " There shall be mockers in the last time who shall walk after their own lusts "* 3^{1,2,3}.

Two of the words which Jude and 2 Peter share are not found elsewhere in the NT: *empaiktēs* and *huperogka*. Another word is not found elsewhere in Biblical Greek: *suneuōcheisthai*, and the following are very rare in Biblical Greek: *zophos, spilas/os*. Both authors use Biblical words, but neither quotes the OT directly, unlike 1 Peter. The proportion of NT hapax in Jude and 2 Peter is the highest in the NT.

2 Peter has a more vibrant, excited style than Jude's and he is also more pretentious and artificial than either Jude or 1 Peter. He is probably more consciously stylistic. Both authors have a rhythmical and rhetorical style, but more of the underlying Jewish Greek appears in 2 Peter than in Jude.

Other Literature :

M. R. James, *2 Peter and Jude* (Cambridge Greek Testament), Cambridge 1912.
B. H. Streeter, *The Primitive Church*, London 1929, 178ff.
J. Chaine, *Les Épîtres catholiques* (Études bibliques), Paris 1939 (Hebraisms on p. 18).
U. Holzmeister, " Vocabularium secundae epistolae S.Petri erroresque quidam de eo divulgati," *Biblica* 30 (1949) 339-355.
G. H. Boobyer, " The Indebtedness of 2 Peter to 1 Peter," *New Testament Essays in Memory of T. W. Manson*, London 1959, 34ff.
E. M. B. Green, *II Peter Reconsidered*, London 1961.
E. M. Sidebottom, *James, Jude and 2 Peter* (Century Bible), London 1967.

CHAPTER THIRTEEN

THE STYLE OF THE BOOK OF REVELATION

§ 1. The Question of Sources

It is an important question, how far the style of Revelation may be affected by the sources employed. It seems to some critics like a book of sources, not well disguised, woven loosely together. First, we may eliminate what seem to be hymns or liturgical quotations, for it has been maintained in very recent times that Revelation contains material taken from earlier liturgical works, for example, by E. Siegman ("Apocalypse," in *New Catholic Encyclopedia*, New York 1967). They have been more precisely identified as liturgies of Asia Minor, by S. Läuchli ("Eine Gottesdienstruktur in der Johannesoffenbarung," *Theologische Zeitschrift*, 16 [1960] 359-378). Such quotations have been classified as Doxologies ($1^6\ 5^{13}\ 7^{12}$), "Worthies" ($4^{11}\ 5^{9.12}$) and the Trisagion (4^{8b}), by J. J. O'Rourke ("The Hymns of the Apocalypse," *CBQ* 30 [1968] 399-409). G. Delling however thinks that these are not taken from previous material, but were specially written for the book, and he notes that they are full of OT matter which helped the seer to understand the visions ("Zum Gottesdienstlichen Stil der Johannes-Apokalypse," *Nov.T.* 3 [1959] 107-137).

A notable feature of some passages is Semitic parallelism: $2^8\ 12^{10-12}$ look like fragments of Semitic song, and there is parallelism in 3^7 7^{15-17}; $11^{17-18}\ 19^{6b-8}$ look like hymns, 15^{3b-4} professes to be a song, and 18 is nearly all poetic.

Besides the liturgical, much of the material is mythological, whether Babylonian (Gunkel), Persian (Bousset), Mandaean Gnostic (Lohmeyer) or Hellenistic astrology (Boll). The OT is never quoted, but much material derives from there and from later Jewish tradition, and this is bound to account in part for the Semitic quality of the language. There are differences of opinion concerning the way this material has been used. On the one hand, it is held that redactors have been at work on the original composition, making interpolations, re-arrangements, and corrections, as indeed has happened to many books in the Bible. On the other hand, the original author himself may have woven the different sources together, Jewish and Jewish Christian.

For instance, the view of Dr. Charles was that the Greek and Hebrew sources include the material in $7^{1-8}\ 11^{1-13}\ 12-13\ (15^{5-8}\ ?)\ 17-18$. (R. H. Charles, *A Critical and Exegetical Commentary on the Revelation of St. John*,

2 vols. ICC Edinburgh 1920, I lxii.) Dr. Charles's more complicated views on authorship (II 144f) were early criticized, justifiably, by Lohmeyer, to the effect that Charles shatters the connection between sources, and then tries to fit them together again in a different way, in order to make a new connection between them (*in loc.* 21⁴).

However, some critics maintain that when the author wove his sources together he imposed upon his book a meaning quite different from that of his sources. Whereas his sources are directed against Rome, I have urged that the final author transferred this attack to faithless Judaism, sometimes omitting to alter his material sufficiently (N. Turner, "The Church's Attitude to the State in the New Testament," *Journal of Theology for Southern Africa*, no. 2, March 1973, 41–52).

There are many doublets in Revelation; cp. e.g. $13^{1-3.8}$ with 17^{3-8}; there are parallels between 4–9 and 12–16, and between 12 and 20. If we would argue for the literary unity of the book, we must suppose that the same author drafted two versions which he later welded into a single text. The theory of M.-E. Boismard was along these lines; he held that there had been conflation of two sources, both of them by the apostle John at different times (" L'Apocalypse ou les Apocalypses de S.Jean," *Revue Biblique* 56 [1949] 507–541). The unity of style throughout the book would support such an hypothesis. At any rate, however many the sources and the redactors, the final redactor has been expert enough to weld the material together so as to make it virtually impossible for critics to agree on the size and nature of the various sources. With few exceptions, the style is uniform, but there are signs that 1–3 stand apart from 4–21; for instance, all six of the occurrences of *oun* are in that part of the book, and the figures for the proportion of *de* : : *kai* are quite remarkable, for in 1–3 the proportion is 4 : : 69 (i.e. 1/17), but in 4–21 it is quite otherwise, 8 : : 586 (i.e. 1/73). Dr. Charles regarded chapters 1–3 as an earlier work of the same author. On the whole, the peculiarities of style cut across all hypothetical source-barriers. Thus, no part is exempt from the characteristic " solecisms " of the final author, and his characteristic tendency to redundancy of expression appears everywhere, as will now be shown.

§ 2. So-called Solecisms

Semitisms will be considered later; what are now in question are either errors which are due to the author's failure to revise, or perhaps the foreshadowing of later Greek (cf. A. N. Jannaris, *A Historical Greek Grammar*, London 1897, § 1181 b).

1. Masculine in place of feminine (11^4 14^{19} 17^3) and neuter (4^8A 5^6S

17^4S* 13^{14} 21^{14} 22^2A); feminine in place of masculine (1^{15} 14^1); feminine for neuter (19^{20}), but probably the latter is a Hebraism, since *fire* is feminine in Hebrew.

2. Accusative in place of nominative (4^4 6^{14} 7^9 10^8 11^3S*A 13^3); and nominative for accusative (2^{20} 14^{14} 20^2); nominative for genitive (2^{13} 3^{12} 7^4 8^9 14^{12}); genitive for dative (1^{15}) and for accusative (21^9); accusative for genitive (1^{20}); nominative for genitive (1^5) or for dative (6^1 9^{14}). However, the nominative in apposition to genitive, accusative, or dative was reckoned a Hebraism by Charles, despite Moulton's efforts to justify it from the Koine (I cxlixf). It might be an Aramaism too.

3. There are the two sense-constructions: " I heard a voice as of a trumpet saying " (*saying* agreeing with *trumpet*) 1^{10}, and " a reed was given to me saying " (but there is LXX precedent) 11^1.

4. There is the modern Greek use of *gemein* with accusative 17^4. Most of the " solecisms " have textual variants reflecting the desire of scribes to correct. However, in course of time, some Greek usage followed the author in his use of participles in discord, always the masculine being preferred, until in modern Greek the participle becomes indeclinable.

" An uneducated writer, like the author of Rev, is foreshadowing the language of the future " (*Grammar* III 315). In some papyri texts also, congruance in apposition is neglected: papyri of A.D. 39, 128, 250.

§ 3. Redundancy of Expression

While there may be deliberate emphasis in some instances, here are some of the more striking examples of redundancy: 3^{12} *to go-out outside*, 18^{22} v.l. *every craftsman of every craft*, 9^7 *the appearances of locusts like horses*, 14^2 *I heard a voice from heaven . . . and the voice which I heard*, 9^{21} *they did not repent of their . . . neither of their . . . neither of their . . . neither of their*, 16^{18} *lightnings and voices and thunders*, 9^{1ff} *the pit of the abyss*, $8^{7.12}$ *the third part . . . the third part*, 8^5 *took . . . and filled*, 14^8 v.l. *another angel, a second*, 18^2 *Babylon . . . is fallen, is fallen*, 3^9 *calling themselves Jews and are not, but they lie*, 16^{19} *fury of wrath*, 2^5 *if not, I will . . . if you do not repent*, 10^{31} *he cried . . . and when he cried, they spoke . . . and when they spoke.*

Instances of polysyndeton are very marked: 5^{12} *and . . . and* (six times), 7^{12} ditto, 9^4 *neither any tree nor any flower*. We may consider 2^{13} an example of Hebraic parallel redundancy also, and it has in addition a Hebrew chiastic pattern of the ABCCBA type:

> . . . *where the throne of Satan is,*
> *and thou keepest my name* (martyrdom)
> *And hast not denied faith in me,*

In the days of Antipas my witness, my faithful one,
Who was slain among you (martyrdom)
Where Satan dwells.

Ten of these characteristic features are found in the sections which Dr. Charles accepted as various sources (7^4 $11^{1,3,4}$ $13^{3,14}$ $17^{3,4}$ $18^{2,22}$), and they, and other features, indicate the thoroughness with which the final editor, redactor or author has imposed his mark everywhere.

§ 4. General Nature of the Greek

The style of Revelation provokes many questions. Do the " solecisms " account entirely for the peculiarity of style ? Was the language a translation, or was it Jewish Greek ? Or is it not translation Greek so much as Greek influenced by the OT and by Semitic sources, together with " a strong feel for memorable titles, epithets, and phrases of a slogan-like nature " which the author worked into his style, as suggested by P. Trudinger (*Nov.T* 14 [1972] 277–279) ?

Was this kind of Greek unique to this particular author ? In writing the article on Revelation in the New Peake Commentary, I was of opinion that " he might have been Semitic-speaking, with a very uncertain grasp of Greek ; or he may have been feeling his way towards a kind of diction more suitable than the normal kind to the impressive nature of his subject " (*Peake's Commentary on the Bible*, ed. Matthew Black, H. H. Rowley, London 1962, § 915 b). The following evidence makes the second alternative more plausible and tends to show that this new kind of diction was one shared by all the NT writers basically, but to an exaggerated extent in this book.

In one point I find it easy to agree with Dr. Charles, namely, when he discovered Moulton's judgment to be not only extravagant but wrong (I cxliii), for Moulton claimed that " apart from places where he may be translating a Semitic document, there is no reason to believe his grammar would have been materially different had he been a native of Oxyrhynchus, assuming the extent of Greek education to be the same " (*Grammar* I 9). But the style of Revelation is much more distinctive than the papyrus letter: the play on words, e.g. 22^{18f} ἐπιθῇ ... ἐπιθήσει ὁ θεός, belongs to a natural orator, rather than to the language of the papyrus letters. Howard appears to have followed Moulton in the opinion that this Greek was a mixture of " wealth of diction " and " grammatical solecism," used by its author all his life as a second language and never from choice, yet still somehow retaining the main elements of the unliterary Greek of the papyri, just as " relaxed " as the papyri in its standards of Greek (*Grammar* II 33f). Howard added the thought that the author's mother-tongue was

Aramaic and that he cast his ideas in that language (as witness the resumptive pronoun after a relative, the co-ordination of a participle and a main verb, and casus pendens). Howard could not have realized that all these were Hebrew features too. However, Howard did see the influence of the LXX and thus thought that three factors solved the mystery of the language of Revelation : (a) the author thought in Aramaic and wrote in vernacular Greek, (b) he used Hebrew sources, (c) he knew the LXX (*Grammar* II 484f). But since Dr. Charles's studies, one must protest that the Greek of Revelation is not "unliterary," but sophisticated, and that it is not full of solecisms but obeys at least his own self-imposed laws, although these laws need not be interpreted so strictly as Charles does, for he tends to relegate to a source all deviations from these strict rules. The Greek of Revelation may need some mastering, but it can be achieved, especially if the valuable assessment of the grammar by Charles is studied (I cxvii–cxlii). We must therefore ignore all previous grammarians and base our own study on that of Dr. Charles.

I do, however, dissent from Dr. Charles's view that the language of Revelation is absolutely unique in Greek literature. He found it difficult to believe that any other Greek *literary* document " exhibits such a vast multitude of solecisms " (I cxliii). The explanation of the solecisms was said to be, that " while he writes in Greek, he thinks in Hebrew " (I cxliii, just as Howard had claimed for Aramaic), besides the fact that his use of Hebrew sources influenced the style. The author renders some Hebrew expressions quite literally. " He never mastered Greek idiomatically " (I cxliv). But Charles proceeded to admit that the author has a better Greek idiom than the Fourth Gospel. " It is more Hebraic than the LXX itself (cxliv). That is so, but the author has some exclusively Aramaic idioms too, which render it more probable that he used a language in which some Hebrew and some Aramaic idioms were already mingled.

What made the style of Revelation appear unique to Dr. Charles and others is a Semitic quality of Greek, which however is only a matter of degree, not kind, in its difference from that of other Biblical Greek authors. The author uses the idioms more frequently, and I suggest that in his case the services of the usual amanuensis, or some other kind of reviser, were not available, especially if he really were on the remote island of Patmos. The part played by the amanuensis is important in all NT letters. Probably such a helper (in the sense that Josephus uses it) normalized the Greek of the Jews who dictated to him, and in particular this may have been the case with the Gospel and the Epistles of John (cf. J. N. Sanders and B. A. Mastin, *A Commentary on the Gospel according to St. John*, London 1968, 26–29, esp. 28). Burney thought that the Epistles may well have been dictated to an amanuensis with good knowledge of Greek, who also translated the Fourth Gospel from Aramaic ; Revelation was dictated by the same person, but in such Greek as he could muster, after he had gone to live in Asia. We need not be so speculative, but it is well to ponder the rôle of the amanuensis (*Aramaic Origin*, 149-152, esp. 149n.).

Burney pointed to numerous resemblances between the Greek of Revelation and of the Fourth Gospel, but as Charles showed, there are significant differences too, especially in the field of word-order, where Rev has its own rigidly observed rules ; thus, as distinct from the F.G., genitives and participal and prepositional phrases never appear between the article and noun. Unlike the F.G., *houtos* always follows its noun (Charles I clvi).

§ 5. ARAMAISMS

There are few Aramaisms which might not also be Hebraisms, although Torrey claimed that Revelation was translated from Aramaic (*The Apocalypse of John*, New Haven 1958, 27-48). Improbable as that may be, some of the sources of the book may have been Aramaic originally. However, the Semitic influence in Revelation is mainly Hebrew.

There is the question of asyndeton to be considered on the other side and it is fairly frequent, especially in the hymns and towards the end of the book : " Thou hast given them blood to drink. They deserve it " (16^6) is a harsh asyndeton. On the other hand, the only instance of " he answered " (7^{13}) has " and " prefixed, which is uncharacteristic of Aramaic ('*ānê*), and so too " he/they say " very rarely lack " and " 22^{20} (C. F. Burney, *Aramaic Origin* 52-54).

The transition-formulae are confined to the very simplest : (*and*) *after this* (7^1 15^5 ; 4^1 7^9 18^1 19^1 20^3), *and* and *and behold*. Asyndeton is frequent enough in Paul and Hebrews ; undoubtedly it is a feature of Biblical Greek, even if the vernacular is tending gradually in that direction too (*Grammar* III 340ff). It seems to have entered Biblical Greek from Aramaic, since Hebrew regularly uses " and."

There is a clear Aramaism in the confusion of *ei mē* and *alla* (Black[3] 114 ; *Grammar* III 330 ; cf. pp. 13, 92, 150). Aramaic '*illâ* was sufficiently like Greek *alla*, to become a homonym, and that must have resulted in a blurring of distinctions in Greek. *But* adversative is required in 21^{27}, not *except*, for " those written in the Lamb's book of life " are not " unclean."

The use of 3rd pers. active impersonal may reflect an Aramaism : 12^6 (cf. pp. 12, 32).

Two cases of some difficulty and doubt should be noted here : 1. *Homoios* followed by accusative instead of the dative, a solecism in Greek : 1^{13} 14^{14} and there are scribal corrections to dative in both instances. It was, according to Bousset, " einer der besten Beweise für den gleichmässigen

Sprachcharakter der Apokalypse "; (W. Bousset, *Offenbarung Johannis*: Meyer's Komm. XVI⁶, Göttingen 1906, 388. Cf. also 159–179 " Die Sprache der Apokalypse "). Charles explained it as the equivalent of *hōs*, not only in sense but in construction (1 36f). It cannot be, as is probably often the case, an unrevised mistake of the author's, for he knew well enough the normal construction, but it seems already to have entered the Biblical language, being found in 1 Enoch 21³ exactly parallel. It may be due to Aramaic influence, since that was probably the initial language of this part of 1 Enoch.

2. Burney thought that the common recurrence of *hina* and *hina mē*, which Rev (11 times) shares with Jn, reflected the Aramaic particle *dî* or *dᵉ*, which is often the conjunction *in that, inasmuch as, because, in order that*, and hence the confusion; and he thought that *hina mē* (for *mēpote*) reflected the Aramaic *dᵉlâ that*... *not*, since the LXX retains *mēpote* for the Hebrew *pen* (C. F. Burney, *Aramaic Origin* 69f; cf. p. 13). Reviewers of Burney's work hastily pointed out that *hina* was rapidly replacing the infinitive as time went on, and that *hina mē* for *lest* is tolerable Greek, without however weakening Burney's contention that its spread in Biblical Greek is out of all proportion to that in secular. The consecutive *hina* was admittedly increasing in Greek as a whole; F. Boll believed the phrase *to conquer* (6²) was emphatic and consecutive, as frequently in later Greek : " having conquered and so that he did (in the future) conquer " (also 13¹³). Cf. *Aus der Offenbarung Johannis : hellenistische Studien zum Weltbild der Apokalypse*, Leipzig 1914, 88 n.1. But among Rev's 42 instances of *hina* are some which are truly final and others imperatival (14¹³). Semitic influence cannot be ruled out in view of " the difficulty of finding anywhere but in Biblical books such a variety in the use of ἵνα, imperatival, causal, consecutive, epexegetical, within so small a space " (*Grammar* III 9). Cf. *Grammatical Insights* 48. W. G. Morrice approves our attribution of 14¹⁸ and 22¹⁴ to imperatival *hina* : *Bible Translator* 23 (1972) 330.

§ 6. HEBRAISMS

These are more numerous, providing some basis for the theory of a Hebrew original (e.g. R. B. Y. Scott, *The Original Language of the Apocalypse*, Toronto 1928 ; A. Lancellotti, *Sintassi ebraica nel greco dell' Apocalisse : I. Uso delle forme verbali*, Assisi 1964).

There are some Biblical idioms in sentence construction : 1. One of them is prolepsis of the subject of a subordinate clause (e.g. " I know thee, who thou art "), which though it can be faintly paralleled in secular writers is a clear Hebrew idiom : Gen 1⁴ *God saw the light, that it was good*, 1 Kgs 5³ 11²⁸ 1 Mac 13⁵³ 2 Mac 2¹ al. In Revelation we have 17⁸ *seeing the Beast, that it was and is not*, 3⁹ *I will make them that they*. . . . The idiom is not peculiar to Revelation, but is in Mark, Matthew, Luke-Acts, John and Paul.

2. Another idiom, possibly also Aramaic (Black³ 108), and foreign to non-Biblical Greek, is the partitive expression appearing as subject (11⁹) or object (2¹⁰ 3⁹ 5⁹) of a sentence, and a further Hebrew idiom is the anarthrous participle, without any appositional noun or pronoun,

as object of the sentence (2^{14}) ; cf. Lk 3^{14}, but elsewhere in NT only in quotations. It occurs in Test Abr 109^{10} ἴδῃς ἐσθίοντα. Cf. Hebrew *môshîa'* = saviour Isa 19^{20}.

3. There is the question of the Hebrew circumstantial clause (Black[3] 87–89), introduced by *waw*, and rendered in Biblical Greek by *kai autos* ; it is very frequent in Revelation (3^{20} $14^{10.17}$ 17^{11} 18^6 19^{15}bis 21^7), and also in Luke-Acts and Paul. Rev 3^{20} *while he sups with me*, 17^{11} *while he is the eighth*.

4. Typical of the antithetical parallelism of Hebrew poetry is 3^9 (*calling themselves Jews and are not : but they lie*), like much in the OT, e.g. Dt 28^{13} (*Yahweh will make you the head and not the tail : and you shall tend upwards only and not downwards*).

Verb. 1. There are two passages where what seems like an anacoluthon is understood on the basis of the LXX Ps $24(25)^{14}$. The idiom *tou* with infinitive is a Biblical Greek alternative for the imperative mood, following *le* " jussive " (Hos 9^{13} 1 Chr 9^{25} Ps $24[25]^{14}$ Eccl 3^{15}), and so Dr. Charles rendered 12^7 " Michael and his angels *must* fight " (I 321f), although another suggestion is that a main verb has dropped out. Without the article, we find infinitive for a future finite verb in 13^{10} (Hebrew *le* with infinitive again) : " If any shall be slain by the sword, by the sword he shall be slain."

2. Moreover, aorist appears for the future in 10^7, on the basis of the Hebrew *waw* converting the normal perfect to the imperfect, and so it is not " it was fulfilled," but " it shall be fulfilled."

3. The future appears as reflecting the Hebrew frequentative imperfect (4^{9-10} 13^8 *all the dwellers upon earth kept worshipping him*).

4. The influence of the Hebrew infinitive absolute is seen in 16^9 (*scorched with a great scorching*), 17^6 (*I marvelled with great marvelling*), 18^6 (*double her double*), forming a Biblical Greek idiom not peculiar to Revelation (i.e. Isa 6^9, Matthew, John, James, 1 Peter), which Burney confessed was not an Aramaism (*Aramaic Origin* 13 ; also W. B. Stevenson, *A Grammar of Palestinian Jewish Aramaic*, Oxford 1924, 53 : infrequent in Palestinian Talmud and Midrashim).

5. There is a striking sentence of only two words in 22^9, ὅρα μή, as the angel rebukes the seer for worshipping him. No doubt following Blass-Debrunner, R.S.V. supposes ποιήσῃς to be understood (" You must not do that ! "). There are no Greek precedents, Biblical or secular, for such an ellipsis, and the two words can only be explained as a Hebrew phrase introduced by *'ak* = *absolutely*, etc. The LXX rendering of *'ak* is ὅρα (-ατε) in Exod 31^{13} Num 1^{49}. The brief exclamation is dramatic and means, " Absolutely no ! "

Nouns. 1. The singular to denote an object which all people possess is a Hebrew idiom, found also in Paul : *their name* for *their names* (Rev 13^8 17^8 ; cf. p. 91). 2. The idiomatic *le* must be considered in

21^8 where the Biblical Greek dative seems to introduce a new subject after the LXX model (cf. the evidence in Charles II 216). Render, "as for ..." (R.S.V.). 3. The Hebrew genitive of quality : 13^1 *names of blasphemy=blasphemous names,* ³ *wound of death=death-blow,* 16^3 *soul of life=living soul.* 4. The Hebrew superlative is expressed by a genitive : 17^{14} 19^{16} *lord of lords, king of kings* (OT Dt 10^{17}). G. Mussies hesitates to accept these as such, referring to Rev 1^5 1 Tim 6^{15} (where it cannot be superlative) and refers to common practice in the Near East, e.g. " king of kings," " lord of all the gods." But Mussies admits as superlative Lk 1^{50}D Heb 9^3 Rev 1^{18} etc. (*ages of the ages*), (*The Morphology of Koine Greek*, Leiden 1971, 96f).

Definite Article. Dr. Charles was of the opinion that sometimes Semitic influence (by which he meant Hebrew) may account for breaches in the author's usually careful use of the definite article. The rule is said to be that phrases are anarthrous when they first appear, then articular, except for " conceptions assumed to be familiar in apocalyptic " (especially $10^{1.3}$). When this is upset, it is due (according to Charles I cxx) either to the author's use of sources or to his lack of adequate revision. Charles gave instances where he thought that the Hebrew construct state had had some effect : 1^{20} $6^{7.16}$ $7^{2.4}$ 15^2 $21^{12.14}$. However, there are sufficient instances in Revelation where a noun in the construct state retains the article, and many other instances where it is omitted for no good reason (except perhaps rhythm). Thus it is only with reservation that one can find definite rules for the use of the definite article in Revelation. The use is as arbitrary as in all Biblical Greek literature.

Particle οὐ μή. Cf. pp. 33, 69. Rev 2^{11} 3^{12} 7^{16} 9^6 15^4 $18^{14.21.23}$ etc.

Vocabulary 1. The persistence of γαρ (17 times) is a Hebraism (*kî*), not an Aramaism. 2. *Hōs=like the sight of* (*k*ᵉ*mar 'ê*) is laboured in Greek: Rev 9^7 19^1 LXX Num 9^{15} Dan 10^{18} where LXX has *hōs*. 3. ἀπό προσώπου= *because of*, as very often does the Hebrew *mipp*ᵉ*nê* : Rev 12^{14} (Charles I 330). 4. μετανοέω ἀπό or ἐκ is a Hebraism (*shûbh min*). With *apo* : LXX Jer 8^6 (quoted in Ac 8^{22}). With *ek* : Rev $2^{21b.22}$ $9^{20.21}$ 16^{11}. 5. ἐπί with κατοικέω is peculiar to Biblical Greek : Rev 3^{10} 6^{10} 8^{13} 11^{10} $13^{8.14ab}$ 17^8 Ac 17^{26} Herm S 1^6 Test Abr 79^{27}. It emanates from the Hebrew preposition '*al* used with *hā'āres* (note ἐπὶ τῆς γῆς in Rev, LXX Num $13^{33(32)}$B al), secular Greek confining itself to the transitive use or to *en*, *kata* ; *en* with *omnumi* is also exclusively a Hebraism : Rev 10^6, Hebrew *b*ᵉ LXX Jg 21^7 etc. (Helbing 72).

6. *Sōtēria* (=victory) as a translation of *y*ᵉ*shû'â* (=salvation, victory), is admitted a Semitism by Bauer, since the Hebrew stem has the double meaning, an idea which B. G. Caird pursues (*A Commentary on the Revelation of St. John the Divine*, London 1966, 100f).

7. υἱὸν ἄρσεν (12^5) recalls the Hebrew idiom of Jer 20^{15} : *bēn zākār*, *a son, a male.* 8. *To be found* (niph. of *māṣâ*) can mean simply *to be,* so that

in Rev we have "no place was found" (12^8 20^{11}), "mountains were not found" (16^{20}), "she shall be found no longer" (18^{21}). 9. Three meanings of Hebrew *nāthan* appear in the non-secular use of *didonai*, *requite, set,* and *appoint.* Thus, *requite*: Ps $27(28)^4$ Rev 2^{23} Set: 3^9 13^{16}. Appoint: Exod 31^6 Num 14^4 Gen 17^{20} Dt 28^1 Rev 9^5 (pass: "orders were given"). Cf. Liddell and Scott s.v. Bauer gives P Lille 28, 11, but it is very little to the point, meaning (as normally) *to grant.*

10. *I will throw upon a bed* (2^{22}) seems meaningless till rendered into Hebrew: "to cause to take to one's bed," i.e. "cause to be ill" (Charles *in loc*).

11. There are two other phrases characteristic of Hebrew: "to avenge the blood of X on (*ek*) Y," unparalleled in secular Greek, is from the OT and was in Christian circulation: Num 31^2 1 Kms 24^{13} Visio Pauli 40 Rev 6^{10} 19^2. The other phrase is *in her heart she says* (Rev 18^7), exactly paralleled in the Greek of Isa 47^8 (*who say in your heart*), while almost the same is "to know in the heart" (Test Abr 110^{23}), like the Hebrew *yāda' belēbhābh.*

12. Sometimes the secondary meaning of a Hebrew word is rendered by the Greek word which normally is equivalent only to the primary meaning: thus 10^1 *his feet* (for *legs*) *were as pillars of fire*, 1^5 *firstborn* (for *chief*), 2^{27} 12^5 19^{15} *he shall shepherd* (for *break*) *them with a rod of iron.*

Word-order. As in Hebrew, the verb is found in first position after the connecting word in nearly all clauses, main or subordinate, in chapters 1–3 (proportion 79 :: 39), but there is an appreciable difference in the rest of the book, where as often as not the verb fails to be in first position (ch. 4–6 29 :: 21 ; ch. 18 22 :: 21).

§ 7. Semitisms

A large number of constructions appear both in Aramaic and Hebrew.

Parataxis. Dr. Black concedes that "the redundant 'and' introducing the apodosis of a conditional sentence, is almost unknown in Aramaic" (Black[3] 67, n.1). There are several constructions involving *kai* which seem to reflect idiomatic uses of *waw*: i.e. *seeing that* (12^{11} 18^3 19^3), adversative *but* ($2^{13.21}$ $3^{1.5.8}$ Fourth Gospel), introducing the apodosis (3^{20}SQ 10^7 14^{10}), consecutive (3^7); incidentally here is a chiasmus ABBA *he that opens so that no one shuts, and shuts so that no one opens.*

Parataxis is a mark of untutored speech, but it is also *literary* Semitic, and here we are dealing with literature and not speech. Revelation is addicted to it, and never once uses genitive absolute. Other examples of parataxis: 11^3 *I will give my two witnesses, and* (final) *they shall prophesy,* 15^5 *I saw, and* (=that) *the temple was opened.*

The Verb. 1. Burney (94f) noted that the present tense of *erchesthai* is used in Revelation and the Fourth Gospel as the equivalent of the Aramaic and Hebrew participle, a *futurum instans*. Of other verbs, too, e.g.: Rev $1^{4.7.8}$ $2^{5.16}$ 3^{11} 4^8 9^{12} $11^{5.9.10.14}$ 14^9 16^{15} $22^{7.12.20}$.

2. The almost superfluous participles and auxiliary verbs correspond to a Hebrew and Aramaic idiom (e.g. Hebrew *wayyēlᵉkû wayyᵉbōʾû* 2 Sam 4^5. Aramaic *wāʾāqûm waʾeʿᵉseh* Dan 8^{27}). In Revelation there is the superfluous *came and* 5^7 8^3 17^1 21^9 and the superfluous *go (take)* 10^8, exactly like *lēk qaḥ* in Gen 27^{13}; also 16^1 *go (and pour)*; also Matthew and the Fourth Gospel.

3. Then there is also an instance of the periphrastic tense γίνου γρηγορῶν (3^2) in spite of Black[3] 130, who would give the first verb full force, " *become* watchful "; the verb, however, never has this sense in Revelation.

4. The indeclinable *saying* (Hebrew *lēʾmōr*, Aramaic *lᵉmēmar* Ezra 5^{11}) comes here: Rev 4^1 5^{12} 11^1v.l. ^{15}v.l. 14^7v.l. 19^6v.l. Also the indeclinable *having*: 10^2 21^{14}.

5. *I have loved you* (3^9) is a Hebrew-Aramaic Stative perfect for *I love you* (LXX Isa 43^4).

6. Another idiom which Revelation shares with the Fourth Gospel is ellipse of the copula in ὄνομα αὐτῷ 6^8 9^{11} Jn 1^6 3^1.

7. An infinitive or a participle becomes a finite verb in the subsequent clause: (a) infinitive 13^{15} (b) participle becoming finite is frequent (*the truth abiding in us and it shall be with us*, 2 Jn[2] AV, RSV, correctly, Col 1^{26}; Luke-Acts frequently, especially in Western readings), in Revelation " relatively of far more frequent occurrence than in the LXX " (Charles, *Studies in the Apocalypse*, Edinburgh 1913, 91): Rev $1^{5f.18}$ $2^{2.9.20.23}$ 3^9 7^{14} 13^{11} 14^{2f} 15^{2f} $20^{(4).20}$, but S corrects the text at 15^{2f} and 046 al at 1^{5f} 2^{20}. Modern editors often miss the point that this is a Semitism and punctuate differently. Charles cited the authority of S. R. Driver (Tenses § 117) that it was a common practice with Hebrew writers to continue a participial construction by means of finite verbs (*Studies* 89ff; *ICC Rev* I cxlivff). In the LXX, Isa $5^{8.23}$ Ezek 22^3 are rendered into normal Greek, but in Gen 27^{33} Isa 14^{17} Ps $17(18)^{33.35}$ the LXX reproduces the Hebrew idiom. In Hebrew, " this change to the finite is *necessary*, when the additional clause is negative " (Davidson, *Hebrew Syntax*[3] 135). On the other hand, W. F. Howard noted that Holden (on Xenophon) cited nine passages in which this construction occurs in Greek (*Grammar* II 428). Howard was compelled to add that the classical examples were not sufficiently like those in Revelation as " to discount Hebraism." But it was C. F. Burney who pointed out that the construction appears in Biblical Aramaic too (e.g. Dan 4^{22}), so that it must be classed with Hebraisms that may equally well be Aramaisms (*Aramic Origin* 96; also Black[3] 68ff, 130).

Case. The nominative is found in apposition to an oblique case very often in Revelation and the Fourth Gospel. It is a mark of

Biblical literature as well as of untutored speech : Rev 1^5 $2^{13.20.26}$ (*he who keeps my words, I will give to him*), $3^{12.21}$ (*he who overcomes, I will give to him*), 6^8 8^9 9^{14} 14^{12} 20^2 (also Matthew, Luke-Acts, John, LXX Exod 9^7. Cf. Charles I cxlix).

Pronoun. 1. The pleonastic pronoun after a relative is a Semitic construction, rare in the Koine but common in the NT : *which no one is able to shut it*, and *where she is to be nurtured there* (the first kind : Rev 3^8 $7^{2.9}$ 12^6 $13^{8.12}$ 20^8. The second : 12^{14} 16^{19} 17^9. Cf. Thackeray, *Grammar* 46. Similarly, Rev 2^{26} $3^{12.21}$ *he that conquers I will give to him*, 6^8 *he that . . . his name*, 2^7 *to him that conquers . . . to him*, etc.).

2. The oblique cases of *autos* (which except in the " source," ch. 18, never precedes the noun) are very numerous, once in three lines of the Nestle text, which is more than most books of the NT, but not remarkably so.

I Acts has one in one, the We sections one in seven, the rest of II Acts one in five, Paul one in nine, the papyri one in 13. Outside the NT, Jewish Greek has about the same proportion : T Abr one in three, T Sol one in four, LXX Gen 1–4 one in three, 4 Kms 1–4 one in two, lines.

Prepositions. 1. *Enōpion* which occurs 34 times, is found infrequently in the Koine, but its common recurrence here has obviously nothing to do with that, but is influenced either by the Hebrew *liphnê* or (less naturally) the Aramaic $q^o d\bar{a}m$ (Dan $2^{2.9.10.11.24.25}$ al). The distribution is uniform through the book, but it is to be noted that there are no examples in ch. 17 or 18 (" sources," according to Charles) while they are in nearly all the other chapters (cf. p. 145).

2. Also Semitic are ἀπὸ προσώπου (6^{16} 12^{14}) and ἔμπροσθεν (4^6 19^{10} 22^8).

3. The instrumental *en* is very frequent in Revelation. Moulton and Geden consider it to be present in 32 instances, as compared with the rest of the NT as follows : Mark 10, Matthew nine, Luke seven, Acts three, Hebrews three, 2 Peter one. Though reluctant to accept so arbitrary a selection, for I believe that Paul also has his share of instrumental *en*, yet the abundance in Revelation is remarkable (cf. N. Turner, " The Preposition *en* in the New Testament," *Bible Translator* 10 [1959] 118f). Both Hebrew and Aramaic have b^e in this sense, and although the Koine was using it, too, to a less extent, this evidence must confirm the rest, to show that the author of Revelation writes the same kind of Semitic Greek as several other NT authors ; the difference is in the degree to which he takes it.

4. A usage of *en* about which there can be little doubt is the Semitic construction which renders literally the *beth pretii* (Rom 3^{25} 5^9 Rev 5^9) : *at the cost of his blood* (N. Turner, 119).

5. The repetition, *between . . . between* 5^6, is a Semitic idiom (*bên . . . ûbên*) found constantly in the LXX (e.g. Gen 1^4).

Numerals. 1. The cardinal appears for the ordinal in 6^1 (*the first of*, not *one of* as RSV), 9^{12} *the first woe*. " It is Jewish Greek " (Black³ 124), and it is not peculiar to Revelation (cf. p. 91). 2. " One " as the indefinite article may be Hebrew or Aramaic (Hebrew '*aḥadh*, Aramaic *ḥadh*, Dan 2^3 al) Rev 5^5 7^{13} 8^{13} 9^{13} 17^1 18^{21} 19^{17} 21^9.

Word-order. 1. In Revelation, as in Biblical Greek generally, the adjective may occur between the article and noun but more often after the noun with repeated article. In Revelation the prepositional phrase, like the dependent genitive and the participial phrase, never occurs between the article and noun. There is one instance (1^{10}) and a further two in Charles's " sources," where the adjective does not follow its articular noun (13^{12} 18^{21}). So Revelation differs from Biblical Greek as a whole only perhaps in the extent of its Semitism, and not in the kind of Semitism.

2. Co-ordinating particles tend not to be in second place in Biblical Greek, following the Semitic order. The proportion of first-place particles to second-place in Revelation is impressive (1 : 0,05), much nearer to Semitic than even LXX Gen 1–4 (1 : 0,16), Tob B 1–4 (1 : 0,18). Contrast the secular Ptolemaic papyri (1 : 2) and Philostratus (1 : 5). Indeed, co-ordinating particles (apart from *kai*) are comparatively rare in Revelation : *gar* = Hebrew *kî* 17, *oun* 6 (all in Rev 1–3), *tote* 0, *men* 0, *te* 1, *alla* 13, total 37.

About the same length as Rev are Heb, Jas, 1 Pet, for which the figures respectively are 118, 24, 4, 24, 22, 37, total 229. Mk, which is slightly longer, has 67, 5, 9, 5, 0, 45, total 131.

Vocabulary. 1. καρποὺς ποιέω (22^2) may be a Hebrew idiom, since '*āsāh* means *yield* as well as *make*, but the idiom is " found in Aramaic, perhaps in imitation of the Hebrew," or it may come from the Hebrew via the LXX (Black³ 138f).

2. Shared by Paul is ἐξουσία ἐπί a very unusual expression in Greek, clearly influenced by the construction with *memshālâ* (Hebrew) or *shallîṭ* (Aramaic).

With genitive : LXX Dan $3^{97(30)}$ 1 Cor 11^{10} Rev 2^{26} 11^{6b} 14^{18}. With accusative : LXX Sir 33^{19} (30^{28}) Lk 9^1 Rev 6^8 13^7. With dative : LXX Dan 4^{23} (Aram), The verb (not noun) has *epi* c. accus at LXX Neh 5^{15} rendering *shāl˒tû 'al*. In these instances in Rev and two in Test Abr (87^{12} 93^9) the authors may be doing justice to the Hebrew '*al*. That '*al* was used with this stem (*shālaṭ*) is shown by Neh 5^{15}. For the possibility of Aramaic influence too, cf. Dan 2^{48} ('*al*).

3. Shared by Mark, John and Colossians is ποιέω (c. infinitive or ἵνα) causative (Hebrew hiphil, Aramaic aphel) : Rev 3^9 $13^{12.15.16}$ Test Abr 110^{20} Mk 1^{17} and LXX. The verb in the causative sense is admittedly

found, rarely, in classical authors and papyri, but never, so far as known, with *hina*.

4. Semitic languages prefer the positive with simple *not* to a more complex negative expression (Burney, *Aramaic Origin* 98). Thus, πᾶς οὐ expressed *no one*, like Hebrew *kōl* ... *lô* and Aramaic *kōl* ... *lâ*: Rev 7^{16} 18^{22} 21^{27} 22^{3}. Cf. Paul (Rom 3^{20} quot., Gal 2^{16} quot.), Eph 4^{29} 5^{5} Mk 13^{20} Lk 1^{37} 2 Pet 1^{20} 1 Jn 2^{21}.

5. An obviously Semitic phrase is "and behold": Rev $4^{1.2}$ $6^{2.5.8}$ 7^{9} 12^{3} $14^{1.14}$ 19^{11} 22^{7}.

Other Literature :

H. B. Swete, *The Apocalypse of St. John*[3], London 1909.
F. Boll, *Aus der Offenbarung Johannis : hellenistische Studien zum Weltbild der Apokalypse*, Leipzig 1914 (especially Anhang 1 : "Zur eschatologischen Rede Jesu" 130-136).
E. Lohmeyer, *Die Offenbarung des Johannes* (HZNT 16) 1926, 2nd ed. 1953.
J. Freundorfer, *Die Apokalypse und die hellenistische Kosmologie und Astrologie* (B.St. XXIII 1) 1929.
E. B. Allo, *St. Jean, L'Apocalypse*[3], Paris 1935, CXXIX-CLIV (Language).
R. J. Brewer, "The Influence of Greek Drama upon the Apocalypse," *ATR* 18 (1936) 74-92.
J. J. Turmel, *L'Apocalypse*, Paris 1938.
P. Gaechter, "Semitic Literary Forms in the Apocalypse and their Import," *Theological Studies* 8 (1947) 547-573.
J. Schmid, *Studien zur Geschichte des griechisches Apokalypse-Textes*, II (Münchener Theologische Studien, 1 Supplement (1955) 173ff.
A. Lancellotti, *Sintassi ebraica nel Greco dell'Apocalisse*, Assisi 1964.
E. H. Peterson, "Apocalypse : the medium is the Message," *Theology Today* 26 (1969) 133-141.

Other General Works on Style

M. Jousse, *Études de psychologie linguistique. Le style oral, rhythmique et mnémotechnique chez les verbo-moteurs*, Paris 1921.
A. Wifstrand, *Stylistic Problems in the Epistles of James and Peter* (Studia Theologica, Lund 1, 1947) 170-182.
E. Pax, "Beobachtungen zum biblischen Sprachtabu," *Studii Biblici Franciscani Liber Annuus* 12 (1962) 66-112.
E. Kamlah, *Die Form der katalogischen Paränese im Neuen Testament*, Tübingen 1964.
E. Pax, "Stylistische Beobachtungen an neutralen Redewendungen im Neuen Testament," *Studii Biblici Franciscani Liber Annuus* 17 (1967) 335-347.
L. Rydbeck, *Fachprosa, vermeintliche volkssprache und Neues Testament,*

Zur Beurteilung der sprachlichen Niveauunterschiede im nachklassischen Griechisch (Acta Universitatis Upsaliensis, 5) Uppsala 1967.*
H. Thesleff, " Besprechung des Buches von L. Rydbeck," *Gnomon* 42 (1970) 551–555.
P. J. du Plessis, " The Meaning of Semantics for the Exegesis of the New Testament," (in Africaans), *Hermeneutica* 1970, 57–64.
O. Linton, " Le *parallelismus membrorum* dans le Nouveau Testament," *Mélanges Bibliques en hommage au R.P.Béda Rigaux*, Gembloux 1970, 489–507.

* This book deserves close study, especially as our two viewpoints are apparently at variance. Rydbeck refers to my raising the question whether NT Greek is a " Spezialsprache," and he seeks to demonstrate its close relationship with contemporary secular Greek. Using a somewhat choice selection of tests, he urges that each NT author stands more or less in a class by himself, and further, that all of them stand over against the non-literary Koine on the one hand, and the literary Koine on the other, forming part of a third class comprising (a) the not-so-unliterary papyri, (b) popular philosophic literature, and (c) technical writings, e.g. the Corpus Hippocraticum. While resisting anything more than a superficial resemblance of NT style with that of contemporary authors, I would still question whether, even on this basis, Rydbeck is justified in placing (e.g.) Luke-Acts and Hebrews in this middle category, for which they are too " literary," and in placing (e.g.) Mark and John there too, since they are too careless of even moderately " literary " standards. The range of NT styles, in fact, is too extensive for their classification together as one category of contemporary Greek, while their varying distinction from all contemporary styles is too great to be passed over.

SUBJECT INDEX

adjective, position, 23f, 55, 94f, 11of, 119
allegory, 87, 108
alliteration, 107, 140
amanuensis, 80, 82, 84, 88, 99f, 104, 127, 130, 149
anacolutha, 86, 142, 146f
antiptosis, 109
antithesis, 96f, 101, 133, 140, 152
Apocalypse of Enoch, 140
Apologists, 103
aposiopesis, 83
Apostolic Fathers, 87, 103
aorist for future, 152
aorist imperative, 128
article, definite, 21, 33, 119, 129, 153
Assumption of Moses, 140
asyndeton, 12, 31, 70, 85, 108, 117, 133, 136, 140, 150
atticizing, 100
atticizing scribes, 39
attributive genitive, position, 17, 96, 137, 141, 143
auxiliary verb, 20, 35, 52, 72

B.&F.B.S. *Diglot*, 18
believe in, 16
Bezae, codex, 30
bilingual, 7, 136
Bunyan, 57

casus pendens, 21, 34, 53, 71, 86, 137, 149
chiasmus, 3, 65, 87, 97f, 116, 147
Christian language, 16f, 62f, 76, 110, 120, 126f, 137, 139
circumstantial clauses, 152
Clementine Homilies, 54
colourful language, 40
construct state, 33, 69, 110, 118, 129, 140, 143, 153

Coptisms, 113

dativus commodi, 90
diatribe, 81f, 96, 107, 114f
digressions, 86
diminutives, 28
doublets, 146

ellipse, 83, 85, 107, 129, 155
Ephesians, style of, 84f
epidiorthosis, 83
epistle, 83, 116

Gattung-criticism, 87f
genitive absolute, 39, 59, 99, 141
genitive before noun, 17, 110, 119
genitive of quality, 48f, 90, 110, 118, 129, 142f, 153
genitive, subjective or objective, 84
Gospel of Thomas, 54

Hellenistic religious terms, 141
higher Koine, 101, 102, 115
historic present, 20, 35
homily, 82, 84, 87, 88, 108
hymn, Christian, 87, 96, 101, 103, 123, 125, 145

imperatival *hina*, 23, 73, 136, 151
impersonal plural, 12, 32, 35, 46, 89
impersonal verb, 129, 150
infinitive absolute, 15, 33, 47f, 69, 84, 89, 118, 129, 135, 142f, 152
infinitive, articular, 16, 43, 47, 67, 90, 109f, 117, 152
infinitive, imperatival, 48, 89
instrumental *en*, 22
irony, 83

Latinisms, 29f, 104, 129
letters, Hellenistic, 132, 134

SUBJECT INDEX

mannerisms, 26
Matthew and Mark, Semitic quality compared, 37f
metaphor, 83, 85, 87
metre, 106, 140
midrash, Christian, 108
Mischsprache, 78
mistranslation, 11, 14, 74
mouth, circumlocution with, 84, 104

negative, strong, 33, 69, 153
negatives, redundant, 26
nominative, in apposition to accusative, 119, 147
nominative, indicating time, 17
numerals, 54, 91

optatives, 62f, 128
ossuaries, 8

paraenesis, 88, 113, 116, 122, 126, 134
paraklesis, 83, 88
paralipsis, 83
parallelism, 82, 83, 96f, 101, 118, 133, 134, 140, 145, 152
parataxis, 19, 34, 50f, 71, 81, 99, 137, 140
parenthesis, 26, 85, 107
paronomasiae, 117
participle, anarthrous, as subject or object, 47, 117
participle, for main verb, 12, 72, 137, 155
participles, heaped up, 26, 90, 124
participle, imperatival, 89, 128
participles, negative, 77, 127
participles, co-ordinating, 17, 96
particles in Hebrews, 111
particles in John, 74f
particles, Matthew's large use, 38
particles in Pastorals, 103
particles, position, 96, 111, 119
partitive expression, 15, 46, 70, 137, 151f
passive voice, 12, 70
periphrastic tenses, 20f, 34, 52, 72, 128, 137
physiognomical expressions, 16, 49, 69, 92, 111, 156
pleonastic *thus*, 23
polysyndeton, 147
positive degree, 22
prepositions, compound, 93
prepositions, John's use, 75f

prepositions, Matthew's use, 36f
preposition, repetition of, 21, 93
prepositional phrase, between article and noun, 139, 141, 157
prodiorthosis, 83
prolepsis, 12, 16, 33, 36, 47, 69, 70, 93, 151
pronouns, personal and demonstrative confused, 53
pronouns, reflexive, 16, 32, 36
pronouns, resumptive, 21, 36, 53, 66, 72, 156
pronouns, superfluous, 35f
Psalms of Solomon, 49

question, for condition, 34
Qumran, 7, 8, 68, 84, 88

rabbinical parallels, 14, 21, 66, 68, 102, 109, 140
redundancy, 19, 26, 32, 39f, 52, 60, 89f, 93, 139, 141, 147, 155
reflexive, Aramaic, 32, 36
reflexive *nephesh* and *psuche*, 16
relative attraction, 59
rhythm, 80, 84, 106, 124, 139, 140

sayings-source, 64
Septuagint, *passim*
signs-source, 65
singular for general objects, 91, 152
stative perfect, 33, 155
Stoicism, 81f
syncrisis, 109
synonyms, 76f, 127, 133

Targums, 6, 68
tenses in John, 77
Testament of Abraham, 13, 49, 52, 53, 54, 67, 78, 111
Testament of Solomon, 53, 78
Testament of the Twelve Patriarchs, 126, 143
trajection, 85, 86, 94
typology, 87

verb, position, 18f, 94
vernacularisms, 38f, 58

Western Text, 13, 21, 22, 30
word-order, *passim*

zeugma, 82, 83

INDEX OF NAMES

Abbott, T. K., 85
Abel, F.-M., 30, 54, 86
Aland, K., 114
Alford, H., 109
Allen, W. C., 14, 16, 20, 38, 39
Argyle, A. W., 9
Aristotle, 106, 139, 142
Arrian, 81

Bahr, G. J., 99
Barrett, C. K., 64, 67
Bauer, W., 50, 60, 118, 153, 154
Beare, F. W., 121, 122ff, 127ff
Benoit, P., 56
Beyer, K., 70, 105
Bigg, C., 123f, 127ff, 139f, 142f
Biesenthal, J. H. R., 112
Bion, 82
Birkeland, H., 9
Bjerkelund, C. J., 83
Black, M., 5, 12ff, 16, 19ff, 30ff, 36, 45, 53, 64, 70ff, 78, 97, 112, 120, 137, 151, 152, 154, 157
Blass-Debrunner, 152
Bligh, W., 97
Bobichon, M., 6
Boismard, M.-E., 122, 123, 146
Boll, F., 135, 151
Bonsirven, J., 109
Boobyer, G. H., 140
Borgen, P., 88
Bornemann, W., 122
Bousset, W., 135, 150
Brooke, A. E., 132, 134
Brown, R. E., 65
Brown, S., 6
Bruce, F. F., 113
Burkill, T. A., 20, 27, 30
Burney, C. F., 11, 13, 14, 34, 67, 71, 73, 93, 136, 149, 150, 151, 152, 154, 155, 158

Butler, B. C., 5
Bultmann, R., 64, 65, 66, 67, 68, 69, 71, 73, 74, 80, 81, 88, 93, 126

Cadbury, H. J., 57
Caird, B. G., 153
Chantraine, P., 21
Charles, R. H., 61, 101, 146ff, 151ff, 154, 155, 156, 157
Cleanthes, 80
Clement, of Alexandria, 82, 106
Clement, of Rome, 48, 116
Collins, J., 97
Colwell, E. C., 6, 73, 91
Couchoud, P. L., 30
Coutts, J., 121
Creed, J. M., 57, 59, 60
Cross, F. L., 84, 122

Dalman, G., 15
Davidson, A. B., 19, 34, 135, 155
Deissmann, A., 17, 83, 90
Delling, G., 135
Demosthenes, 4
de Zwaan, J., 20, 62
Dibelius, M., 84, 115, 118, 120, 132
Dio Chrysostom, 81
Dodd, C. H., 64, 114, 132
Dover, K. J., 1, 18
Driver, S. R., 19, 72, 155

Emerton, J. A., 9
Epictetus, 57, 66, 81, 82, 83, 102, 107, 140
Epicurus, 82
Epimenides, 96

Fitzmyer, J., 6
Funk, R. W., 134

Giavini, G., 98

163

INDEX OF NAMES

Grayston, K., 102
Grundman, H., 61
Guilding, A., 108
Gundry, R. H., 8

Harrison, P. N., 101, 103
Helbing, J., 50, 112, 153
Herdan, G., 102
Héring, J., 107, 110, 111
Herodotus, 18, 53
Higgins, A. J. B., 9
Hitchcock, F. R. M., 102
Hort, F. J. A., 127
Howard, G., 109
Howard, W. F., 11, 13, 49, 56, 60, 71, 72, 76, 132, 134, 148, 149, 155
Hunkin, J., 20

Irenaeus, 7
Isocrates, 106

Jannaris, A. N., 146
Jerome, 5, 7
Jewett, J., 80
Johannessohn, M., 19
Josephus, 8, 48, 55, 56, 87, 100, 115, 119, 124, 139, 142

Kahane, P., 8
Kautzsch, E., 18, 19
Kehl, N., 98
Kelly, J. N. D., 104
Kirby, J. C., 84
Kistemaker, S., 109
Kittel, G., 114, 115
Kümmel, W. G., 56, 108, 112, 133, 135

Lagrange, M.-J., 5, 12, 13, 19, 20, 71
Lamsa, G. M., 5
Lancellotti, A., 151
Läuchli, S., 145
Léon-Dufour, X., 65
Lifshitz, B., 8
Lightfoot, J. B., 82
Lock, W., 102, 103
Lohmeyer, E., 15, 135, 146
Lohse, E., 123, 124
Lund, N. W., 87, 97

Malherbe, A. J., 81, 82
Manson, T. W., 14, 67, 136
Manson, W., 112
Mastin, B. A., 149
Martin, R. A., 57
Martin, R. P., 97, 122

Mayor, J. B., 115, 116, 117, 120, 139, 140, 141
Mayser, E., 24, 47, 59, 75, 95, 96
McCown, C. C., 49
Menander, 96, 140
Meyer, A., 117
Milligan, G., 83
Mitton, C. L., 84
Moffatt, J., 101, 106, 107, 109
Morrice, W. G., 23, 73, 151
Moule, C. F. D., 122
Moulton, J. H., 13, 49, 57, 60, 88, 89, 132, 147, 148
Moulton and Milligan, 49
Mullins, T. Y., 83
Mussies, G., 7, 153

Norden, E., 60, 81, 82, 86, 94, 99, 106, 115

Oepke, A., 17
O'Rourke, J. J., 135

Parker, P., 5
Percy, E., 90
Perdelwitz, R., 121
Pernot, H., 66, 74
Philo, 82, 107, 108, 115, 116, 124, 139, 142
Philostratus, 23, 24, 72, 110, 111, 119
Phrynichus, 60, 96
Plato, 80
Plummer, A., 56, 57
Plutarch, 57, 115, 139, 142
Polemon of Ilion, 82
Polybius, 57, 96
Preisker, H., 122, 124

Rabin, C., 108
Radermacher, L., 16, 49, 90
Rawlinson, A. E. J., 11, 28
Rife, J. M., 24
Robertson, A. T., 88
Roetzel, C., 88
Robinson, J. M., 87, 98
Ropes, J. H., 114, 115, 116, 118
Ruckstuhl, E., 66
Rydbeck, L., 12, 157

Sanders, E. P., 30, 31, 34, 35, 36, 40, 41, 57
Sanders, J. N., 84, 149
Schenkl, H., 81
Schlatter, A., 7

INDEX OF SEMITIC, GREEK AND LATIN WORDS

'ak, 152
'āmar, 31
'ªsher lô, 21, 72
'aḥadh, 35, 72, 157
'illâ, 13, 150
abba, 5, 9, 57
agalliasis, 62
aiōnes, 91
aischunesthai apo, 136
alisgēma, 62
alla, 13, 74, 92, 103, 150
alleluia, 9
anēr (indef.), 35
amen, 9, 57
antapodoma, 62
anthrōpos (indef.), 35, 72, 91
ara oun, 84
autos (oblique cases), 21, 53, 56, 64, 91, 119, 156

Barnabas, 9
bayyāmîm hāhēm, 16
Beelzebub, 33, 57
berakah, 84
Boanerges, 9

Cananaean, 57
Cephas, 9
consilium facere, 29

dābhār, 49
dᵉ, 14, 15, 70, 72, 73, 151
dî, 52, 74, 151
doxa, 69
duci eum iussit, 29

ean mē, 13
egeneto, 47
ei (interrogative), 54, 92

ei mē, 13, 92, 150
eis (great load in Mk), 28
eis to, 90
ek (" some of "), 15, 46, 137, 151
ekeinos, 25, 66, 95
eloi . . ., 5
elpizein epi, 130
elthōn (redundant), 84, 89
en (Christian), 17, 22, 137
en tō, 47, 90
enōpion, 49, 69, 92, 111, 119, 156
ephphatha, 5, 9
epi to auto, 62
erōtān, 69
euthus, 29
exousia epi, 93, 157

gehenna, 57
genua ponere, 29
Golgotha, 57

ḥadh, 35, 72, 157
hamartanein, 60, 93
hā'ōlām hazzê, 108
ḥāphēṣ bᵉ, 16, 93
hªwâ, 52
heis, 35
heis . . . heis, 36
hen, 13
heneka (-en), 96
hina, 38, 73, 74, 130, 135
hina (causal), 130
hina (epexegetic), 23, 36
hina (imper.), 23, 73, 92, 136
hina mē, 13, 151
hōs (like the sight of), 153
hōs (when), 66, 70, 74
hosanna, 57
hōsper, hoste, 103
hotan, 39, 74, 135

166

INDEX OF SEMITIC, GREEK AND LATIN WORDS 167

hoti, 29, 45, 66
hoti (recit.), 29, 52
hoti (when), 70
houtos, 66, 95, 150
hupagein, 14

idou, 53, 60
incipere, 20
iter facere, 29

yāda' bᵉlēbhābh, 154
y'l, 20
yôm wăyôm, 92
ysp, 15, 48

kai autos, 152
kata prosōpon, 92
katenanti, 13, 92
kathōs, 74, 130, 133
katoikein, 50
kî, 52, 153
kî 'im, 92
kōl . . . lô, 158

lambanein, 71
legion, 30
lêlōhîm, 91
lᵉmâdhî, 13
lêmōr, 52, 155
lᵉ'ênî, 49
lᵉ'ôlām, 16
lᵉqubhla, 36
lᵉwāth, 13, 71, 93
limmûdhî Yahweh, 90
liphnê, 16, 69, 92, 156
lô . . . kol, 73
logisthēnai, 93
loipon, 13, 92
lutrōtes, 62

mah-lî wālāk, 17, 68
mammon, 57
marana tha, 5, 9
mᵉla, 14
membrana, 104
men . . . de, 38, 59, 75, 103
mēpote, 13, 151
mikkᵉ' an, 13

nāsâ pānîm, 127

omnumi en, 153
oros, 14
ou mē, 33, 69, 153

'āsâ 'ᵉmeth, 135

palin, 29, 32, 38
pas, 95, 104, 130, 136
pascha, 9, 57
peripatein, 69, 93
pîstᵉqâ, 14
pistis/pisteuein eis/en, 74, 93, 104, 127
plērōma, 14
poiein, 14
poiein hina, 73, 90
polis, 74
polla, 13, 38, 92, 117
pro prosōpou, 16
pros (with verbs of speaking), 28, 54, 111
pros (with), 13, 71, 93

rabbi, 57
rabboni, 5, 57
rationes conferre, 30
rhēma, 49
rsh, 16

satan, 57
satisfacere, 29
shārî, 20, 46
shûbh, 60, 153
sikera, 57
sōtēria, 153
splagchna, 93
splagchnizesthai, 50, 60

talitha cum, 5, 9
tḥl, 20
ti emoi kai soi, 68
ti gar emoi, 92
tote, 46
ṭura, 14

verberibus recipere, 29

wayᵉhî 'îsh, 68
wayya'an w, 51, 69
wayyēlek, 51

SELECTIVE INDEX OF NEW TESTAMENT REFERENCES

Matthew	PAGE		PAGE		PAGE
1^{18}	. 39	10^{25}	33, 33	20^{21}	. 38
1^{20}	33, 39	10^{29}	. 42	21^{19}	33, 35
1^{23}	. 34	11^{1}	. 43	21^{23}	35, 39
2^{10}	33, 48	11^{8}	. 35	21^{28}	. 35
2^{13}	33, 43	11^{19}	. 35	21^{32}	. 43
2^{23}	43, 74	12^{4}	. 92	21^{41}	. 38
3^{4}	. 36	12^{11}	35, 35	22^{2}	. 33
3^{10}	. 43	12^{12}	. 33	22^{4}	. 32
3^{12}	21, 36	12^{24}	. 37	22^{11}	. 35
3^{13}	. 43	12^{25}	. 37	22^{25}	. 31
4^{1}	. 39	12^{35}	. 33	23^{2}	. 33
4^{3}	36, 38	12^{41}	. 35	23^{9}	. 32
4^{8}	. 32	12^{42}	31, 33	23^{31}	. 32
4^{17}	. 32	12^{43}	. 35	23^{34}	. 32
4^{25}	. 43	13^{19}	. 37	24^{36}	. 92
5^{1}	. 39	13^{20}	. 37	24^{40}	. 36
5^{15}	32, 33	13^{24}	. 33	24^{45}	. 34
5^{18}	. 33	13^{26}	. 43	25^{8}	. 32
5^{20}	. 33	13^{28}	. 35	25^{14}	. 31
5^{26}	. 33	13^{31}	. 35	25^{22}	. 31
6^{12}	. 33	13^{44}	. 35	25^{24}	33, 35, 69
6^{14}	. 31	13^{45}	. 35	26^{23}	. 37
6^{19}	. 36	13^{52}	. 35	26^{25}	. 45
7^{9}	. 35	14^{30}	. 32	26^{51}	. 35
7^{12}	36, 43	14^{31}	. 33	26^{63}	. 38
7^{24}	. 35	14^{36}	. 38	27^{14}	. 36
7^{26}	. 35	15^{5}	. 33	27^{17}	. 39
8^{1}	. 39	15^{11}	. 37	27^{32}	. 35
8^{5}	. 39	15^{28}	. 32	27^{42}	. 37
8^{9}	. 35	15^{29}	. 33	27^{44}	. 43
8^{15}	. 39	16^{18}	. 38	27^{48}	35, 35
8^{28}	. 39	16^{22}	. 33	27^{57}	. 35
8^{29}	. 17	17^{14}	. 35	27^{60}	. 39
		17^{18}	. 32	28^{10}	36, 38
9^{2}	. 33	17^{27}	32, 36		
9^{9}	. 35	18^{14}	. 36		
9^{10}	. 35	18^{15}	. 36	Mark	
9^{17}	. 35	18^{19}	32, 33	1^{2}	. 16
9^{18}	. 39	18^{20}	32, 36	1^{7}	. 21
9^{22}	. 32	18^{23}	30, 35	1^{8}	. 16
9^{25}	. 39	18^{24}	32, 35, 39	1^{9}	. 16
9^{32}	. 35	19^{3}	. 40	1^{11}	. 16
10^{6}	. 49	19^{22}	. 31	1^{15}	. 16
10^{11}	21, 36	20^{8}	. 32	1^{23}	. 22

168

SELECTIVE INDEX OF NEW TESTAMENT REFERENCES 169

	PAGE			PAGE			PAGE
1^{24}	16, 16	8^2	.	. 17	16^8	.	. 26
1^{31}	. 26	8^{31}	.	. 22	$16^{9.20}$	.	. 11
1^{34}	. 21	8^{36}	.	. 16			
1^{41}	. 26	8^{38}	.	. 22			
1^{44}	. 26	9^8	.	13, 26	*Luke*		
2^{1-12}	. 11	9^{19}	.	. 13	1^{15}	.	. 57
2^2	. 26	9^{20}	.	. 28	1^{29}	.	. 62
2^7	. 22	9^{37}	.	. 15	1^{36}	.	. 53
2^8	. 22	9^{38}	.	. 27	1^{38}	.	. 62
2^{11}	. 58	9^{43}	.	. 22	1^{46}	.	. 50
2^{15}	. 26	10^{18}	.	. 22	1^{51}	.	. 50
2^{15f}	. 18	10^{26}	.	. 29	1^{58}	.	50, 50
2^{21}	. 14	10^{40}	.	. 13	1^{62}	.	. 62
2^{23}	. 29	10^{51}	.	. 23	1^{70}	.	. 55
2^{24}	. 22	11^1	.	. 22	1^{72}	.	. 50
3^6	. 29	11^{14}	.	. 26	2^3	.	. 55
3^7	. 21	11^{28}	.	. 23	2^9	.	. 47
3^{13}	. 14	11^{31}	.	. 29	2^{26}	.	52, 59
3^{20}	. 26	11^{32}	.	. 16	2^{31}	.	. 49
3^{27}	. 26	12^2	.	. 15	2^{38}	.	. 53
3^{29}	. 16	12^6	.	. 29	3^{14}	.	47, 152
4^{22}	13, 14	12^7	.	. 28	3^{15}	.	. 62
4^{30}	. 22	12^{10}	.	. 21	4^{41}	.	. 46
4^{40}	. 22	12^{12}	.	. 29	4^{43}	.	. 53
4^{41}	15, 29	12^{14}	.	. 26	5^{22}	.	. 22
5^1	. 21	12^{34}	.	16, 26	5^{24}	.	52, 58
5^2	. 22	13^{11}	.	. 21	5^{34}	.	. 49
5^3	. 26	13^{26}	.	. 22	5^{41}	.	. 22
5^7	. 17	13^{32}	.	13, 92	6^2	.	. 22
5^{15}	. 27	14^1	.	. 22	6^{11}	.	. 62
5^{18}	. 27	14^3	.	. 14	7^{21}	.	. 53
5^{19}	. 27	14^{19}	.	. 23	7^{34}	.	. 49
5^{23}	. 23	14^{20}	.	. 22	8^2	.	. 46
5^{25ff}	. 26	14^{21}	.	14, 22	8^9	.	. 62
5^{27}	. 22	14^{23}	.	. 15	8^{12}	.	21, 53
5^{37}	. 26	14^{25}	.	15, 26, 48	8^{25}	.	. 45
5^{43}	. 29	14^{41}	.	14, 14	8^{28}	.	. 17
6^2	. 23	14^{43}	.	. 22	8^{35}	.	. 46
6^3	. 13	14^{49}	.	13, 66	9^{46}	.	. 62
6^5	. 26	14^{60}	.	. 26	10^1	.	. 50
6^{16}	. 21	14^{65}	.	. 29	10^6	.	. 49
6^{26}	19, 21	14^{67}	.	. 26	10^7	.	. 53
6^{34}	. 22	14^{68}	.	. 14	10^{21}	.	. 53
6^{41}	13, 27	15^1	.	. 29	10^{37}	.	. 50
6^{43}	. 15	15^5	.	. 26	11^{49}	.	. 46
6^{45}	. 14	15^{11}	.	. 40	12^{12}	.	. 53
6^{48}	. 22	15^{15}	.	. 29	12^{20}	.	. 46
6^{56}	22, 39	15^{19}	.	. 29	12^{43}	.	21, 53
7^2	. 16	15^{23}	.	. 27	13^1	.	. 53
7^4	. 32	15^{43}	.	. 26	13^{23}	.	. 54
7^{11}	. 26	15^{44f}	.	. 27	13^{31}	.	. 53
7^{20}	. 21	16^2	.	. 22	15^6	.	. 55
7^{25}	. 21	16^3	.	. 28	15^{14}	.	. 60

SELECTIVE INDEX OF NEW TESTAMENT REFERENCES

Luke (contd.)

Reference	PAGE
15^{15}	60
15^{16}	60
15^{17}	60
15^{18}	60, 60, 60
15^{20}	60, 60
15^{21}	60, 60
15^{22}	60
15^{23}	55
15^{26}	62
15^{27}	55
15^{29}	60, 60
16^{8}	48
18^{6}	48
18^{35}	62
19^{11}	48
19^{38}	48
20^{11}	48
20^{19}	53
20^{36}	49
22^{11}	19
22^{15}	47
22^{23}	62
22^{41}	29
22^{42}	48
22^{49}	54
23^{12}	53
24^{7}	47
24^{13}	53
24^{33}	53

John

Reference	PAGE
1^{1}	71
1^{5}	69
1^{14}	68, 69
1^{27}	21
1^{32}	69
1^{33}	21, 66
1^{39}	71
1^{44}	77
1^{49}	69, 77
2^{4}	17, 68
3^{8}	76
3^{17}	66
3^{21}	68
3^{22f}	77
3^{25}	69
3^{27}	72
3^{29}	48, 69
4^{2}	74
4^{5}	69
5^{4}	74
5^{5}	68

Reference	PAGE
5^{7}	73
5^{9}	68
5^{25}	76
5^{27}	69
5^{28}	76
5^{36}	72
5^{37}	76
5^{44}	69
6^{36-40}	65
7^{38}	74
7^{40}	70
7^{46}	72
8^{2}	67
8^{34}	71
9^{3}	66
9^{5}	69
9^{7}	72
9^{8}	70
9^{13}	70
9^{18}	70
9^{22}	66
10^{3}	76
10^{12}	77
10^{16}	76
10^{18}	67
10^{24}	67
11^{1}	77
11^{3}	68
11^{7}	19
11^{31}	71
11^{37}	73
11^{52}	66
11^{56}	68
11^{57}	74
12^{9}	66
12^{23}	74
12^{38}	68
12^{41}	70
12^{42}	66, 74
12^{46f}	77
12^{47}	66
13^{1}	74
13^{18}	66
13^{26}	21
13^{34}	73
14^{21}	66, 68
14^{31}	66
15^{6}	70
15^{17}	73
16^{2}	66, 74
16^{14}	70
16^{15}	70
16^{17}	70

Reference	PAGE
16^{20}	70
16^{32}	74
17^{11}	69
17^{12}	69
17^{15}	66
18^{9}	21
19^{17}	32
19^{38}	68
20^{1}	72
20^{2}	70
20^{12}	70
20^{19}	72
20^{30}	69, 77
21^{6}	67
21^{10}	70
21^{20}	67

Acts

Reference	PAGE
1^{6}	54
1^{17}	45
2^{12}	62
3^{10}	47
3^{13}	49
4^{17}	47
5^{13}	50
5^{24}	62
5^{28}	48
6^{1}	8
6^{9}	8
7^{1}	54
7^{39}	45
7^{52}	53
7^{60}	29
8^{20}	62
9^{40}	29
10^{15}	19
10^{17}	62
10^{46}	50
11^{27}	53
12^{3}	48
13^{10}	49
13^{24}	49
13^{32}	47
14^{10}	9
14^{27}	50
15^{4}	50
15^{23}	48
15^{36}	47
16^{3}	47
16^{6}	47
16^{15}	52
16^{17}	55

SELECTIVE INDEX OF NEW TESTAMENT REFERENCES

Ref	PAGE	Ref	PAGE	Ref	PAGE
16^{18}	53	7^3	93	15^{42f}	97
16^{25}	52	7^{24}	83, 90	16^2	91
17^9	30	8^3	86, 87	16^{12}	86, 92
17^{11}	62	8^{18}	94	16^{19}	92
17^{18}	62	9^2	97		
17^{20}	62	9^{21}	94		
17^{26}	50	10^{9f}	92	**2 Corinthians**	
17^{36}	49	11^3	85	1^7	89
18^{21}	19	11^{13}	94	2^4	94
19^1	47, 47	12^3	85, 90, 94	2^{14}	85
19^2	54	12^9	89	3^1	85
19^{17}	50	12^{15}	89	3^{13}	85
19^{33}	46	14^9	81	4^{18}	99
19^{34f}	30	15^6	92	6^{11}	92
20^{22}	53	15^{13}	90	8^{24}	89
20^{25}	53	16^6	93	$9^{11,13}$	89
20^{26}	29	16^{12}	93	10^4	89, 91
21^1	47	16^{22}	83	10^{10}	81
21^5	29, 47			11^{19}	83
21^{11}	55			11^{33}	92
21^{16}	46	**1 Corinthians**		12^7	94
21^{23}	62	1^{10}	13	12^{17}	86
21^{37}	54	1^{15}	13	12^{21}	99
22^{13}	53	1^{16}	92	13^{11}	92
22^{25}	54	1^{17}	13		
23^{14}	48	2^{13}	90		
23^{26}	48	3^2	82	**Galatians**	
24^{19}	62	3^5	94	1^5	91
25^{16}	59	3^{20}	93	1^{11}	93
25^{20}	62	3^{21}	81	1^{17}	19
26^5	47	4^1	91	2^6	86
26^{22}	61	4^2	92	2^{10}	94
26^{29}	62	4^6	70, 93	2^{16}	91
27^{10}	52, 52	4^8	81, 83	3^{15}	85
27^{24}	50, 53	5^{12}	92	3^{19}	93
27^{33}	50	6^4	94	3^{23}	93
27^{35}	49	7^{13}	101	4^9	19
27^{44}	47	7^{17}	94	4^{18}	90
28^4	54	7^{26}	91	4^{22}	70
28^8	47	7^{29}	92		
		7^{35}	81		
		9^{25}	81	**Ephesians**	
Romans		10^{11}	86	1^4	84
1^{20}	85	10^{12}	96	2^2	84, 90
2^8	86	10^{20}	89	2^5	85
2^{25}	93	11^{21}	90	2^6	85
3^9	86	11^{28}	91	2^7	91
3^{19}	92	12^{22}	94	2^{14}	84
4^{17}	93	13^1	94	2^{17}	89
4^{20}	93	14^7	85	3^5	84
5^6	85	14^{19}	92	3^{11}	91
5^{10f}	89	14^{34}	82	3^{17}	89
5^{19}	85	15^{33}	96	4^1	85

172 SELECTIVE INDEX OF NEW TESTAMENT REFERENCES

Ephesians (contd.)	PAGE
4^2	89
4^8	84
4^9	84
4^{10}	91
4^{29}	84, 84, 92
5^5	84, 86
5^6	84, 90
5^{14}	96
$5^{22\text{-}33}$	84
6^2	84
6^{10}	92
$6^{10\text{-}20}$	81
6^{12}	81
6^{19}	84, 92

Philippians	PAGE
1^{22}	83
1^{29f}	89
3^1	92
3^2	80, 85
3^{16}	89
3^{21}	90
4^8	92

Colossians	PAGE
1^{13}	90, 91
2^2	89
$3^{1\text{-}6}$	89
3^3	97
3^6	90
3^8	92
3^{11}	81
3^{14}	86
3^{16}	93
4^{16}	90

1 Thessalonians	PAGE
1^6	94
2^{13}	85
3^9	69
4^1	92
5^5	90
5^{11}	70

2 Thessalonians	PAGE
2^7	85, 93
3^1	92

Philemon	PAGE
5	97
19	83

1 Timothy	PAGE
1^{3ff}	86
1^8	102
1^{12}	104
2^{12}	82
3^6	94
3^{13}	104
3^{16}	96, 97, 101
4^3	82
5^6	102
5^{24}	104
6^{17f}	102

2 Timothy	PAGE
2^1	104
3^{15}	104
4^8	92, 104
4^{11}	104
4^{17}	92, 104

Titus	PAGE
1^{12}	96
2^{10}	104

Hebrews	PAGE
1^1	107, 110, 111
1^3	110
1^4	109
1^8	118
2^3	107, 109
2^6	107
2^{10}	111
2^{15}	109
2^{16}	107
2^{17}	107
3^1	107
3^3	109
3^{12}	107, 110
3^{15}	109
4^3	107
4^4	107, 108
4^{16}	110
5^7	110, 111
5^{12}	109
6^{14}	107

Hebrews (contd.)	PAGE
6^{18}	112
7^4	107
7^9	107
7^{27}	111, 112
8^5	108
8^7	109
9^2	109
9^{13}	111
9^{14}	109
10^{32}	107
11^{11}	112
11^{17}	109
11^{28}	107
11^{37}	108
12^4	109
12^7	112, 125
12^{11}	107
12^{13}	106
13^5	108, 111
13^8	107
13^{22}	108

James	PAGE
1^1	48
1^4	115
1^8	120
1^{11}	120
1^{16}	115
1^{17}	115, 118
1^{19}	115
1^{22}	120
1^{23}	118
1^{25}	118
2^1	118, 120
2^4	114, 118
2^5	114
2^9	120, 120
2^{13}	120
2^{14}	114
2^{16}	120
2^{18}	115
2^{23}	120
3^2	117
3^6	118
3^9	119
3^{11}	114
3^{12}	114
3^{13}	114, 118
3^{17}	115
3^{18}	120
4^4	114
4^5	114

SELECTIVE INDEX OF NEW TESTAMENT REFERENCES

	PAGE		PAGE		PAGE
4^{10}	. . 119	2 Peter		6 . . 69	
4^{11}	. . 120	1^{3f}	. . 141	10 . . 68	
4^{14}	. . 114	1^4	. 141, 141		
4^{17}	. . 117	1^{14}	. . 141		
5^1	. . 115	1^{17}	. . 143	Jude	
5^3	. . 120	1^{19}	. . 142	1 . . 139	
5^{5ff}	. . 120	1^{20}	. . 143	3 . 139, 139	
5^{13f}	. . 114	1^{21}	. . 143	4 . . 139	
5^{17}	. 48, 117, 118	2^1	. . 142	5 . . 139	
		2^3	. . 140	9 . . 140	
		2^4	. . 142	15 . . 139	
		2^{10}	. . 142	16 . . 139	
		2^{11}	. . 141	17 . . 139	
1 Peter		2^{12}	. 141, 143	19 . . 139	
1^2	. . 128	2^{14}	. . 142	24 . 96, 139	
1^3	. . 125	2^{21}	. . 142		
1^4	. 125, 130	2^{22}	. . 140		
1^6	. 121, 125	3^3	. . 143	Revelation	
1^8	77, 125, 127, 127	3^{15}	. . 141	1^{5f} . . 155	
1^{11}	. 125, 127, 129	4^6	. . 140	1^{10} . . 147	
1^{13}	. 125, 130			1^{13} . . 150	
1^{14}	. . 129			2^{10} . . 151	
1^{15}	. . 125	1 John		2^{13} . . 147	
1^{19}	. 124, 125	1^1	. . 135	2^{14} . . 152	
1^{23}	. . 125	1^2	. . 71	2^{20} . . 155	
1^{25}	. 129, 130	1^3	. . 133	2^{22} . . 154	
2^3	. . 124	1^6	. . 68	3^7 . . 154	
2^6	. . 129	2^2	. .. 66	3^8 . 21, 60	
2^{16}	. 125, 129	2^5	. 77, 137	3^9 151, 152, 152, 155	
2^{17}	. . 128	2^{12f}	. . 135	3^{20} . . 152	
2^{20}	. . 128	2^{16}	. . 135	5^9 . 151, 156	
2^{21}	. . 124	2^{18}	. . 133	6^2 . . 151	
2^{24}	. . 129	2^{19}	. 66, 136	6^{10} . . 154	
3^1	. 42, 128, 130	2^{21}	. . 73	7^2 . . 21	
3^6	. . 129	2^{24}	. 72, 137	7^9 . . 21	
3^8	. . 129	2^{28}	. . 136	7^{13} . . 150	
3^{14}	. 48, 128	3^1	. . 66	8^5 . . 60	
3^{16}	. . 125	3^4	. . 71	8^{11} . . 70	
3^{17}	. . 128	3^5	. . 66	10^6 . . 153	
4^3	. . 126	3^{12}	. . 133	10^7 . . 152	
4^6	. 129, 130	3^{15}	. . 66	11^1 . . 147	
4^9	. . 42	3^{22}	. . 69	11^9 . . 151	
4^{11}	3, 121, 124, 125, 129, 130	4^{12}	. . 77	12^5 . . 153	
		5^6	. . 66	12^6 . 21, 150	
4^{13}	. . 129	5^{16f}	. 76, 135	12^7 . . 152	
4^{14}	. . 130	5^{21}	. . 136	12^{14} . . 21	
4^{15}	. . 126			13^1 . . 153	
4^{17f}	. . 125			13^3 . . 153	
5^4	. . 129	2 John		13^8 . 21, 152	
5^9	. . 128	2	. 137, 155	13^{10} . . 152	
5^{10}	. . 128			13^{12} . . 21	
5^{11}	. . 129			14^4 . 39, 150	
5^{12}	. 99, 129	3 John		14^{13} . . 151	

Revelation (contd.)

		PAGE			PAGE			PAGE
15^{2f}	.	. 155	17^8	.	61, 151, 152	19^{16}	.	. 153
16^3	.	. 153	17^9	.	. 21	20^8	.	. 21
16^6	.	. 150	17^{11}	.	. 152	21^8	.	. 153
16^9	.	48, 152	17^{14}	.	. 153	21^{27}	.	. 150
16^{19}	.	21, 70	18^6	.	. 152	22^2	.	43, 157
17^4	.	. 146	18^7	.	. 154	22^9	.	. 152
17^6	.	. 152	19^2	.	. 154	22^{14}	.	. 151
						22^{18f}	.	. 148

www.ingramcontent.com/pod-product-compliance
Lightning Source LLC
Chambersburg PA
CBHW050138240426
43673CB00043B/1718